Environmental Crime

Environmental Crime
A Sourcebook

Ronald G. Burns and Michael J. Lynch

LFB Scholarly Publishing LLC
New York 2004

Library of Congress Cataloging-in-Publication Data

Burns, Ronald G., 1968-
  Environmental crime : a sourcebook / Ronald G. Burns, Michael J. Lynch.
     p. cm.
  ISBN 1-59332-000-0 (alk. paper)
  1. Offenses against the environment--United States. 2. Environmental law--United States--Criminal provisions. I. Lynch, Michael J. II. Title.
  HV6403.B87 2004
  364.1--dc22

2003026271

ISBN 1-59332-000-0

Printed on acid-free 250-year-life paper.

Manufactured in the United States of America.

4/05

Table of Contents

Foreword

Unfortunately, in our daily preoccupation with administrative criminology there is often a feeling we do not have the time or the willing audience to explore the basic construction of crime definitions and images. Our focus on measuring and treating crime allows us to avoid critiquing the process by which problems are identified and to neglect the subtle nuances of assumptions which are fundamental to the meaning of our work.

For example, why is it that street criminals become infamous by name (Ted Bundy, Charles Manson), but environmental criminals avoid such a stigma.
Bhopal and Love Canal remain etched in our minds as if somehow the place had absorbed guilt in the same way it absorbed toxic fumes and chemical spills. The labeling of the locale instead of the offender speaks to the responsibility as if it were some type of geographic fate, void of human intent, individual malfeasance, and executive cover-up.

Distancing one's self from crime is significant in the attribution of guilt (responsibility). Corporate dynasties not only mastermind their ability to avoid detection, but pander to our willingness to criminalize protestors, critics and activists in terms we easily recognize as trespassing, disorderly conduct, and "eco-terrorism." This ability to provide "spin" is merely another approach to blaming the victim.

As Burns and Lynch explain, the accountability process has evolved in a shamefully slow trickle of piecemeal legislation that seems destined to insure that we remain far behind the pace of the destruction of resources. Yet the potential of the internet to provide a valuable tool for students to investigate environmental crime is the most potent weapon in the arsenal of crime fighting today.

We are extremely proud to be associated with this exciting resource. It is important not only to write about environmental crime, but also to teach activism as crime fighting. This is a manifesto – a clearly written appeal to students to investigate their world and to engage in research so meaningful, that our very existence depends on it. This is not giving the student a fish, it is teaching them to fish and it could not be a more timely shift in our methodology. We must teach students to ask the right questions and to define terms differently, away from the bias of industry controlled media.

Marilyn McShane and Frank P. Williams III

Preface

In 1971, Dr. Seuss published *The Lorax*. The mustachioed Lorax was nature's spokesperson, and Seuss used him to examine corporate greed, its impact on society and the environment, and to sensitize children to pollution issues. Addressing Onceler—the short-sighted capitalist in this story, who consumed environmental resources at a rapid rate, leaving behind polluted water and air ways—the Lorax spoke his widely known phrase: "I am the Lorax. I speak for the trees. I speak for the trees, for the trees have no tongues." Later, he also spoke for the animals as well. In a similar sense, this book is here to speak for environmental data because it has no tongue—it speaks only through those who use it. Our main message is that those who study crime and justice do not use these data enough, effectively cutting off the tongue of environmental data. The purpose of this book is to help give environmental data a voice.

We refer to Dr. Seuss's story to make another point. *The Lorax* story incorporates a widespread stereotype about environmental harms and crimes: that they only damage nature. The neglected harms that hide behind the damage caused by pollution also impacts humans. While the damage done to nature is significant, this book highlights the harms that environmental crimes cause to people, because these harms make the damages caused by ordinary crime look rather small. We estimate that each year in the United States, up to ten times as many people die from environmental crimes, such as exposure to toxins in the workplace, home, and school, as die by homicide. Hundreds of thousands, perhaps a million more people suffer debilitating diseases and injuries from these exposures each year. These estimates do not include those related to pesticide exposure, which would result in 50,000 more deaths, and hundreds of thousands of illnesses and injuries. Little attention is given to these deaths, injuries, and illnesses in the press, or in the academic literature on crime and justice. But, these deaths, injuries, and illnesses are more common, and have a greater impact on the average person than ordinary crime. This book examines sources of environmental crime data to move the study of environmental crime to the forefront of crime studies.

To be sure, discussions of environmental harms to humans are addressed in academic literature, primarily in the medical and environmental sciences. Unfortunately, the fields in which crime, law, and justice are the primary issues—criminology, criminal justice, legal studies, and law (our "home" disciplines)—have devoted little attention to the topic of environmental crime. Criminologists have kept themselves busy focusing on the crime most likely to be committed by much less powerful people, and draw on widely available crime data published by police, court, and correctional agencies. Criminologists often attest "If only there was comparable data on environmental crime...."

The primary purpose of this book is to demonstrate to criminologists that there is sufficient data available to study environmental crime. This book identifies where these data are found, and provides illustrations of these data and how they can be employed in an effort to stimulate the study of environmental crime within criminology and criminal justice (though we believe this book will be useful to researchers in other fields as well).

In writing this book, we owe a debt of gratitude to Paul B. Stretesky who, several years ago, helped hatch the idea for this book when the three of us discussed the possibility of an even larger project: "The Sourcebook on Corporate Crime." Stretesky, busy with his own studies of environmental crime, justice, and the administration of environmental law, wished us well when we invited him to participate in this project. We are sure that the book would have benefited from his knowledge of environmental crime data. We also wish to recognize the TCU Office of Research and Sponsored Projects, which provided a seed grant for an earlier version of this work, and Wes Longhofer and Roneka Patterson for their contributions. Thanks are also owed to our manuscript editor, Lori Cavanaugh, and to Marilyn McShane and Frank Williams, the series editors, for their comments and suggestions. We also wish to thank Leo Balk for his assistance with this work and more generally, his appreciation of recent scholarship.

And, of course, no book is written without the help or sacrifices of ones' families, including Lisa and Ryan Burns, and Liz Cass and Vincent Lynch.

Ronald G. Burns dedicates this book to his late mother, Catherine Burns, whose love, guidance, and support is appreciated every day.

Michael J. Lynch dedicates this book to his grandmother, Violet Tamburrino, who has witnessed a great many changes in her ninety-plus years.

CHAPTER 1

Introduction: Thinking About Environmental Crime

Any effort to understand involves contemplation or deep thinking. In this effort to understand, one must contemplate the nature of the thing, event, or behavior, its relationship to other things, events, and behaviors, and its meaning. No doubt, these are huge tasks; however, before understanding can be achieved it is necessary to consider the big picture when the problem being examined involves social relationships (Mills, 1959).

To facilitate the type of thinking that leads to understanding, we must first know something about the thing/event/behavior we are contemplating. Whether we derive this knowledge through direct observation, or by becoming familiar with our subject matter by reading and studying someone else's description and observations, we are, in effect, collecting data. We cannot contemplate anything in the absence of some form of data. In short, without data of some kind, contemplation is impossible.

While we need data to learn about the world around us, not all data are equivalent. It is possible, for instance, that the selected data may be biased in some way, possibly as a result of its means of collection, or because it only tells part of the story, or because some relevant facts are not counted or recorded. Biased or "bad" data can cause us to think we understand something when, in fact, we really know nothing because we have only been exposed to misleading or false data. The problem is that we do not always recognize this situation when it arises (i.e., we think we know something when we do not).

The observation that data may be biased does not mean that we should discount the validity of data altogether. The less data we have before us, and the more we rely on our own speculative ideas, the more likely we are to error in crafting our understanding of something. In summary, when researching a topic, one must: (1) be careful when using data, (2) use it appropriately and with caution, and (3) avoid reaching unwarranted conclusions. For valid research, one must collect a variety of data capable of connecting different events, structures, and behaviors. In a larger sense, this means that when we contemplate we must also think deeply about the meaning and usefulness of the data in front of us.

DATA ACCESS AND THE ACT OF CONTEMPLATION

In recent years, the expansion of the Internet has created new opportunities to gain access to data, which in turn has accelerated our ability to think deeply about a variety of topics. In their research, Lynch, Stretesky, and McGurrin (2002) examine toxic crimes and crimes of environmental justice to demonstrate, among other things, the weakness of claims that there is a lack of data that can be used to study corporate crime. For example, the Internet provides easy access to governmental data, enabling the public to learn more about the day-to-day functions of various governmental agencies and the events and behaviors they regulate. These government data archives are rich sources of information for contemplation and are often available to measure behavior trends over an extended time period. One should, however, exercise caution when using government-provided data. As an example, let us briefly consider crime data.

Crime statistics can fluctuate for a variety of reasons. Agencies may change how they record behaviors, or they may have adopted policies that change the behavior of agents charged with discovering, responding to, or reporting criminal events. In these cases, the number or rate of crimes may not have really decreased; what has changed is how crimes are recognized and reported. If we use these data and observe that crime has declined but fail to pay adequate attention to how policies have affected crime rates, we could easily reach the wrong conclusion about a decline in crime and why it has occurred. For these reasons, the kinds of aggregate crime data available on government Web sites may be useful for examining trends in behavior or even changes in an agency's behavior, but not necessarily for pin-pointing the level of a criminal behavior with any degree of accuracy. It is only by becoming aware of the big picture and the context in which crime data are produced that we can begin to understand what that data means. Therefore, we must know the context of the issue before we can analyze government data.

When treated appropriately, government data is useful for research and analysis. It also serves a second purpose in that it makes the government more accountable to the public. By becoming aware of these data sources, we (the public) are not only in a position to think more deeply about a problem, but we also obtain the information we need to act in ways that direct the government to serve us better. For example, by becoming familiar with data on environmental pollution, we can not only thoroughly understand the impacts of pollution on humans, animals, plants, waterways, the air, or even the weather, we can also search for policy responses that will mitigate the problems we uncover.

The reasons we are discussing data, contemplation and access to government data via the Internet is that each shaped the material collected to produce this book. Our general interest in the topic of environmental crime was stimulated by the fact that we have spent a good deal of time contemplating the causes and extent of corporate crime. There is a significant amount of corporate crime in the world today. In fact, there appears to be much more corporate crime than most people can imagine, and much more corporate crime than the ordinary street crimes that appear in the daily news (Reiman, 2001; Lynch, Michalowski & Groves, 2000; Frank & Lynch, 1992; Simon, 2000). Unfortunately, corporate and environmental crimes are not widely discussed in the media, which is the source of many people's knowledge about crime. Furthermore, environmental crime is overlooked by criminologists as an area of interest that requires deep thinking and explanation.

THE NEGLECT OF CORPORATE AND ENVIRONMENTAL CRIME

Until recently, neglect of corporate crime research was understandable because criminologists who wanted to study corporate or environmental crime lacked access to data on the nature of, extent of, or trends in these acts. With access to new sources of environmental crime and pollution data on the Internet, however, criminologists can now begin to research these activities and events with the hope of understanding and preventing them.

Contemplating environmental and corporate crime may lead us to ask: "why do criminologists pay more attention to street crime than environmental crime?" Jeffrey Reiman (1979, 2001) explained this lack of interest in his classic book, *The Rich Get Richer and the Poor Get Prison*. He argued that the typical corporate offense lacks the circumstances or characteristics we have come to associate with crime. As a society, we have constructed a stereotype of crime, especially violent crime. Environmental crime does not fit the image of the typical violent crime we have stored in our collective heads. In brief, our image of crime involves the following inaccurate elements.

First, violent crimes include direct and immediate physical confrontations typically involving acts such as murder, rape, robbery, and assault, or one-on-one harms. Environmental crimes and pollution lack these direct confrontational acts of violence. Also, we see environmental pollution and crime as acts committed by organizations, not people. Likewise, the violence associated with environmental pollution and crime can take years to emerge. For example, it takes years of persistent exposure to pollutants before someone contracts cancer. Because of the length of time involved, we may not link the outcome (cancer) to unseen pollutants (Lynch & Stretesky, 2001). Finally, acts such as burying hazardous waste or diverting it to waterways are qualitatively different from directly threatening someone with a gun or knife. For example, unhealthy work environments contaminated with unseen gases or particle matter do not appear to pose an imminent danger to us. Likewise, living near a toxic waste site does not arouse the same fear in us as living near a crack house.

Second, when we are asked to imagine an act of environmental crime, we don't ordinarily think of an act of violence. Yet, when corporations pollute the environment, they are presenting us with a violent and physical toxic threat to our health and well-being. Sometimes we assume that corporations would not purposefully expose us to chemicals that they know are harmful to human health. Other times we assume that because the government has issued a permit to dump chemical waste into a waterway, that the pollutant must not be harmful to human health. Finally, we may also assume that because a chemical is in regular, everyday use and is easily available that it must not be harmful to human health. To place the violent threat to our health and well being in perspective, let us consider just one form of environmental toxin exposure that many of us overlook—exposure to pesticides.

Many people routinely use pesticides in their home, and believe that these products are safe (either because they are used as directed, or because humans are not pests). Furthermore, pesticides are readily available in all types of stores, from the grocery store, to discount stores, and hardware and home improvement centers. In addition, the government regulates pesticides, and pesticide containers are labeled with numerous warnings and directions. We also observe lawn maintenance and public works personnel applying pesticides on a regular basis. Our exposure to all these routine activities gives us the impression that pesticides must be safe. Each year, however, nearly

12,000 people in the United States die from pesticide poisoning. The true number may be twice as high due to underreporting. One way this occurs is that reporting physicians fail to appropriately classify long-term pesticide exposure deaths. Depending on the estimate we employ, we can assume that pesticide exposure kills anywhere from 50% to 100% as many Americans as homicides in a given year. Yet, we rarely hear about these events on the news, nor is there a national fervor over pesticide poisoning. Our point is that if we combine all the deaths caused by environmental exposure to toxic pollutants, the figure would be many times the homicide rate. Despite these facts, most people are much more concerned with their potential for being a homicide victim than they are with their exposure to toxic pollutants and the likelihood that they may become ill or die from such exposure. This may be because people do not understand the threat posed by toxic crimes and pollution because they are not regularly exposed to data related to these problems. When toxic crimes occur, they are not lead news stories; homicides often are. Also, there is no centralized reporting system for toxic crimes, while there is for ordinary crime.

WHY A SOURCEBOOK?

Until recently, researchers interested in environmental crimes had to piece together disparate articles estimating the extent of these activities and the harms they create, or they had to spend a good deal of effort to collect data from numerous agencies to create their own estimates. Access to Internet data has begun to solve this problem, though researchers must still collect data from various agencies to arrive at a conclusion. Despite the fact that these kinds of data are more readily available, researchers still face the problem of what to look for and where to look when they study environmental crime. In contrast, those who study street crimes have a wealth of information and resources available to them. For example, beginning in the 1930s, the Federal Bureau of Investigation (FBI) has published annual crime data for the United States collected from police departments across the country. Similar data can be obtained from the Bureau of Justice Statistics (BJS), or from individual states. Data from a variety of criminal justice agencies are also collected and presented each year in the Bureau of Justice Statistics' *Sourcebook of Criminal Justice Statistics*, which has been in print for thirty years. Each edition includes data collected from more than 100 sources covering all aspects of crime and criminal justice in the United States. These data are presented in over 600 tables. Compiling data from numerous state and federal agencies, the

Sourcebook provides various indicators of crime and justice across jurisdictions. Unfortunately, no similar sources exist for environmental crime, or corporate crime more generally.

In examining the state of environmental crime research, Rebovich (1998, p. 349) argues that "A major barrier to the effective control of environmental crime is the absence of an effective, centralized information-sharing mechanism. Such a mechanism would allow federal, state, and local environmental law enforcers to assist each other in identifying environmental crime." This book, which is designed as a guide and introduction to environmental crime data and laws, marks one step toward the broader project of creating a sourcebook on corporate crime. Because of the enormous scope of that task, we have focused our attention here on environmental crime. The chapters in this book address a variety of issues related to environmental crime and law. Discussions of environmental issues are supplemented with some environmental crime data and analyses of these data. In places, we illustrate the use of environmental crime data by providing original analyses of some of the data. It should be noted that we do not claim to identify all sources of data for studying environmental crimes/harms, nor do we propose to provide a comprehensive account of environmental crime data. The book, instead, is primarily designed to highlight available data and encourage research on this important topic.

English novelist Aldous Huxley once noted: "Facts do not cease to exist because they are ignored." In compiling this book, we hope to stimulate further research into environmental crime, and to provide a useful guide to environmental crime and law data for researchers, government officials, public policy specialists, teachers, students, and the public. It is hoped that the presentation of examples of available data sources in this area, as well as functioning and accessible data sets will: (1) further highlight the existence and importance of these incidents, (2) prompt greater societal response to such acts, and (3) demonstrate to researchers and policymakers alike that such data are available, and can be presented in much the same manner as data concerning street crime. The project also provides a foundation upon which additional, related white-collar crime data can be added. Expansion of this project should identify and include data sources from regulatory and enforcement agencies (among other entities) in other areas, such as those charged with overseeing occupational, automobile, and food and drug regulations (please see Appendix A for a partial list of other agencies that could be included).

CHAPTER 2

Defining Environmental Crime

In 1996, leaked internal Shell Oil Company documents revealed that the company had knowingly engaged in the illegal injection of oil waste into the aquifer of the city of Diyarbakir, Turkey. The documents contained evidence that Shell Oil executives knew that they were in violation of Turkish and European Union environmental statutes. The documents acknowledged injecting more than 475 million barrels of waste into the aquifer between 1974 and 1994. In addition, the documents indicated the intention to dump an additional 175 million barrels of waste oil into the aquifer by 2001. Indicating the extent of Shell's knowledge of the problem were case outcome scenarios. According to internal documents, the most likely case scenario was that the waste oil pollution would affect the water supply of Diyarbakir (population of the province in which Diyarbakir is located is over 1 million) for a period of 840 to 1000 years! At one point, Shell attempted to reduce the problem, but withdrew resources when it became clear that it would sell the operation to Perenco.

This chapter examines why situations such as this should be recognized as a crime. The discussion begins with an examination of how environmental crime fits under the umbrella term "white-collar crime," and continues with more elaborate examinations of white-collar, corporate, and environmental crime terminology. The chapter concludes with a discussion of social and environmental justice issues that should be of significant concern to anyone interested in understanding harms to the environment and the betterment of society.

IDENTIFYING ENVIRONMENTAL CRIME AS WHITE-COLLAR CRIME

Defining white-collar crime has challenged researchers since Edwin Sutherland coined the term in the 1930s. Researchers have offered numerous definitions of this term, each with its own limitations. Among other things, the varied nature of white-collar offenses and offenders results in white-collar crime being more difficult to define than street crime. In 1996, a workshop cosponsored by West Virginia University and the National White Collar Crime Center drew together 15 white-collar crime experts for the purpose of attempting to solve the white-collar crime definition dilemma. Following three days of presentations and debate, the group agreed to the following definition of white-collar crime: "Illegal or unethical acts that violate fiduciary responsibility or public trust, committed by an individual or organization, usually during the course of legitimate occupational activity, by persons of high or respectable social status for personal or organizational gain" (Helmkamp, Ball, & Townsend, 1996, p. 330). Although agreement was reached, the task was not an easy one.

David Friedrichs addresses the difficulty of clearly identifying white-collar crime in his work *Trusted Criminals* (1996, pp. 5–17). Friedrichs' typology of white-collar crime includes five subcategories: corporate crime; occupational crime; government crime; state-corporate crime, finance and techno-crime; and enterprise crime, contrepreneurial crime, and avocational crime. We focus on Friedrichs' discussion of corporate crime involving environmental harms. Friedrichs (1996, p. 9) defines corporate crime as "illegal and harmful acts committed by officers and employees of corporations to promote corporate (and personal) interests," and argued that there are two types: corporate violence and economic exploitation (which includes abuse of power and frauds). Friedrichs categorizes corporate violence according to the targets of the harmful activities, although he recognizes that there are different ways to classify the term (e.g., according to product or service provided). He notes that corporate violence can be targeted toward: (1) the public, particularly in the form of unsafe environmental practices (e.g., toxic waste, air pollution, corporate destruction of a community, etc.); (2) consumers, through the consumption of unsafe food products, harmful pharmaceutical products, unsafe transportation products and services; and (3) workers, particularly in the form of unsafe working conditions.

One of the problems with defining crime *of any kind* in a theoretical sense is that there is always some disagreement concerning the scope of the definition chosen. Legal definitions have the advantage of being rather straightforward, narrow, and well-defined (as long as the law that applies in a particular case is precise). When we use a legal definition, we say that crime is a behavior that violates the law. But, what *kind* of law must be violated? Some argue that the violation must be of the criminal law. Others, especially those who study corporate, white-collar, or environmental crimes, wish to go beyond the limits of legal definitions to examine behaviors that violate laws and codes of a noncriminal nature (e.g., administrative and regulatory laws). Still others do not wish to be "shackled by the confines" of criminal law (Sellin, 1938). Sellin, who made this point with reference to cross-cultural research, argued that legal definitions were artificial, and that these definitions constrained the kind of research criminologists could conduct. This argument has important implications for the study of environmental crime.

Definitions of environmental crime are in a constant state of flux. To some extent, the changing nature of these laws has something to do with the fact that environmental law is a relatively recent creation, and is constantly being reevaluated and modified by new legal precedence or the identification of new harms. The creation of environmental law, however, is also affected by the interests of powerful corporations to whom these laws apply. Chemical, oil, pharmaceutical, and automobile companies maintain trade and lobby associations that review proposed changes to environmental statutes and apply pressure to legislators or regulators involved in the process of making these laws to restructure or nullify laws perceived as detrimental to corporate profit-making abilities. Part of the study of environmental law, therefore, involves research that examines the process of environmental law making; or identifying how a behavior that was previously unregulated becomes identified as a harm (or how a behavior that is currently recognized as a harm in law, is removed from the books).

As noted, the concept of environmental crime is a rather recent and specific phenomenon that is related to white-collar and corporate crime. Thus, we begin our discussion of environmental crime by briefly examining the definitions of white-collar and corporate crime. After exploring these ideas and defining environmental crime, we also examine the idea of environmental justice, which has become a central component of some forms of environmental law.

WHITE-COLLAR CRIME

Crime has generally been viewed as a behavior engaged in by the lower classes (Chevalier, 1973; Brace, 1880; Carpenter, 1851). The greed and avarice exhibited by the "Robber Barons" (Josephson, 1934), captured in the writings of "muckraking journalists" (late 1800s–early 1900s; e.g. Sinclair, 1906), along with rising worker resistance to poor working conditions and low wages (1870s–1900) sensitized the population to the immoral and dangerous acts of the powerful. These concerns were heightened by President Theodore Roosevelt and his focus on regulating corporate behavior ("trust busting") and protecting the environment. The first academic to touch on these issues was Edward A. Ross (1907). But, it was not until the late 1940s, with the publication of Edwin H. Sutherland's work on white-collar criminals that the idea of elite crime began to take hold.

Sutherland defined white-collar crime as "a crime committed by a person of respectability and high social status in the course of his occupation" (Sutherland, 1983, p. 7). While there has been much debate about the meaning of the phrase "high social status," and whether crimes exist outside of criminal law (Tappan, 1947), two things are clear. First, Sutherland's definition clearly excluded the ordinary crimes that businesspersons might commit, such as murder, robbery, family violence, or assault because these acts do not require access to an occupation. Second, Sutherland drew attention to the neglected area of upper-world crime.

While much has been made of Sutherland's failure to define the phrase "high social status," debate about this phrase has been more mystifying than elucidatory. The manner in which the FBI counts white-collar crime has contributed to these uncertainties. Consider the following: a bank teller (earning $11/hour or $23,000/year) embezzles a few pennies from each check s/he receives; a store clerk (earning $5.25/hour or $11,000/year) purposefully makes incorrect change and pockets the profit; a bank president (earning $25/hour or $52,000/year) diverts funds into a foreign bank account; and an auto-mechanic (earning $25/hour or $52,000/year) overcharges for parts. Who is the white-collar criminal? We would select the bank manager because of his/her high social status. The remaining offenders have engaged in frauds, but they are not necessarily white-collar crimes.

How does a white-collar crime differ from a corporate crime? In an effort to distinguish white-collar and corporate crimes, Frank and Lynch (1992, p. 17) argued that white-collar crimes are committed for personal gain while corporate crimes are committed to benefit the corporation (the individual may benefit indirectly). Let us clarify this argument by way of example.

In the 1980s, two former white-collar offenders were brought to public attention: Ivan Boesky and Michael Milken. Boesky was an arbitrage specialist whose business invested in corporations that were potential takeover targets for mergers and acquisitions. Following a significant loss on an attempted Gulf Oil takeover of City Services (CITGO), Boesky enlisted the help of Martin Siegel (of Kidder Peabody) and Dennis Levine (of Drexel, Burnham, and Lambert) to improve his odds of success. Unfortunately, receiving the kind of "insider" information Levine and Siegel provided is illegal, and in

1986, the Securities and Exchange Commission (SEC) charged Boesky with numerous "insider trading" violations. Boesky entered into a plea agreement. He received a 3½ year prison sentence, and a $100 million fine. The SEC also agreed not to make Boesky reveal the assets he held in foreign bank accounts. In return, Boesky agreed to provide evidence on other insider traders by allowing the SEC to tap his phones. Milken was the primary target.

Milken, an employee at the now defunct Drexel, Burnham, and Lambert, is recognized as the inventor of "junk bonds" or high-yield, speculative bond investments. However, Milken achieved his success in a less than scrupulous manner. For example, Milken cooperated with Boesky, and the two swapped ownership of securities to hide their origins (a practice called "parking") so that Milken could trade stocks in companies in which Drexel had confidential interests. The SEC charged Milken in a 98-count criminal indictment that included insider trading, price manipulation, falsifying records, filing false reports, racketeering, and defrauding customers. Milken pled guilty to six relatively minor securities violations, and received a $600 million fine and 10-year prison sentence (he served 22 months), and was barred from the securities industry for life (although he subsequently engaged in security trading after his release from prison).

These acts, which involved large sums of money and harmed an uncounted number of investors (though some also became extremely wealthy), are unquestionably serious crimes because they threaten the system of trust that underlies the securities market. The individuals who perpetrate these crimes also have their own enrichment as their primary goal. White-collar crimes are quite different from corporate crimes in this regard, as illustrated in the aforementioned example involving the Shell Oil Company's destruction of the environment. Endangering the health of over 1 million people by illegally injecting oil waste into an aquifer is qualitatively different from the financial crimes of Boesky and Milken. The other difference is that the managers of the Shell refinery who engaged in these acts did so for the direct benefit of Shell, not themselves. But the largest difference is that the persons who engage in corporate crimes are often hidden behind the scenes. Notice that when we discuss corporate crimes (the Shell case) we do not make direct mention of the names of the individuals involved. One reason we neglect the people who are behind these crimes is that we may not know the identity of these people. Another is that these kinds of crimes involve the cooperation of many people, making it simpler to refer to a corporation than to 10, 20, or 100 individuals.

Having clarified the distinction between white-collar and corporate crime, we briefly discuss some corporate crime research. It was this research, which first began the discussion of corporate violence, that allowed researchers the latitude to investigate environmental crime.

CORPORATE VIOLENCE

It was not until the late 1970s that criminologists began to turn their attention from the financial harms associated with corporate and white-collar crime to its violent aspects. In brief, this movement began to pinpoint the ways in which corporations acted violently. Attention was initially focused on violence in the workplace, or violence committed by corporations against workers. (Interestingly, this term was later corrupted by corporate interests, and redefined to include acts of violence committed by coworkers, such as workplace homicides and assaults). These acts of violence include unsafe working conditions that violate the law, and lead to injury, disease, and death. In a recent book, Leigh, Markowitz, Fahs, and Landrigan (2000), place the total number of U.S. workplace injuries, diseases, and deaths at more than 14.5 million annually. Of course, not all of these injuries, diseases, and deaths are caused by violations of law, and it is impossible to estimate exactly how many of these harms are due to violations of law. Many, however, are due to negligence or purposeful avoidance of laws and regulations designed to protect the health of workers, and numerous researchers have addressed these issues.

Jeffrey Reiman was among the first to tackle this issue in his 1979 book, *The Rich Get Richer and the Poor Get Prison*. His work, probably more so than any other, paved the way for criminologists to reorient the study of corporate crime from its financial to its violent aspects. This was no easy redirection, and many denied that corporations committed violent acts.

Before Reiman, Ralph Nader sensitized Americans to the issue of corporate violence in 1965 with the publication of his book, *Unsafe at Any Speed*. His congressional testimony on unsafe automobile designs, and his later work on environmental and workplace pollution, brought the discussion of corporate violence into the open. And, no discussion of the topic of corporate violence would be complete without reference to Rachel Carson's 1962 book, *Silent Spring*, in which she predicted the coming environmental damage related to uncontrolled use and production of synthetic pesticides. Brief summaries of several noteworthy books that highlight the ways in which corporations committed acts of violence are found in Table 2-1.

Table 2-1: Early Books that Highlight Corporate Violence

Arthur Kallet and F.J. Schlink. (1933). *1,000,000 Guinea Pigs: Dangers in Everyday Foods, Drugs and Cosmetics.* One of the earliest books to detail the health dangers in foods, drugs, and cosmetics.

Ralph Nader. (1965). *Unsafe at Any Speed.* Exposes unsafe automobile design practices, focusing attention specifically on the Chevrolet Corvair. This book, which led to Nader's testimony on automobile safety in the U.S. Congress, was credited with providing a climate conducive for passing automobile safety legislation.

Samuel Epstein. (1979). *The Politics of Cancer.* Examines the environmental causes of cancer in foods, drugs, and the workplace.

Marshall Sapo. (1979). *A Nation of Guinea Pigs.* Reviews a variety of health concerns in foods and drugs to which Americans are routinely exposed.

Ralph Nader, Ronald Brownstein, and John Richard. (1981), *Who's Poisoning America.* Examines the widespread problem of toxins in the U.S. environment and the responsibility of corporations for placing them there.

Milton Silverman, Phillip R. Lee, and Mia Lydecker (1982). *Prescription For Death.* Physicians expose the pharmaceutical company practice of marketing drugs banned in the United States for health reasons in nations where such regulations had yet to be passed.

David Weir and Mark Shapiro. (1982). *Circle of Poison.* Details how corporations that manufacture pesticides that are banned in the United States due to health concerns continue to produce these products for use in overseas markets where use of these chemicals is not restricted, and how these dangerous pesticides are reimported into the United States on the foods we eat.

Stuart Hill. (1987). *Corporate Violence—Injury and Death for Profit.* Describes numerous cases where corporate profit is placed ahead of human health.

Francis T. Cullen, William J. Maakestad, and Gray Cavender. (1987). *Corporate Crime Under Attack.* An in-depth study of the Ford Pinto case.

Michael H. Brown. (1980). *Laying Waste: The Poisoning of America by Toxic Chemicals.* Primarily focuses on the Love Canal incident, but includes information on numerous other toxic waste hazards found across the United States.

Countless books have recently been published that are useful for understanding the association between environmental pollution and corporate violence. Brief descriptions of some of the more important and useful of these books are provided in Table 2-2.

Table 2-2: Recent Books on Environmental Pollution and Human Health Consequences

Marc Lappe. (1991). *Chemical Deception: Exposing Ten Myths that Endanger Us.* Lappe, a former Chief of the Hazards Evaluation System for the State of California, examines 10 myths about toxins in the environment that, when accepted, allow corporations to continue to victimize human health.

Joseph V. Rodericks. (1992). *Calculated Risks: The Toxicity and Human Health Risks of Chemicals in Our Environment.* Provides a detailed discussion of scientific evidence on environmental health risks and regulatory policy.

Theo Colborn, Dianne Dumanoski, and John P. Myers. (1997). *Our Stolen Future: Are We Threatening Our Fertility, Intelligence and Survival? A Scientific Detective Story.* Among the best books on the effects of synthetic pesticides on human health. Specifically discusses how one scientist (Colborn) discovered the connection between synthetic chemicals as hormone disruptors, and the subsequent human health effects.

Sandra Steingraber. (1997). *Living Downstream.* The personal story of a scientist who has been the victim of pesticide-related disease, and her effort to expose and understand the threats pesticides pose to human health.

John Wargo. (1998). *Our Children's Toxic Legacy.* Wargo, an environmental policy researcher, examines the history of pesticide laws and their failure to protect current and future generations from harm.

Devra Davis. (2002). *When Smoke Ran Like Water.* Internationally recognized cancer expert Devra Davis, who performed groundbreaking research on the environmental causes of breast cancer and other chronic diseases, reviews her career battling environmental pollution.

Criminological interest in corporate crimes of violence broadened throughout the late 1980s and early 1990s. The focus expanded to include workplace violence, health and safety, and environmental crimes of violence (Frank & Lynch 1992). With the 21st century, criminologists have begun to take issues of environmental crime and human health consequences more seriously.

Contemporary research on environmental crime can be traced back to the work of scholars and activists who directed our attention first to white-collar crime, then to corporate crimes, and then to a subset of corporate crimes, corporate crimes of violence. Today, criminologists treat environmental crimes as a special case of corporate violence. But, we still have yet to define the term "environmental crime." Let us begin with a general legal definition provided by Clifford and Edwards (1998, p. 26): "An environmental crime is any act that violates an environmental crime statute." Specifically identifying what constitutes an environmental crime, however, provides many unexpected challenges.

ENVIRONMENTAL CRIME

As noted elsewhere in this work, recognizing harms against the environment as criminal is a relatively new practice. Rebovich (2002) notes that although societal recognition of particular human behaviors as criminal typically takes an extended period of time and involves continuous momentum and pressure from special interest groups, the recognition of pollution as official crimes against the environment occurred quickly. He suggests that high-profile incidents such as those occurring at Love Canal in the late 1970s and at Times Beach, Missouri (which involved dioxin contamination) in the early 1980s attracted extensive public attention to the harms associated with the illegal dumping of hazardous waste and was responsible for the quick passage of federal and state laws designed to protect the environment and people. These incidents, along with media coverage and continued environmentalist efforts played a role in the criminalization of harms against the environment. Lowe, Ward, Seymour, and Clark (1996) note that historically, pollution and pollutants were recognized as technical problems instead of environmental crimes. They credit the recent environmental movement and widely publicized events with reframing the public's opinion of pollution as a crime.

In an insightful account of the difficulties involved with defining "environmental crime," Clifford and Edwards (1998) suggest that even though many of us (including politicians, news reporters, pollsters, and researchers) have heard and used the term, there exists no clear understanding as to what it exactly constitutes. The varied derivatives of the term environmental crime (e.g., "offenses against the environment," "harms to the environment"), they argue, serve to further complicate matters. They add:

> The term environmental crime has been used almost indiscriminately and without any universally accepted definition. Laws, organizations, government agencies, academics, lawyers, and others have added to the confusion by using the term without specifying what they mean (p. 6).

To demonstrate their argument, Clifford and Edwards identify the confusion that exists in differentiating what most consider environmental crime (e.g., illegalities committed in relation to the environment) and the established body of environmental criminology. Environmental criminology, which examines the relationship between social ecology/structural factors and crime, has little, if anything to do with what is called environmental crime. Some researchers, however, have offered terms signifying harms against the environment and identify what is meant by the term.

Lynch and colleagues (2002, p. 111), for instance, suggest that toxic crimes are "corporate behaviors that unnecessarily harm or place humans and the environment at risk of harm through the production and management of hazardous waste in the course of a legitimate business enterprise." Others address corporate violence, which could be considered a subcategory of environmental crime. For instance, Stretesky and Lynch (1999) recognize polluting the environment as an act of corporate violence, while Frank and Lynch (1992, Chapter Six) identify various forms of violence against the environment.

Specifically identifying environmental harms as corporate crime can be somewhat challenging. For instance, some harms to the environment are not necessarily recognized as crimes in a legal sense, and would thus be excluded from definitions that require breaking the law. Clifford and Edwards (1998) suggest that the term environmental crime involves a behavior that violates the law, even though it is often used to describe incidents in which no criminal charges are filed. To elaborate, consider that many acts we currently consider environmental crimes were committed prior to passage of modern environmental legislation. Should those acts be recognized as "offenses against the environment," yet not as "environmental crimes?" The problem is that immoral acts are not considered illegal if they are not addressed by the law. The area of environmental crime, as we note later, is still evolving due to changes in environmental laws. Behaviors that today are "legal but immoral" will become crimes tomorrow, that is, once they are defined in law as a crime. Still, the definition of crime involves a constantly changing interpretation of which harmful behaviors should carry the label crime. Part of the work of those who research environmental crimes is pushing that boundary so that a larger number of acts that threaten human health become recognized as crimes by the legal system.

Using select definitions and particular incidents, we identify how an environmental crime can, and should be recognized as corporate and white-collar crimes. To begin, let us turn to David Friedrichs's (1996, p. 10) definition of white-collar crime:

> a generic term for the whole range of illegal, prohibited, and demonstrably harmful activities involving a violation of a private or public trust, committed by institutions and individuals occupying a legitimate respectable status, and directed toward financial advantage or the maintenance and extension of power and privilege.

Friedrichs's (1996, p. 71) suggestion that "...corporations' contributions to the polluting and poisoning of the environment may well be the most common form of corporate violence" is echoed by Rosoff, Pontell, and Tillman (2002), who suggest that much of our poisoned water comes not from illegal hauling of dangerous waste products, but from the criminal negligence of corporations themselves. They cite the example of the FBI's 1989 raid of Colorado's Rocky Flats nuclear weapons plant, in which a Department of Energy facility operated by Rockwell International had become contaminated to the point that it would take 24,000 years (Brever, 1993) and $2 billion (Sachs, 1993) to cleanup the facility. Further, it was found that

Rockwell was dumping radioactive materials into local rivers ("The Rocky Flats Cover-up...," 1992).

Clearly, Rockwell's behavior contains the elements required by Friedrichs's (1996) definition of white-collar crime. Polluting rivers is clearly "illegal, prohibited, and demonstrably harmful" and covered by the legal requirements of the Clean Water Act. Further, Rockwell (an institution of legitimate and respectable status) engaged in activities that involved a violation of a private or public trust, thus meeting another requirement of Friedrichs's definition. Friedrichs's final requirement is that white-collar crimes be "directed toward financial advantage or the maintenance and extension of power and privilege." Issues surrounding motivation and intent often make it difficult to meet this requirement. For instance, in our example, how do we identify or decide on Rockwell's motivation and intent to commit harm? Short of working closely with Rockwell administrators, we cannot be assured that they polluted rivers out of a need for profit. Perhaps their behavior was the result of absolute ignorance (e.g., they didn't' realize they were harming the environment—although this would be difficult to imagine given the pollutants that were involved). Along these lines, how do we know Rockwell behaved the way it did for the sake of extending its power and privilege?

Without convincing testimony or documentation we cannot determine the motives behind Rockwell's behavior. We can, however, speculate that their pollution of the environment was unnecessary, and even if it is attributable to ignorance, Rockwell is accountable for its actions. One could make a strong argument, based on historical acts of corporate deviance, that Rockwell behaved in a careless manner and contaminated their immediate environment because following proper procedure would have been more time-consuming, labor-intensive, and ultimately, more expensive. The ability of a corporation to grow, as is well known, is based on its ability to generate profits. Further, generating extensive profits enhances the corporation's position in society.

It is easier to fit Rockwell's behavior into other perspectives on corporate crime. Albanese, for example, would label Rockwell's behavior as a "regulatory offense." Clearly, this behavior violates an environmental regulation, and there is no need to discuss the actors' intentions to fit Rockwell's behavior into Albanese's typology (see Albanese, 1995).

In his discussion of corporate environmental crimes, Simon (2000) helps contextualize crimes against the environment, citing the corporate institutionalization of many illegal and deviant environmentally based acts, adding that such acts occur with "alarming frequency" (p. 634), are often international in scope, and involve corruption (including the illegal bribery of officials of foreign governments). Simon adds that the U.S. government, sometimes in cooperation with major industrial corporations, "... is frequently a major environmental polluter" (p. 634), a finding supported by Caldicott (1992). Simon also noted that most environmental violations occur in select industries, including petrochemicals, automobiles, petroleum, and electrical products.

The laws surrounding environmental crimes are continuously evolving, leading to the identification of new forms of environmental crimes. Sometimes, behaviors that have been common become illegal when new scientific evidence of harm is produced. Often, however, such evidence has existed for decades, but has been covered up by corporations (Fagin & Lavelle, 1996). Corporations also use their economic power to lobby lawmakers in an effort to persuade them not to criminalize acts of environmental pollution, such as deep well injection of toxic waste. What do we do when we find evidence that a corporation knew they were harming people, but continued to do so because the behavior in question was not a violation of law while they were doing it? Consider the case of the herbicide (weed killer), atrazine, a long-acting, long-lasting, water insoluble herbicide.

Invented in the 1950s by researchers at what is now Ciba-Geigy, atrazine became the most widely used herbicide in the world. Not surprisingly, atrazine sales make up a significant portion of Ciba-Geigy's chemical sales. Documents contained in files housed at the EPA indicate that Ciba-Geigy submitted evidence of atrazine's carcinogenic (cancer-causing) effects in the 1970s (Fagin & Lavelle 1992, p. 19). Following a series of newly released research, the EPA finally recognized atrazine's negative health impacts in 1984. Other evidence presented to the EPA by Ciba-Geigy noted the widespread distribution of atrazine in U.S. waterways, including the Mississippi River. The U.S. Geological Survey found atrazine in 990 of 1,604 water samples taken from Midwestern rivers, streams, reservoirs, and aquifers between 1989 and 1994. Several foreign nations then banned the use of atrazine. However, in the United States, atrazine's biggest market, it was still legal, though its use was restricted beginning in 1990. While the EPA attempted to further limit the use of atrazine, Ciba-Geigy turned in mountains of paperwork to the agency that attempted to demonstrate atrazine's safety. One report, filed in March of 1995, is 92 volumes, and over 14,000 pages long (Fagin & Lavelle, 1992, p. 22). It was estimated that, since 1983, Ciba-Geigy has spent more than $25 million on research supporting atrazine as "safe and effective."

These facts omit one crucial detail: what about the farmers and people who live near farms in the Midwest who have been exposed to atrazine all these years? At one point, the EPA estimated that a farmer who mixes and applies atrazine had a 1 in 863 lifetime chance of developing cancer, while non-farmers had a 1 in 20,747 chance of developing cancer (EPA Public Docket document, Atrazine, November 9, 1994). It should be noted that it is EPA policy to take action against a chemical when the lifetime chances of it causing cancer are less than 1 in 1,000,000. Even in light of new evidence of atrazine's impact on amphibians' sexual organs (www.ourstolenfuture.org/NewScience/ wildlife/frogs/20020416hayesetal.htm) the EPA has failed to ban its use, and continued registration of the chemical pending further review (set for October, 2003; see www.epa.gov/oppsrrd1/REDs/ atrazine_ired.pdf).

Clearly, the mounting evidence on atrazine's negative health impacts—that it causes cancer in mice; is a suspected human carcinogen; alters the sexual organs of frogs; and has been banned by numerous countries—should cause the EPA to take action as an agency of the federal government charged with protecting public health. Perhaps equally disturbing, however, is the action of Ciba-Geigy executives, scientists, and other industry-funded groups who promote the use of atrazine. While atrazine use remains legal, how are we to view the actions of those who, knowing its dangers, promote its applications to lawns and crops?

Another emerging issue environmental criminology addresses involves environmental justice, or the distribution of environmental harms relative to the race, class, and ethnic composition of local areas. Research on environmental justice, a social justice issue, is arguably a subcategory of environmental crime.

SOCIAL AND ENVIRONMENTAL JUSTICE

Environmental crimes, from a legal standpoint, involve environmentally based acts that fail to meet statutory requirements. Addressing environmental harms from a legal view is a popular approach. However, some analyze environmental issues from social and environmental justice approaches. Ryan (1982), for instance, notes that social justice advocates support equal treatment and equal opportunity for all, while holding constant the qualitative and quantitative options for all. These issues can, and have been addressed with regard to environmental concerns.

Evidence of unequally distributed pollutants dates back to 1971, when research indicated that minority communities were disproportionately exposed to hazardous risks (U.S. Council on Environmental Equity, 1971). Origins of the environmental justice movement can also be traced to the 1972 ruling that resulted from protests in North Carolina over a proposed hazardous waste site in the poorest county in the state. The court recognized the placement of this site as a violation of residents' civil rights and a threat to public health (Ringquist, 2003).

Claims of environmental injustice failed to receive public support until the late 1980s when a series of research studies identified inequities in the distribution of environmental harms disproportionately affecting poor and minority communities (Ringquist, 2003). Ringquist argues that early environmental groups sought to remain distinct from social justice concerns because they were primarily interested in conserving wildlife; not reducing harms in our inner cities. They feared that an alliance with social justice advocates would negatively impact membership levels, particularly since poor minorities certainly do not constitute the bulk of environmental group memberships (Shabecoff, 1990). Regardless, Ringquist notes that there has always been, and remains potential for an alliance between the two groups.

Stretesky and Lynch (1999) note that criminologists have begun to incorporate environmental justice issues, a subcategory of social justice involving, among other things, the study of the relationship between the proximity of racial and ethnic minorities to environmental hazards, into their discipline. Sometimes referred to as "distributive justice" (Kasperson & Dow, 1991), "environmental equity" (EPA, 1990), and/or "environmental racism" (Bullard, 1996), environmental justice research has largely focused on the "spatial relationship between race, ethnicity, economics and hazardous waste facilities" (Stretesky & Hogan, 1998, p. 268). Environmental justice research has predominantly focused on the proximity of industrial pollution to minority communities (e.g., Bullard, 1990; Bullard & Wright, 1992, 1993). Environmental justice, however, "… is also concerned with the social and economic processes that shape racial, ethnic, and economic demographic patterns around existing hazardous waste sites" (Stretesky & Hogan, 1998, p. 268). Stretesky and Hogan (1998, p. 268) suggest that:

Environmental justice means two things. First, it means that environmental hazards should be distributed equally across society and that no individual group, or community should bear a disproportionate burden from this type of health threat. Second, and more ideally, it means that no one should be forced to suffer from the adverse effects of environmental hazards.

Having emerged primarily through the efforts of civil rights activists, environmental justice is largely concerned with reducing the disparities in toxic chemical exposure between minority and non-minority groups (Capek, 1993). However, as Burby and Strong (1997, p. 469) note, environmental justice is not only concerned with race-linked disproportionate exposure to harmful environmental hazards, but also considers "... the exclusion of the views of minorities from policy formulation, and the under-representation of minorities in environmental regulatory agencies" as discriminatory and well within the definition of environmental crime.

The EPA recognized the existence of issues pertaining to environmental justice, with the establishment of the EPA's Office of Environmental Justice. Instead of using the term "environmental justice," the EPA opts for the term "environmental equity" to identify the distribution of environmental risks across various groups/populations and EPA policy responses to those risks (EPA, 1990). In accordance with many environmental justice researchers, an EPA task force found that minority communities are more often exposed to environmental risks than are non-minority communities.

Simon (2000, p. 633) is among those who use the term "environmental racism" to "describe the victimization of people of color by corporate polluters" while Bullard (1996, p. 497) defines environmental racism as "...any policy, practice, or directive that differentially affects or disadvantages (whether intended or unintended) individuals, groups, or communities based on race or color." These and other terms are used to describe practices that, evidence suggests, are clearly discriminatory, although difficult (due to legal constraints) to specifically identify as criminal.

In sum, establishing adequate definitions of environmental crime, environmental justice, and related terms has proven quite difficult. Downey (1998) noted that the lack of consistency in defining the term "environmental justice" has resulted in researchers drawing different conclusions from similar findings. He adds that using the same term to describe different models restricts scientific progress, which in turn requires some consensus on the variety of terms used to describe what is often considered environmental justice. Ringquist (2003, p. 270) echoes these concerns, suggesting that "... we will have no standards with which to judge either the adequacy or the effectiveness of government efforts to ensure environmental equity" until we agree what constitutes discrimination and equity with regard to environmental protection.

Clarification of what constitutes environmental crime and environmental justice (and their derivatives) will likely emerge as research in this area continues. One must avoid becoming overly optimistic, however, that consensus will be reached with regard to any of these terms, as there remains uncertainty regarding what, specifically, constitutes a crime; a term that has existed for a much longer time and undergone much greater scrutiny and examination (e.g., Quinney, 1970; Robinson, 2002) than, for instance, the term "environmental justice." It is hoped that agreement, or at least further clarification, can soon be reached with the intent to focus research energies on issues related to the environment instead of syntax.

CHAPTER 3

History of the Environmental Movement

This chapter examines the history of environmental movements. Our goal is not to provide an exhaustive review of this area, but to provide readers with adequate background materials needed to understand the main issues and engage in independent investigation into environmentalism. In our view, readers who want to learn more about environmental crime issues need to read extensively in the areas of social justice, white-collar crime, and environmental justice, among other areas. Our purpose in this chapter is to review major issues surrounding the development of U.S. environmentalism with the intent to place the remainder of this work into perspective.

Only recently has there been continuous and strong support for the conservation and preservation of the environment. The environmental movement initiated in the 1960s has retained momentum through the turn of the century. This movement is unique in that never before has there been such protracted concern for protecting the environment. Prior to the 1960s, however, several events demonstrate that people in earlier eras recognized the need to protect the environment for the pleasure, health, and well-being of society. As suggested by Frank and Lynch (1992, p. 83), "There have been various environmental movements throughout history which have affected the way we conceptualize the harms done to the environment, plants and animals (e.g., Theodore Roosevelt's 'conservationist movement' in the late nineteenth to early twentieth century)." None of these events, however, impacted society to the extent that post-1960s environmental efforts have (although one could make the argument that each individual event in environmental history contributed in some manner to the recent, notable environmental developments we've experienced, and at the very least, each contributed to protecting the environment).

Clearly, identifying the roots of environmentalism has undoubtedly challenged all who have attempted the task (Athanasiou, 2002). Edwards (1998, p. 31) is among those who identify the difficulties in

25

signifying events largely impacting the current status of environmentalism, suggesting that "The roots of the modern environmental movement are as deeply fractured as environmental activism is today." Such a fractured heritage results in difficulties in any attempt to describe the history of environmentalism. Our attempt, although certainly not comprehensive, highlights historical and current events that have shaped how society views and treats the environment.

THE EARLY HISTORY OF ENVIRONMENTALISM

Although it is likely that earlier societies recognized the value of the environment, documented concern for the environment dates back to 1290 when King Edward I of England, disturbed by the smoke-filled air of London, prohibited the burning of coal while Parliament was sitting. Years later, a German researcher noted the detrimental effects of exposure to various gas and metal pollutants (Bellini, 1986).

The attempt to protect what would become U.S. lands dates back to 1626 when citizens of Plymouth Colony passed ordinances with the intent to moderate the cutting and sale of trees. Similar efforts in this area and around this period, including William Penn's 1681 forest conservation efforts in Pennsylvania (Nash, 1990), demonstrate that concern for the environment is not necessarily a recent phenomena.

Friedrichs (1996) noted that the environmental movement can be traced to the actions of conservationists during the latter part of the nineteenth and the beginning of the twentieth century. At that time, Americans changed their focus from the countryside to the cities, spurred largely by the introduction of labor-saving agricultural machinery, a burgeoning industry, and a surge in urban populations (Nash, 1967). Cities became host to an expanding number of families, and the countryside was no longer recognized as something that required clearing, but something that could instead be the source of recreation.

Switzer and Bryner (1998) noted that most historians recognize the turn of the century as the beginning of an actual environmental movement, at a time when conservationist ideals influenced events of the Progressive Era. Conservation, based on the idea that valuable natural resources must be protected for the sake of future generations, was the primary concern among most early environmental protection efforts, as evidenced in the Progressive Conservation Movement, which took place in the 1890s and 1900s (Edwards, 1998). The Movement would eventually branch in two distinct directions, primarily due to differences in member beliefs regarding the best method to protect the environment. Some promoted the *preservation* of natural resources, which centered around protecting environmental resources because of their intrinsic values and not their economic values. In contrast, others supported the *conservation* approach, which was concerned with quality of life issues for future generations. Conservationists focused on maintaining environmental resources for economic reasons, and in the end would largely prevail over preservationists (Cable & Cable, 1995).

A significant event that impacted environmentalism during this period occurred when the U.S. Census Bureau declared the American frontier closed. This announcement increased concern for preserving the environment (Cable & Cable, 1995) and Americans' perceptions of classical liberalism and the protection of individual rights (Edwards, 1998). Edwards (1998) adds that this event was further impacted by American society transforming from an agrarian-based economy to an industrial one, noting that "Securing economic benefits from natural resources was a major focus of federal laws enacted during this period in history" although "the conservation of natural resources for future generations was one of the most significant priorities" (p. 34).

Several writers from this period offered their input regarding whether to protect the environment and how best to do so. Among the preservationist writers was Henry David Thoreau who believed that "humans required wilderness in order to remain civilized. By communing with nature, humans could stay in touch with their spiritual self. For this to happen, though, nature needed to remain undisturbed by human activity" (Edwards, 1998, p. 34). Other preservationists included: George Catlin, an artist, writer, and advocate for national parks to preserve the American wilderness; and John Muir who argued that "Humans could only sustain their spirituality through exposure to God's undisturbed creations" (Edwards, 1998, p. 34). Later, in 1949, Aldo Leopold wrote *A Sand County Almanac*, which impacted subsequent environmental movements through encouraging readers to form a better appreciation of our environment. Leopold's work is recognized as "...probably the most influential book on conservation ever written" (Schindler, 1995, p. 32).

Other notable conservationists include George Perkins Marsh (1801–1882), whose *Man and Nature; or Physical Geography As Modified by Human Action* (1864) suggested that earlier civilizations perished as a result of destroying their environment; Frederick Law Olmsted (1822–1903), who promoted the development of urban parks for public use and recreation; and John Wesley Powell (1834–1902), whose work was influential in the Reclamation Act of 1902 (Nash,

1976), which established the federal water storage and irrigation policies still in use today (Edwards, 1998).

Gifford Pinchot (1865–1946), a conservationist who impacted environmental efforts through his Washington, DC connections (particularly through his relationship with President Theodore Roosevelt), is often credited with focusing American environmental efforts on conservation as opposed to preservation (Switzer & Bryner, 1998). Pinchot's influence is evident, for example, in a White House Conference on Resource Management he organized in May 1908, which drew 1,000 national leaders. The conference resulted in the leaders asking the federal government to develop a National Conservation Commission to document all U.S. natural resources (Switzer & Bryner, 1998). The conservationist approach became quite popular, particularly among those involved with the federal government.

The Progressive Era (circa 1890–1920) was clearly a period of significant environmental concern, particularly due to the efforts of Theodore Roosevelt, who has been deemed "The undisputed political leader of the Progressive Conservation Movement" (Edwards, 1998, p. 37). Roosevelt's conservationist approach led to his support of strong scientific management of environmental resources. To encourage orderly growth, Roosevelt appointed a Public Lands Commission in 1903 and developed the Inland Waterways Commission in 1907 to best utilize the resources provided by the nation's rivers (Switzer & Bryner, 1998; Edwards, 1998). Similarly, Congress created the National Park Service (1916), established new forests, and passed laws to protect migratory birds and historic sites during the presidencies of Theodore Roosevelt, William Howard Taft, and Woodrow Wilson (Switzer & Bryner, 1998). The Progressive Era is also credited with the establishment of conservation groups such as the National Audubon Society (1901), the Save-the-Redwoods League (1918), the National Parks and Conservation Association (1919), and the Izaak Walton League (1922).

A 1908 White House "Governor's Conference" on conservation and resources is recognized as one of the earliest formal, politically sponsored, environmentally based gatherings. The conference "established extraction rates for renewable resources as well as policies on soil and water conservation and the protection of natural areas" (O'Riordan, Clark, & Kates, 1995, p. 6). Hays (1959) notes, however, that the conference was little more than a political gesture to rationalize unacceptable resource use during the late nineteenth century. Despite its political appearance, the conference was also recognized as the beginning of a period of federal government intervention in natural resource management and pollution control, practices which had been underway in many parts of Europe for about fifty years (O'Riordan et al., 1995).

Despite great progress with regard to environmental issues, the Progressive Era did not occur without controversy. For instance, Edwards (1998, p. 37) notes, "… scientific management of natural resources meant the end of business as usual, and a backlash against the conservation movement . . . ." Groups in the eastern and western parts of the United States were affected differently by the developing environmental legislation and environmental concerns. Westerners, whose lifestyle and economic subsistence were often impacted by environmental legislation, perceived eastern politicians (whose lifestyle and constituents often were unaffected by environmental policy) to be elitist bureaucrats (Edwards, 1998). These conflicts set the stage for the environmental activism in the 1970s through the 1990s. Such was the case with the late 1970s Sagebrush Rebellion in which, after years of frustration with federal land management rules, several western states enacted laws that provided them ownership of all federal lands within their boundaries (Edwards, 1998).

ENVIRONMENTALISM & ECONOMICS, 1910–1930s

Despite the environmental developments during their tenures in the White House, the presidencies of William Taft and Woodrow Wilson were marked by decreased concern for conservation (Edwards, 1998). Taft and Wilson appeared more concerned with other issues (e.g., business), which perpetuated western Americans' belief that easterners were elitist, and created further division between American environmental groups in the East and West. Conflicts among eastern and western Americans generated enhanced concern for environmental issues at the local level, and contributed to the development of grassroots environmental efforts.

In addition to economic stability, environmental policy was a concern to the federal government during the Great Depression (Switzer & Bryner, 1998). President Franklin D. Roosevelt, elected to office in 1932 shortly after the beginning of The Great Depression, brought renewed vigor to the conservationist approach at the federal level (Edwards, 1998). The federal government's focus on conservation was evidenced in the creation of several agencies, including the Tennessee Valley Authority (1933), the Soil Conservation Service (1935), and the Civilian Conservation Corps (1933–1942), with the latter designed to promote the conservationist approach while simultaneously stimulating the economy by employing 2 million previously unemployed young men (Switzer & Bryner, 1998). Legislation enacted during this period included the Taylor Grazing Act of 1934, which provided the federal government regulatory control over public lands in the Western portion of the United States (Edwards, 1998).

In discussing the "apex of the conservation movement," Edwards notes that 1930s environmental practices "were human centered and intended to serve economic needs. The laws were enacted, for the most part, to conserve, protect, reconstruct, or prolong natural resources in order to support their use for economic purposes" (1998, p. 42). The 1930s also brought the development of two important preservationist groups: The Wilderness Society (1935) and The National Wildlife Federation (1936) (Dunlap & Mertig, 1992).

DECLINING ENVIRONMENTALISM, 1941–1960

The end of World War II and postwar America are recognized as proud times in American history. Wartime success and economic dominance generated much national pride. Along with economic dominance, however, came environmental destruction. American economic dominance was largely the result of increased emphasis on, and developments in industry. Industrialization accelerated development of synthetic chemicals, nuclear power, and toxic pollutants. Friedrichs (1996, p. 71) argues that modern pollution problems are attributable, in part to the "dramatic increase in the production of toxic wastes, especially since World War II."

The 1950s have been characterized as "… a heady time, rich in excitement, danger and promise" (Schindler, 1995, p. 32). Switzer and Bryner (1998) note that Americans shifted their interest in the environment following World War II, with recreational concerns taking precedent over concerns for scientific management. They note that "Over thirty million Americans toured the national parks in 1950" (1998, p. 7), which left a great need for the government to update, preserve, and protect these natural resources. In response, the National Park Service provided a 10-year improvement program "wish list," that would serve as a guide for the development of national parks and recreational areas. Aside from government-sponsored efforts, several other groups contributed to protecting the environment. For instance, the Defenders of Wildlife (founded in 1947) was concerned with habitat protection, while in the early 1950s The Nature Conservancy began to acquire tracts of land to protect the habitats of endangered species (Switzer & Bryner, 1998).

Schindler (1995, p. 32) notes that during the 1950s, "The public was beginning to be sensitized. Warnings of deteriorating environment were coming in from all over." These warnings began to shift public attitudes toward the environment, eventually culminating in the beginning of the modern environmental movement.

RECLAIMING THE ENVIRONMENT, THE 1960s

During the 1960s, environmental issues involved conflict between proponents of industrial growth and environmentalists and their supporters. Parks and wilderness areas were of concern not only to environmentalists, but to much of society. It was during the 1960s that the foundations of many current environmental laws were passed. The decade is also credited with substantial development in environmental groups (Switzer & Bryner, 1998). Authors Rachel Carson (*Silent Spring*) and Paul Ehrlich (*The Population Bomb*) drew attention to environmental issues in the 1960s, highlighting harms associated with pesticides and the dangers associated with explosive population growth. Carson's work, in particular, is recognized as a primary motivation for many to examine the environmental harms associated with industry, especially the chemical industry. As evidence of the tension and conflict between environmentalists and industry during this period, the chemical industry accused Carson of involvement in a "communist plot" to undermine U.S. agriculture (Athanasiou, 2002). Switzer and Bryner (1998) note that other authors (e.g., Murray Bookchin) offered pessimistic predictions of environmental harms, resulting in a gloomy societal outlook for the environment.

In addition to the influence of writers highlighting environmental concerns, several incidents drew substantial attention to the need to preserve/conserve the environment. Events such as two oil spills less than six miles off the coast of Santa Barbara, California, the 1969 declaration that Lake Erie was "dead" as a result of industrial pollution (Markham, 1994), and the fire that engulfed the Cuyahoga River when it spontaneously burst into flames (Cockrell, 1992) underscored the need to better protect the environment. Frank and Lynch (1992) argue that environmental movements of the 1960s introduced the idea that environmental harms such as those noted above should be recognized as violence. Friedrichs (1996) adds that media coverage of these incidents, a growing awareness of environmental harms in the politically active middle class of America, and the technological advances designed to identify industrial pollution greatly contributed to increased societal concern for the environment.

Events of the 1960s contributed favorably to the subsequent move to criminalize environmental harms (Yeager, 1991). Accordingly, significant and substantial environmental legislation made its way through Washington, DC during this period. The first Clean Air Act (1963; later amended to the Air Quality Act in 1967) and the Water Quality Act (1965) are two of the hallmark pieces of environmental legislation passed during this period. Along with increased legislation came an expanding number of environmental groups and greater participation in existing groups, which forced the federal government to "take a more pervasive role in solving what was beginning to be called 'the environmental crisis.' The limited partnership between the federal government and the states was insufficient to solve what was already being spoken of in global terms" (Switzer & Bryner, 1998, p. 10). As a result, the latter part of the 1960s "... was marked by social unrest and the public's misgivings about governments' commitment to the causes of peace and social justice" (O'Riordan et al., 1995, p. 6).

UNSTABLE ENVIRONMENTALISM, THE 1970s

For Switzer and Bryner (1998), society's unstable attitude with regard to concerns for the environment is best exemplified by the decade of the 1970s. Environmental concerns at this time were impacted by: (1) several significant incidents resulting in harm to the environment; (2) political actions in response to societal recognition of harms to the environment; and (3) the institutionalization of environmental groups. One could argue that this period signifies the beginning of modern environmental protection efforts (Athanasiou, 2002), marked by the initial celebration of Earth Day in 1970. Although societal concerns for the environment were attenuated by frustrations over the war in Vietnam and a struggling economy, public recognition of the environment as a major issue continued throughout the decade. Overwhelming public support for the first Earth Day is recognized as having "solidified popular demand for an increase in environmental protection efforts" (Edwards, 1998, p. 43).

During the first Earth Day, millions demonstrated in support of the environment, citing the harms associated with environmental abuses, and generating support for the passage of landmark environmental legislation including the Endangered Species Act (1973), the Safe Drinking Water Act (1974), and a Presidential order that created the EPA (1970). Although widespread public interest in environmental issues quickly dissipated after Earth Day 1970 due to continuing economic problems and the war in Vietnam, "The 20 years following the first Earth Day saw unprecedented increases in public awareness, scientific knowledge, and government actions on environmental issues, not only in the United States but around the world" (O'Riordan et al., 1995, p. 6). Politicians quickly seized the opportunity to capitalize on public support for the environment.

Both President Nixon and Congress quickly recognized and adapted to the public's concern for the environment. Nixon created the National Environmental Policy Act in 1970, recognized as a move "... to integrate the economy and the environment into 'productive harmony'" (O'Riordan et al., 1995, p. 6). Nixon declared the 1970s "the environmental decade," (similar declarations were made by both George H. and George W. Bush) and urged his staff to expeditiously process new legislative proposals. When Congress failed to implement the legislation needed to create a federal environmental agency to develop and enforce environmental regulations, Nixon established the EPA through executive order (Switzer & Bryner, 1998). Congress, meanwhile, enacted over 20 major pieces of environmental protection legislation. Many refined earlier bills, while others created new areas of environmental protection, including marine mammal protection and pesticide and toxic substance regulation (Switzer & Bryner, 1998). Many of these major pieces of legislation remain in place today.

As in the 1960s, several high-profile events that resulted in substantial harm to the environment shifted public concern toward environmental protection during the 1970s. The 1973 Arab oil embargo, the 1979 meltdown at the Three Mile Island nuclear plant, and extensive media coverage of the harm caused by toxic dumping at Love Canal in Niagara Falls, New York, were among these incidents (Switzer & Bryner, 1998). These high-profile events continued to occur along with "hundreds, if not thousands, of more local, less newsworthy events" (Couch & Kroll-Smith, 1997, p. 187).

Aside from high-profile incidents and political posturing over environmental harms, the 1970s environmental movement was also impacted by the continued development of increasingly powerful environmental interest groups. Greater numbers of individuals were associating themselves with the growing variety of environmental groups. Edwards (1998) is among those who recognize the early 1970s as a time when the environmental movement became institutionalized. While the growth in size and scope of environmental interest groups would seem to result in substantial benefits for supporters of environmental protection, several events during the 1970s (and 1980s) shaped the environmental movement; events which have also impacted modern environmental efforts.

The 1970s saw the beginning of industry and business involvement in environmental issues, which changed the playing field with regard to pro-environmental efforts, legislation, and support. Switzer and Bryner (1998, p. 28) suggest that "As the goals of the movement began to expand from conservation to environmentalism in the late 1960s and early 1970s, so too did the potential impact on business and industry, which had never really felt threatened before." Environmental interest groups were also being affected by the increasingly wide range of environmental topics requiring attention, and the need for extensive financial resources and technical expertise to promote particular causes. These increased burdens resulted in business and industry maintaining a notable advantage over many environmental organizations (Switzer & Bryner, 1998). The resultant fragmentation among environmental interest groups led to expansive interpretations of the term environmentalism.

Such pressures explain, in large part, why many mainstream environmental groups relocated to Washington, DC and used lobbying as a means of self-promotion. Edwards (1998, p. 44) notes that these groups were recognized as the voice of environmental policies on Capitol Hill and "Eventually, the Washingtonization of these groups had a profound impact on the environmental movement itself, both in Washington and in the rest of the country." Their efforts, however, would soon lead to a split within the environmental movement.

Dunlap and Mertig (1992) note that membership in and financial contributions to mainstream environmental groups continued to grow during the 1970s. By the 1980s, the membership of many environmentally conscious groups had doubled (Dowie, 1995). The increase is attributed, in large part, to the Reagan administration's move to limit environmental enforcement efforts by reducing the budgets of the EPA and other environmental-based efforts, and appointing people who favored businesses at the expense of the environment to influential governmental positions (Dunlap & Mertig, 1992; Lester, 1989; Switzer & Bryner, 1998). Nevertheless, having succeeded in the nation's capital, and with increased membership, mainstream environmental groups drew the admiration and support of many, and maintained an important place in protecting the environment.

While environmental groups were gaining ground in Washington, they were losing favor at the local level. Individuals felt that localized issues were being ignored by environmentalists in Washington, DC.

This feeling eventually created a distrust between local and national environmental groups (Edwards, 1998). Dowie (1995) suggests that environmentalists in Washington, DC became indistinguishable from other political figures, a position supported by Ferkiss (1995), who suggests that in addition to previous accusations of elitism was the claim that DC environmental groups had become another group of well-paid bureaucrats who had lost touch with their constituents.

Perhaps one of the most significant and radical branches of the environmental movement also appeared in the 1970s. According to Athanasiou (2002), the anti-nuclear movement, which drew massive public support and has hard-line environmental connections, was founded in 1974.

Toward the end of the 1970s, newly elected President Jimmy Carter, who had strong environmental tendencies, found it difficult to achieve much on this front as the American economy slipped deeper into recession. A depressed economy would create more difficult times for the environmental movement during the 1980s, especially under the Reagan White House.

WHERE HAVE ALL THE ENVIRONMENTALISTS GONE: THE 1980s

Switzer and Bryner (1998) suggest that the Reagan administration's concern for deregulation, budget cuts, downsizing government, and installing people into government posts who held their more conservative worldview hampered many environmentally based legislative initiatives, and significantly and detrimentally impacted environmental policy for the next ten years.

Reagan's penchant for deregulation and tax cuts had a tremendous impact on the EPA, and its ability to act on environmental matters of grave concern. Simultaneously, environmental activism adopted a grassroots approach. The Reagan administration and other politicians overlooked the substantial growth and potential impact of these groups on efforts to protect the environment (Edwards, 1998). Throughout the 1980s, while Reagan was attempting to deregulate at the federal level, local activists were forcing increased regulation at the local level.

Deeming himself "the environmental president" during his 1988 campaign, George H. Bush faced repairing the damage caused by the Reagan administration (both in terms of public support and actual environmental reparations) and several new environmental problems. Among the problems was global warming, which had important international implications (Switzer & Bryner, 1998). Despite his reluctance to accept the existence of global warming, the George H. Bush administration is credited with passing two major pieces of legislation (the Clean Air Act Amendments of 1990 and the 1992 Energy Policy Act), which symbolized a break from congressional legislative actions under Republican administrations (Switzer & Bryner, 1998).

Frank and Lynch (1992, p. 83) note that renewed interest in the environment continued into the 1990s; a decade originally termed the "Era of Environmentalism." The 1990s brought about "green political parties" (whose platforms are structured by environmental concerns) in numerous countries, including the United States (Frank & Lynch, 1992; Postrel, 1990; Walijassper, 1990), and recycling programs designed to reduce environmental harms caused by household waste. As Frank and Lynch (1992) note, marketing strategies in some American companies used recycling and environmental concerns to attract consumers.

THE ENVIRONMENT RETURNS: THE 1990s

At the close of the 1980s, membership in national environmental organizations leveled off and began to decline (Szasz, 1994). During the early 1990s, people began to shift their allegiance from large, national environmental groups, to local, grassroots organizations involved in, among other issues, struggles for environmental justice. This movement, captured by Ralph Nader's political position and several groups he sponsored, such as Democracy Rising, influenced the development of the American Green Party.

Several events around this time, however, would further boost environmental activism, including Earth Day 1990 and the 1992 Earth Summit. Compared to the 1970 Earth Day, the 1990 celebration (the twentieth anniversary) was much broader in scope, involving a wider array of groups, such as the business community and ethnic minorities, and generating a more upbeat mood. The 1990 Earth Day is credited with garnering support for legislation that otherwise may not have passed (O'Riordan et al., 1995).

The 1992 Earth Summit, formally titled the "U.N. Conference on Environment and Development," was held in Rio de Janeiro, Brazil. This conference also generated increased concern for the environment. This groundbreaking meeting highlighted the need for global responses to environmental issues, and identified the differences between industrialized and developing nations in terms of their contributions to, and expectations about their response to environmental pollution (Switzer & Bryner, 1998). This meeting has been recognized as a starting point for establishing global environmental policies and approaches. It was the second of three United Nations conferences designed to address environmental issues (the others are addressed later in this chapter). Among other accomplishments, these meetings facilitated cooperation between international groups, as well as government organizations and non-government groups (O'Riordan et al., 1995). It was around this time that a change in the American political structure appeared to enhance pro-environmental efforts.

Environmentalists expressed great excitement at the 1992 presidential election of Democrat Bill Clinton and Vice President Al Gore, the latter known for his particularly pro-environment stance. Clinton soon appointed Bruce Babbitt (former head of the League of Conservation Voters) Secretary of the Interior, Carol Browner to the EPA, and several other pro-environment professionals to various influential positions within his cabinet. Environmentalists believed their hard work had finally paid dividends as they now had in place one of—if not the—"greenest" administrations ever (Dowie, 1995).

Their excitement would soon diminish, however, as the new Clinton administration failed to approach the expectations of environmentalists. For instance, the administration chose to compromise with congressional opponents on many environmental issues as opposed to asserting its authority (Ferkiss, 1995). Dowie (1995) cites a diminished environmental influence in Washington, DC as a primary reason behind the Clinton administration passing only one meaningful piece of legislation during Clinton's first two years in office, adding that the administration continuously failed to protest anti-environmental efforts by industry, special interest groups, and Congress. For instance, the Clinton administration is charged with failing to provide ample support for Babbitt's move to reassume control of public lands from ranchers (Ferkiss, 1995).

The 1994 election of a Republican Congress once again challenged the historical and notable environmentalist accomplishments painstakingly pieced together over the previous decade. The new Congress drew attention to the financial cost and regulatory burdens associated with environmental protection, and Republican House Leader Newt Gingrich's "Contract with America" echoed Reaganism in that it called for reduced government regulation and the promotion of economic development as opposed to preservation (Switzer & Bryner, 1998). Switzer and Bryner (1998, p. 16) note that "Republicans in Congress sought to reduce environmental regulation through cutting EPA and Interior Department budgets, attaching riders to appropriations bills that reduced specific protections, and introducing major rewrites of the leading environmental laws."

The Republican stronghold on environmental regulation, however, did not have the impact many anticipated. Facing attacks from concerned environmentalists across the country, an inspired President Clinton challenged the Republican agenda and subsequently watched his popularity climb. Republicans soon ceased their attacks on environmental regulation and laws (Switzer & Bryner, 1998). Switzer and Bryner (1998) suggest that Clinton's reelection in 1996 was due in part to his willingness to oppose the congressional Republicans' deregulation approach, adding that Bruce Babbitt was instrumental in the president's newfound concern for environmental issues.

Membership in environmental groups was stagnant in the early 1990s. Environmentalists attributed this lack of growth to the ongoing recession (Dowie, 1995). Dowie (1995), however, argues that the problem was the result of self-inflicted wounds. Specifically, he cites the lack of an effective DC presence as a primary cause. This concern is echoed by others, including Ferkiss (1995) who suggests that mainstream environmental groups often share different views on national politics and poorly coordinate their lobbying efforts. Ferkiss adds that the struggle over the North American Free Trade Agreement (NAFTA) notably divided mainstream environmental groups. Years later, the problem remained, as Goldstein (2002) notes, that despite substantial improvements to the environment since 1970 and a substantial increase in donations to environmental groups around the turn of the century (donations to environmental groups alone increased to over $6.4 billion in 2001), the Earth's most serious concerns remain "as intractable as ever, making environmentalists vulnerable to charges that green groups have prospered while the earth has not" (Goldstein, 2002, p. 58). Goldstein questions whether environmental tactics are appropriate to address pressing issues such as global warming, loss of biodiversity, and marine depletion. The lack of coordination and focus at the national level encouraged a notable shift in environmentalist efforts toward local-level participation.

Athanasiou (2002) adds that part of the problem was a change in the strategy of corporations. During the 1970s, corporations strongly opposed environmental groups. By the 1980s, they learned to cooperate with, and contribute to them. By the 1990s, however, corporations had changed tactics, creating their own "environmental front groups," and donating to these groups instead. These groups have names that make them appear environmentally friendly while their work reflects the nature of their corporate sponsorship (see Karliner, 1997). Table 3-1 includes a selection of these groups.

Table 3-1: Selection of Groups That Sound Environmentally Friendly, Yet Support Industries Operating in the United States (Source: Greenpeace)

Alliance for Environment and Resources. Founded in 1985 by the California Forestry Association, this group is supported by the timber industry in its attempts to reduce logging restrictions.

B.C. Forest Alliance. Founded in 1991, this group includes the 13 largest Canadian lumber companies seeking to improve the image of the Canadian lumber industry.

Business Council for Sustainable Development. Founded in 1991 and supported by Swiss billionaire-industrialist Stephen Schmidheiny, this group was created to address environmental policies and weaken treaties and alliances that would be formed at the 1992 Earth Summit.

Citizens for the Environment. Formed in 1990 by the Citizens for a Sound Economy and funded by major corporations, this lobby group/think tank has no citizen members. It promotes deregulation of the economy as a means for solving environmental problems.

The Global Climate Coalition. This group, founded in 1989, represents business interests in an attempt to convince people, especially Congress, that global warming is a myth.

Information Council for the Environment. Founded in 1991, this group represents the interests of major coal companies in garnering support for coal power and detracting attention from alternative energy sources by convincing people that global warming is a myth.

National Wetlands Coalition. Founded in 1989 by the law firm Van Ness, Feldman, and Curtis, this lobby group represents miners, utilities, and real estate developers that seek to open wetlands for development and reduce wetland development restrictions.

The shift away from widespread support of national environmental issues to local-level, grassroots environmental concerns is a recent movement within the larger environmental movement (Brown & Mikkelsen, 1990; Goldman, 1991). Cable and Benson (1993) note that community-based grassroots environmental groups primarily focus on local environmental concerns, as opposed to the nationally based groups that are more concerned with national environmental policy and legislation. They add that these groups are smaller in size, tend to draw members from lower educational and status groups, and promote enforcement of existing laws and environmental justice as opposed to seeking the creation of new environmental laws or environmental reform (Clark, Lab, & Stoddard, 1995). Edwards (1998) notes that these smaller, grassroot groups are often referred to as NIMBY ("not in my backyard") groups that organize to halt environmental degradation in their communities. While most grassroots efforts do not involve the direct action tactics assumed by more radical environmental groups such as Earth First! and Greenpeace, grassroots groups have undoubtedly helped highlight societal concern for environmental harms and have impacted responses to such acts (Cable & Benson, 1993).

THINK GLOBALLY, ACT LOCALLY

More recent changes in the environmental movement reflect the recognition and adoption of global issues. In identifying how American environmentalist efforts have confronted the global economy, Conca (2000, p. 72) notes:

> Anyone old enough to remember gas lines, Love Canal, or Three Mile Island will recall a time when the environmental movement focused mainly on domestic issues. To be sure, the idea of a fragile planet was always part of the logic of ecology. But the actual work of lobbying for clean air and water, defending endangered species, protecting wilderness, and challenging toxic polluters was mainly a local and national affair.

The American environmental movement adopted a global outlook during the Reagan era. The global outlook was largely encouraged by recognition of the ozone hole and the loss of biodiversity (Conca, 2000). Conca notes, however, that mainstream American environmentalism is unprepared to address economic globalism, as evidenced in their split into competing camps when faced with the difficulties posed by neoliberal globalism, and their ineffective influence during the debate over NAFTA. This unwillingness to address global issues exists despite the claims of scientists in the 1960s who noted the global interconnectedness of critical environmental issues, warning that humans were destroying the Earth; and a 1972 U.N. Conference on the Human Environment in Stockholm, Sweden, in which delegates from around the globe met to discuss these warnings and produced a series of recommendations for government action (Runyan & Norderhaug, 2002).

Concern for global environmentalism is evident in the 2002 United Nations' "World Summit on Sustainable Development," held in Johannesburg, South Africa. The Summit focused on the environmental threats impacting the planet, while examining the extent of 30 years of efforts to protect the environment and offering a look to the future. The event drew considerable interest and was well attended, as evidenced by the 100 world leaders who addressed the Summit, and the roughly 22,000 people who participated including thousands of delegates, non-governmental organizations (NGOs), and members of the media (www.johannesburgsummit.org). The term "sustainable development," as used in the title of the Summit, is widely defined as "that which meets the needs of the present without compromising the ability of future generations to meet their own needs" (Taylor, 2002, p. 29). Time will tell if the Summit has any impact on environmental efforts.

The 2000 presidential election of George W. Bush was seen as a renewed challenge to the environmental movement, which as of 2001 consisted of 30 large organizations with roughly 20 million dues-paying members and thousands of regional and local activist groups (Helvarg, 2001). Helvarg (2001, p. 5) notes:

> Bush's hard line on the environment, including decisions on carbon dioxide, oil drilling, arsenic, mining, forests, oceans and energy, as well as budget cuts that target agencies like the EPA and the Interior Department and law like the Endangered Species Act, is mobilizing the environmental movement in a broader, deeper way than has been seen since the first Earth Day thirty-one years ago.

The challenge exists for instance, in the impending showdown between environmentalists and President Bush, Vice President Cheney and the Republican leadership concerning drilling in the Arctic National Wildlife Refuge (Helvarg, 2001). Similarly, in 2001 Bush announced that the United States would not ratify the Kyoto Protocol (which mandates reductions of 6–8% from emission levels by the years 2008 to 2012 for industrial countries), stating that the United States cannot afford to reduce carbon dioxide emission (Runyan & Norderhaug, 2002). Environmentalists face additional challenges due to the 2002 election of a Republican Senate, and the change in directorship of the Environment and Public Works Committee from Independent Jim Jeffords (a supporter of environmental causes) to Jim Inhofe whose 2002 major campaign contributor was the oil and gas industry (Helvarg, 2001).

Summing up the nature of the modern, and to some extent historical, environmental movement, O'Riordan (1995, p. 9) notes:

> …evidence from opinion polls across the world shows that environmental concern waxes and wanes, depending on the particular driving forces and circumstances. Events of great movement, dramatizing the consequences of misregulation or uncaring greed as well as the sufferings of innocent people and the agony of our own internal contradictions, briefly create martyrs and attract media attention. Pressure groups then capitalize on this to lobby for reform, possibly with the assistance of those in the academic, business, and regulatory communities. But such events are relatively rare; most environmental degradation takes place quietly, far removed from public consciousness.

Couch and Kroll-Smith (1997) argue that similar to the feminist, labor, and civil rights movements, the environmental movement generally appeals to issues of justice and rights to promote particular concerns. One primary benefit of the environmental movement is the recognition, most notably by legislators and politicians, of the threats posed and damage done to the environment. Such recognition resulted in environmental harms becoming "criminalized" and subsequently subject to penalty. Accordingly, the evolution of terms such as "environmental crime," "environmental justice," and "environmental racism," became part of the vocabularies of politicians, researchers, activists, and the public in general. However, some question whether we truly understand these often-used terms.

CHAPTER 4

Environmental Laws: An Overview

This chapter provides some background material useful for navigating the intricacies of environmental law. Environmental law is complex for a number of reasons. First, numerous laws often come into play when environmental violations are at issue. To make this clear, let us compare a potential environmental law violation to a potential criminal law violation. When a behavior violates the penal code, we generally know where to look for a description of the infraction: in the state penal or criminal law statutes. Even though numerous behaviors are described in criminal law, we can find the law violation by using the criminal law index. When an environmental law is broken, however, the description of the rule of law and penalties could be in one of several different environmental statutes at the federal, state, or local level. To locate the exact legal violation where an environmental crime is suspected, we may have to examine a number of different environmental law indices. And, once we have found the appropriate statute(s), there are likely to be jurisdictional issues to settle.

Second, as a form of law, environmental law is relatively new. Consequently, there will be fewer experts in this area, and many lawyers may not even be exposed to courses that teach them about environmental law in law school. Since many key environmental statutes are less than two decades old, the fine points of these laws may not have been completely resolved in the courts. New challenges to these laws emerge on a routine basis, and environmental law is in a constant process of evolution. Therefore, this chapter simply provides an overview of some key features of environmental law. In addition, as social scientists, we are interested in the principles and theoretical perspectives that inform particular positions within the law. Consequently, we also review some of these issues.

THE EMERGENCE OF CONTEMPORARY ENVIRONMENTAL LAW

Prior to the creation of the EPA in 1970, there were few laws, statutes, or acts that directly defined or dealt with environmental crimes. Many of the activities that are now regulated by environmental law were previously addressed with common law remedies. Why the sudden change?

Prior to the 1960s, there was less concern with behaviors that directly threatened the natural environment, or public health as a consequence of degraded environmental conditions. During the 1960s and 1970s, however, levels of pollution increased dramatically, and the effects of pollution were more readily observable. Major events, such as large fish kills, rivers that burst into flames, and human tragedies, such as Love Canal, captured news headlines. Equally important was the emergence of scientific study of the potential human consequences associated with environmental pollution. Chief among these works was Rachel Carson's book, *Silent Spring*, published in 1962. Carson's work detailed the environmental damage being inflicted by widespread applications of unregulated pesticides. Its publication coincided with publicity generated by many other tragedies related to the devastating potential of man-made chemicals, such as Thalidomide, which was responsible for a number of birth defects in the early 1960s.

Carson's book, which was also excerpted in the *New York Times*, created a national controversy concerning the safety of synthetic chemicals such as pesticides. It drew the attention of researchers who began to look at the harmful consequences of synthetic chemicals more earnestly, corporations which produced and defended synthetic chemicals, and the government's responsibility for protecting public health. Increased concern over environmental pollution spread to the general public, which began to worry about how it might be impacted. Because of the increasing frequency of chemical disasters, the plight of animal populations pushed toward extinction by exposure to synthetic chemical pollutants, and increasing rates of diseases among humans that could be attributed to synthetic chemicals in the environment (Colborn, Dumanoski, & Myers, 1998), it became clear that some form of environmental regulation would be needed. In short, contrary to widely argued and popular positions, when left to regulate themselves in a free market, corporate leaders failed miserably in their responsibility to stem the growing tide of industrial pollution.

FROM FREE TO REGULATED MARKETS

Historically, the guiding source of economic regulation in the United States is found in Adam Smith's analysis of free markets and the notion that free markets are guided by the "invisible hand" of competitive market relations. Prior to the 1970s, environmental pollution issues were largely left to be addressed by the functions of the free market economy. The few exceptions to this rule involved regulations aimed at preserving wilderness areas that established federal and state parks in the early 1900s.

Free market economic perspectives assume that consumers would be able to influence manufacturing decisions that negatively impacted the environment by selecting products made by manufacturers who did less damage to the environment. In this way, consumers would act as a balancing market force by redirecting their purchasing power to environmentally friendly products, thus influencing the behavior of manufacturers. This assumption, however, is tied to a second assumption: that in a free market, manufacturers would respond to consumer preferences and demands and produce things in different ways, and thereby provide consumers with alternative choices. If environmental pollution was a consumer concern, then among the choices consumers would have at their disposal was the option of selecting products produced by manufacturers who had made wise environmental-impact decisions. This option, however, can only occur if manufacturers offer these alternatives. The problem was that until recently—and still on a limited basis—manufacturers typically did not offer these alternatives to consumers. Environmentally friendly products tend to be marketed as upscale consumer products. Thus, in contrast to free market assumptions, manufacturers were not responding to consumer demand. To some extent, market freedom appeared to take the form of freedom to ignore consumer and public demands.

As Findley and Farber (2000, pp. 81–84) argue, a free market economic system was not up to the task of protecting the environment. For much of the past century, consumers did not have consumption options when it came to purchasing decisions. For example, until recently there were no "clean cars" in the marketplace. Consumers could not select solar- or wind-powered generation over more conventional fossil fuel alternatives. Indeed, even today, fossil fuels are the preferred choice of manufacturers. This preference has been supported most recently by policy initiatives pursued by George W.

Bush's presidential administration, which has close links to the fossil fuel industry.

In making their argument that the free market failed to protect the environment and human health, Findley and Farber (2000) discuss two key free market issues that impact environmental protection: external costs and external benefits.

External costs are monetary losses or potential expenditures incurred by someone other than the manufacturer of a commodity. We illustrate this point using a fictional example. The *Wood Company* (a fictional company) produces lumber products. It harvests raw wood from national forests under a contract with the federal government. It processes the raw wood employing the local water resources in *Little Town*, and empties the water it used in the production process into the local river. This method of disposing of waste water alters the PH of *Little Town River* because *Wood Company* adds acid products in the production process which, when expelled into the river, lowers the PH of the river water. Furthermore, *Wood Company's* production process employs machinery that generates a strong odor, and air pollution composed of smoke, particle matter, carbon monoxide, sulfur dioxide, and dioxin. These air pollutants degrade local air quality, cause various diseases and, when combined with the odor, make areas adjacent to the facility uninhabitable. The declining river PH causes the death of aquatic plants and insects, affecting the downstream water quality for many miles. Because of the deteriorating water quality conditions, the local fish population begins to die which, in turn, impacts *Little Town's* fishing industry. Further, the harvesting of trees from the national forest leads to the extinction of rare, local bird species that has been the subject of *Little Town's* tourism industry. With the tourism and fishing industries in a state of decline, the local economy falters, unemployment increases, and property values fall. At the same time, profits for *Wood Company* increase, and the value of its stock rises. In fact, with the demise of rare, local bird species, the federal government allows *Wood Company* to increase its tree harvest.

The fictional scenario depicted above illustrates a variety of external costs related to *Wood Company's* actions. From the financial perspective of *Wood Company*, nothing is wrong with this scenario: the company is economically healthier today than a few years earlier. Its production practices, which have negatively affected the local environment, people, and economy, have little direct impact on *Wood Company*. Indeed, this happens because the costs of its production process are externalized, that is, borne by others outside the corporation. From an economic standpoint, *Wood Company* has no incentive to reduce the level of environmental damage it creates. In fact, *Wood Company* benefits from the environmental damage.

In response to this kind of situation, Findley and Farber (2000, p. 83) note that "because the free market provides inadequate incentives [to reduce polluting behavior], the government must intervene to limit external costs and facilitate production of external benefits and collective goods." Given that corporate behavior is economically motivated, the question becomes: how can we introduce some factor that alters *Wood Company's* polluting behavior in ways that produce external benefits? This is precisely the role that environmental laws are designed to fulfill.

Environmental laws, regulations, and punishments generate external benefits or socially valued outcomes through a variety of mechanisms. One mechanism transforms external costs into internal costs. Simply put, environmental laws and regulations accomplish this task by providing incentives to reduce pollution and disincentives for polluting. These incentives and disincentives can be easily turned into monetary outcomes that become part of the cost-benefit analysis corporations make with respect to behaviors that may impact the environment.

Typically, environmental laws make corporations take notice of behaviors that impact the environment in one of three ways: (1) penalties and fees; (2) taxes and subsidies; and (3) flexible market incentives (Ferrey, 1997, pp. 8–11; Findlay & Farber, 2000, pp. 83–84). We describe each of these environmental protection strategies below.

INTERNALIZING EXTERNAL COSTS: THE ROLE OF REGULATION

Penalties and Fees

Penalties and fees attached to polluting behavior require polluters to pay at least some (but usually not all) of the costs associated with polluting activities. By attaching a penalty or fee to a polluting activity, environmental regulations effectively transform the external costs of polluting (e.g., environmental harms that impact entities outside the corporation) into internalized costs of production that must be included in a corporation's business costs.

In theory, penalties and fees would appear to be a useful mechanism for controlling polluting behavior because they turn the socialized costs of polluting (i.e., externalized costs) into concrete economic losses for businesses. If, for instance, a corporation must pay a $1 penalty or fee for each pound of pollution it produces, and the corporation produces a millions pounds of pollution a year, then it will lose an additional $1 million. It does not really matter to the corporation whether this economic loss is a penalty (e.g., a fine for an activity) or a fee (e.g., the cost of disposing of waste into a river). What matters is that the government's response causes the corporation to log a loss against its profits.

Despite the fact that penalties and fees appear to make logical sense as mechanisms for controlling polluting behavior, these reactions tend to have less effect than intended for three reasons. First, penalties and fees tend to be small relative to profits and, consequently, are not an effective means for transforming external costs into sufficiently large internal costs that impact polluting behavior—they rarely approach the $1 million mark used in the example above.

Second, environmental regulations are often not enforced stringently, or are enforced irregularly, resulting in a low apprehension rate. Because they are unlikely to get caught, corporate executives can assume that the penalty or fee is unlikely to impact their business's profits. Unfortunately, this outcome has much to do with the nature of economic production and budgetary constraints faced by environmental protection agencies. There are a large number of businesses that produce pollutants, but relatively few environmental law enforcement agents to detect these violations. As a result, environmental law enforcement agencies have instituted programs that seek the voluntary compliance and reporting of polluting activities by polluters. In other words, the EPA asks polluters to self-report how much and what types of pollution they release into the environment. The effort to achieve compliance with self-reporting policies related to polluting activities and violations are integral elements of taxes and subsidies, and flexible market incentive responses. EPA enforcement practices are further discussed in Chapter 6.

Third, corporations shift penalties and fees onto consumers who end up paying the corporation's financial pollution liabilities. Consumers are not told, of course, that the extra cost of the product they have been consuming now goes to pay an environmental penalty. If they were, they might use this information as if the market were really free and competitive, and switch to more environmentally friendly products.

Taxes and Subsidies

Taxes and subsidies offer different mechanisms for internalizing pollution costs that also reward efforts at pollution reduction (Ferrey, 1997, p. 8). Pollution taxes endeavor to internalize the costs of polluting by taxing polluters when they emit pollutants in excess of a specified threshold (a specific or acceptable pollution amount). These taxes are designed to encourage pollution generators to seek alternative means of production (e.g., Lynch and Stretesky, 2001) that reduce pollution outputs. Subsidies that reimburse costs for installing pollution control devices, for example, serve the same purpose. To some extent, taxes are similar to penalties, while subsidies serve the same function as rewards for pollution reduction. Ferrey (1997) suggests that one of the benefits of taxes and subsidies is that they can be easily adjusted to reflect changing environmental conditions. If, for instance, pollution reduction efforts are not meeting expectations, both taxes and subsidies can be raised by the EPA. In contrast, the EPA does not always have such tight control over the penalties meted out for pollution violations, especially in cases for which a judge renders the penalty decision.

Like penalties, tax and subsidy systems also have limitations. The primary problem is establishing an effective external control or monitoring mechanism. An additional problem involves translating the harms caused by pollution into monetary costs (e.g., quantifying the costs of pollution; Ferrey, 1997, p. 9). Another problem stems from the effort to determine the level at which taxes and subsidies will accomplish their stated goal. How large a tax (or subsidy) is needed to get polluters to change their behavior? Accomplishing this task may require a good deal of trial and error. Finally, the income that results from a pollution tax may be insufficient to fund the governmental monitoring system needed to oversee a program of pollution reduction. To address these deficiencies, other alternatives, such as flexible market incentives, are also used by the EPA.

Flexible Market Incentives

Flexible market incentives (FMIs) operate in much the same way as taxes and subsidies at a very general level. Corporations, however, have greater control over FMIs, while they have much less control over taxes and subsidies. FMIs are similar to a credit and debit system. A corporation can earn pollution credits by generating less pollution than environmental regulations specify, while their "pollution account" with the EPA is debited when it exceeds those legal limits. The corporation must pay off its pollution debits with either cash or pollution credits.

FMIs are typically constructed on a regional basis to reflect localized pollution issues. Thus, in contrast to some EPA rules, which are standardized for the nation, FMI rules contain flexible standards and criteria that depend on the location of pollution emitters and levels of pollution in the region in which a manufacturer is located. In this flexible market scheme, the EPA may, for example, determine that a specific region has an elevated level of pollutant X, and that it is in the interest of public health to reduce the output of pollutant X in that region. To do so, the EPA first studies the extent of the problem, determines the current level of pollutant X outputs, estimates the health consequences associated with that level of output, and then sets a pollution reduction target that will enhance public or environmental health. To achieve this pollution reduction target, the EPA must also determine how much of pollutant X will be allowed to be emitted in the region under examination. Once they have determined the aggregate level of pollutant X output that will be allowed, the EPA then divides this sum and distributes pollution allowances to individual manufacturers of pollutant X. Each individual company must then decide what it will do to stay within its allowance for pollutant X. To do so, some companies may decide to close down a plant or limit production of commodities that generate pollutant X. Other companies may install pollution control devices, while still others may seek alternative methods of production that allow it to continue its current level of operation without generating pollutant X.

But, what if *Company A* decides to exceed its pollution allowance for pollutant X? Or, what if *Company A* experiences increased demand for its product, and in the process of meeting that increased demand exceeds its pollution allowance? Built into the FMI system is an allowance for buying, selling, and trading pollution. In effect, if *Company A* exceeds its allowance for pollutant X, it may buy unused pollution credits (or it may trade its own unused pollution credits for a different pollutant) from another company. This outcome does not necessarily reduce the overall emission of pollutant X within the region, but it establishes incentives to reduce pollution for some companies because they can profit by selling their credits. In other words, companies that are successful at reducing levels of pollution may reap a financial reward by selling their credits to competitors.

Some FMI programs also allow companies to accumulate credits for future use. For instance, the fictitious *Corporation Planned Growth* has laid out a development program for future facility expansion. At the same time, its leadership decides that it will begin to curtail production at a few existing plants. Knowing that it will possibly exceed its pollution credit allowance in the future, *Corporation Planned Growth* executives decide not to sell the pollution credits it has saved through curtailed production, and instead saves these credits for future use at its new facilities.

The kind of system described above cannot work, however, unless there is also a penalty for failing to reduce the aggregate level of a pollutant within a region. What, for instance, could the EPA do if all companies that produced pollutant X within the region met and agreed that they would ignore the EPA's regulation and continue to produce unacceptable levels of pollutant X? If all companies acted in this way there would be no pollution credits to buy, which would mean each company would have a pollution debit with the EPA. To dissuade companies from acting this way, the EPA turns pollution debits into fines, and in some cases, may even be able to prosecute violators in other ways.

Another means of achieving pollution reductions under FMI is through the use of pollution offset requirements. Offset requirements differ from the more general system described above because they only allow trading of pollutant levels within a company and within a region. Let us say, for example, that the fictitious *Big Corporation* wants to build a new facility that will increase its production of pollutant X. The proposed plant's pollutant X output would have to either be offset by reductions in pollutant X at other plants in the region owned by *Big Corporation*, or offset by the reduction of some other pollutant at *Big Corporation* plants in the region as indicated by the EPA. Offset requirements, therefore, are more stringent than general market trading allowances because they force pollution producers to reduce emissions without recourse to pollution credits that may be available in the broader regional marketplace.

In theory, FMIs, like subsidies, provide incentives for exceeding the expectations for pollution production set forth in regulation. This kind of social control response is quite different from that encountered by criminologists when they study criminal law penalties for rule violations. There are no incentives for not behaving criminally in criminal law; the criminal law, for example, does not allow a burglar to trade the number of burglaries s/he did not commit for a burglary they did commit. Thus, it should be clear that corporations that violate rules and regulations are not treated in the same ways that we treat other rule violators. What is similar across these two groups of violators (criminal law and environmental law violators) is the idea that we are trying to obtain their compliance with the law, and that often times we use mechanisms that are designed to deter them from socially disapproved behaviors.

Deterrence and Compliance

The primary goals of the social control mechanisms employed to reduce pollution operate through the connected ideas of compliance and deterrence. To some degree, the ideas of compliance and deterrence comprise opposite mechanisms in environmental law. Under EPA rules, compliance is often achieved by offering incentives or rewards for fulfilling obligations stated in law. Examples include subsidies and FMI structures. In contrast, the EPA employs the notion of deterrence when it sets out penalties for violations of rules, such as fines, taxes, or imprisonment. Compliance and deterrence mechanisms resemble the ideas found in the theory of utilitarian calculus set forth by philosopher Jeremy Bentham.

The utilitarian calculus is based on the assumption that rational actors will base their behaviors on the costs and rewards associated with different behavioral options or choices. In theory, these assumptions mean that we can manipulate the behavior of actors by altering the costs and rewards of different behavioral choices. This idea also informed the earlier work of Enlightenment theorists who examined ideas such as rationality. A prime example is found in Adam Smith's (1776) classic analysis of capitalism, *The Wealth of Nations*.

Smith's argument implies that external regulations were unnecessary in capitalist markets because in a free-market system, the actions of individual decision-makers were influenced by the rational actions of self-interested individuals who would calculate the costs and rewards of their behaviors. Theoretically, a marketplace driven by the free competition of various self-interests would create long-term equilibrium without creating an advantage for any particular actor over another. Throughout most of U.S. history, this view dominated the way economic markets were understood, which explains why there were few environmental laws until recently. The history of environmental degradation that characterized the twentieth century, however, indicates that Smith's theory is flawed and a free market economy, like the one in the United States, is incapable of creating a balance of interests. If that explanation is not acceptable, than only two other explanations of the inability of the market to achieve balance and prevent pollution are possible. First, the U.S. economy was, and is, not a truly free market economy. Many radical economists would agree. Second, it is possible that the self-interest of producers is such an overriding concern that it cannot be balanced by the interests of the general public. That is to say, individual wealth goals are more important than social goals concerning a healthy environment.

Regardless of which explanation is adopted, the history of environmental pollution teaches us that self-regulation and self-interest do not provide adequate protection for the environment. As a result, government intervention became necessary to balance the self-interest of producers with public interest in a clean environment. To explain how this system is supposed to operate, we need to briefly return to the work of Bentham.

Bentham applied assumptions about rationality developed by Enlightenment scholars to an analysis of the relationship between crime and punishment. For Bentham, every behavior had potential costs and rewards. Rational actors possessed the ability to examine these costs and rewards, and would select the behavioral option that yielded them the greatest benefit. Rational actors, in other words, choose rewards over costs, and in theory, we can determine which behavior rational actors will select by knowing the costs and rewards associated with each behavioral choice. Further, under this assumption, behaviors could be manipulated by exerting outside influences that altered the costs and rewards associated with each behavioral choice.

Bentham applied these observations to criminal behavior, and argued that criminals could be deterred from committing socially harmful acts by increasing the costs of those acts so that the costs of crime outweighed its rewards. This could be accomplished by increasing the level of punishment associated with socially disapproved behavior.

Applying this idea to pollution prevention, polluting behavior can be deterred or prevented by adding punishments that cause the costs of polluting to rise above its rewards. This idea is similar to the environmental argument that pollution can be prevented by mechanisms that transform external costs into internal costs. In other words, when rational corporate actors make production decisions that generate pollution in a free market for which the costs of pollution are externalized, there is no mechanism that forces them to consider external costs as part of their accounting practices. If, however, the government intervenes and imposes a fine or other penalty for polluting, then the costs of that penalty must be registered against potential profits associated with that production practice.

Theoretically, this idea makes a great deal of sense, especially in capitalist economies in which the primary motivation for production is profit. In practice, however, the idea that penalties are useful mechanisms for deterring polluting behavior has met with limited success. On one hand, the penalties may not be great enough to influence corporate decision-making in the ways predicted by Bentham's theory of utilitarian calculus. On the other hand, it is possible that other conditions outlined by Beccaria in his book, *On Crimes and Punishment* also come into play. These additional conditions include the certainty and swiftness of punishment. First, fines and other penalties are relatively rare in cases of environmental pollution violations. Second, these penalties tend to be disproportionately small compared to corporate profits (and to the harm done, though this is not a consideration in deterrence theory). Third, the meting out of penalties for polluting behavior is not typically swift, and the time lag between the offense and the penalty may include a significant number of years, especially when the legality of the penalty is challenged by the offender. Each of these penalty-related outcomes reduces the assumed effectiveness of deterrence strategies.

In sum, deterrence has the potential to be a useful mechanism for controlling corporate behavior given that corporations are rational actors that calculate the costs and rewards of their behaviors. Indeed, these kinds of calculations are an integral part of planning in a capitalist economy. For this reason, the EPA endorses deterrence as a major mechanism for controlling polluting behavior. In practice, however, deterrence often fails to accomplish the mission of significant pollution reductions. In turn, the EPA also relies on mechanisms of social control that attempt to gain the compliance of corporations without having to resort to the use of punishment or coercive means of social control. Compliance is a complex pollution control mechanism, and we discuss this practice further below.

Compliance Strategies

The federal Clean Air Act, originally passed in 1963, was amended in 1990. One key feature of the amendments involved the addition of compliance provisions in the National Ambient Air Quality Standards (NAAQS). The compliance provisions in NAAQS involve an effort to make state governments more responsible for addressing air pollution and air quality issues falling within their legal boundaries. This revision forced states to become more active in ensuring that levels of air pollution and air quality were brought within acceptable limits delineated in the Clean Air Act. States could do this in a number of ways as long as their plans were approved by the EPA.

The EPA air monitoring program instituted under NAAQS identifies geographic areas that are either in compliance with (compliance areas), or not in compliance with (in noncompliance, or noncompliance areas) EPA air quality standards for specific pollutants. States containing noncompliance areas must submit a plan for achieving compliance to the EPA. If the state fails to submit a workable plan, or if the plan fails to achieve compliance by a specified date, then the state can be penalized. These penalties include reductions in federal funding for highways and the imposition of offset requirements within a region or area.

As noted earlier, an offset requirement involves a condition that limits the addition of new pollution sources (e.g., new production facilities, or expansion of existing production and pollution outputs) within a noncontainment area (an area where an identified pollutant is above EPA threshold levels) *unless* there is an equivalent reduction in pollution emissions at existing facilities. To determine whether emitted pollutants in an area fall within legal requirements, facilities are required to monitor the airborne pollutant outputs they generate and report this information to the EPA. The EPA can then take each of these individual reports and sum up the total level of pollution being produced in a region.

What happens when the sum of pollution reported by individual manufacturers in a region exceeds the pollution limit for that region? If an area within a state (or larger region) continues to remain in noncompliance by a specified deadline, then remediation is required. Remediation is a remedy which, in this case is designed to fix a pollution-related problem. The remedy may take numerous forms.

More serious environmental problems require that the EPA be able to access law enforcement tools with broader powers and scope. Such tools are available, for example, when pollution violations fall under the purview of the Comprehensive Environmental Response Compensation Liability Act (CERCLA, also known as the Superfund Act), which deals with hazardous waste sites.

CERCLA Enforcement Tools: An Example of Compliance
Under CERCLA or the Superfund Act, the EPA has broad enforcement powers to protect public and environmental health by "forcing" the cleanup (remediation) of hazardous waste sites. In cases where a hazardous waste site presents an "imminent hazard," for instance, the EPA is authorized to take any steps necessary to protect public health and the environment. In responding to hazardous waste sites, the EPA has recourse in the form of civil injunctions and unilateral administrative orders. Civil injunctions require court action, while unilateral administrative orders may be pursued on direct order of the EPA. The advantage of a unilateral administrative order is that the

order must be carried out by the offending party by a specified date under threat of penalty ($25,000 per day for each day the offender is not in compliance with the order), *unless*: (1) the order is reviewable as stated in EPA regulations (Ferrey, 1997, p. 320), or (2) a sufficient cause for noncompliance defense can be offered. Noncompliance with a unilateral administrative order may also result in punitive damage assessments in addition to remediation costs and noncompliance fines.

Provisions in CERCLA also allow the EPA to sue defendants for (1) expenses incurred by the federal government when cleanup or other remediation actions are needed; and/or (2) to obtain restitution for damages and injuries. In other words, the EPA may employ civil remedies to recover remediation costs in cases where a corporation or individual has created a hazardous waste site.

In most cases, usually as an action of first resort, the EPA will attempt to gain the voluntary compliance of offenders through a process of informal negotiations and settlements. In these proceedings, the EPA may threaten other actions, such as the civil or administrative procedures described above to "persuade" offenders to comply with a hazardous waste site cleanup request.

SUMMARY OF MAJOR FEDERAL LEGISLATION

The sections that follow provide a summary of major federal legislation employed by the EPA to regulate environmental pollution. These materials provide only basic information about specific laws and regulations, and offer guidance to further investigation of these regulations. Since this is not a book about environmental law, certain features of regulations have been excluded. Likewise, not every applicable law is discussed. We restrict our discussion to the following: the Clean Air Act; the Clean Water Act; the Comprehensive Environmental Response Compensation and Liability Act; and the Resource Conservation and Recovery Act. More extensive details may be found by consulting these laws directly (see also; Ferrey, 1997; Findlay & Farber, 2000; Jalley, Moores, Henninger, & Maragani, 2002).

The Clean Air Act (CAA. 1963. Amended 1970, 1977, 1990)

Primary Goals:
The Clean Air Act was designed to reduce the level of air pollution by establishing national, uniform standards for ambient (outdoor) air quality. Prior to 1963, air pollution was addressed in a piecemeal

manner. Some states and smaller political units had instituted air pollution legislation. The Clean Air Act, originally passed in 1963, has been updated several times in efforts to improve air quality, reduce environmental harm, and improve public health. One of the main tools for accomplishing these tasks is technology-based standards for pollution emissions.

Summary of Related Statutes:

National Ambient Air Quality Standards (NAAQS, 1977, Amended 1990). Under NAAQS (Clean Air Act Section 109–110), the EPA was tasked with creating air quality standards for "criteria" air pollutants. The standards for criteria air pollutants may vary by region. These regions are referred to as air quality control regions (AQCRs). There are currently over 250 AQCRs in the United States. NAAQS regulate existing sources of air pollution under the rule of "reasonably available control technology" (RACT; Clean Air Act Section 172). There are currently eight criteria air pollutants identified in this legislation. In typical concentrations, these chemicals are nontoxic. In certain regions, however, heavy concentrations of these chemicals present health threats to the environment and humans. These pollutants include: sulfur dioxide (SO_2; contributes to acid rain), lead (Pb; associated with brain dysfunctions and other central nervous system and behavioral disruptions), carbon monoxide (CO; constituent of smog), nitrogen oxides ($NO_{(x)}$; associated with smog and global warming), ozone (O_3; related to the formation of smog), hydrocarbons (HC; ozone precursor), particle matter -10 (PM-10, or less than 10 microns in size), and particle matter -2.5 (particle matter less than 2.5 microns; respiratory irritation and illness).

New Source Performance Standards (NSPS; Clean Air Act Section 111). NSPS regulate new sources of air pollution, which include new facilities, technologies, and points of emissions. NSPS output levels are judged according to "best available control technology" (BACT) criteria. BACT criteria apply uniformly across states, establishing a situation in which individual states are not at liberty to alter these criteria in an effort to attract new businesses that emit regulated pollutants. BACT rules require that the efficacy of pollution control efforts and technological requirements be balanced against the cost of instituting new technologies and controls so that economic production is not adversely impacted. Amendments to the CAA in 1977 designated AQCRs as either "attainment" or "nonattainment" areas. NSPS issues are also addressed under two additional regulations: Prevention of Significant Deterioration and New Source Review.

<u>Prevention of Significant Deterioration</u> (PSD; CAA 1990 Section 112). Prevention of Significant Deterioration requirements apply to NSPS attainment areas, and are designed to prevent areas that have obtained clean air status from experiencing a decline in improved air quality. The level of acceptable air quality deterioration is determined by a classification system (Class I, II, and III), with Class I areas facing the most severe restrictions. Major new or modified stationary pollution sources are required to apply for a permit. Permit outcomes depend on the applicant's overall impact on air quality in the attainment area and the attainment area's Class rating.

<u>New Source Review</u> (NSR; CAA Section 111). Proposed major new or modified stationary sources of air pollution in a NSPS noncontainment area must apply for a preconstruction permit (CAA Section 111(a)(4)). A preconstruction permit may be issued if the proposed site's new pollutants are offset by the closing of existing facilities, or the State has an approved State Implementation Plan (SIP), or the site employs Lowest Achievable Control Technology (LACT).

<u>National Emission Standards for Hazardous Air Pollution</u> (NESHAP; CAA Title III, 1990). NESHAP is designed to control the emission of numerous toxic air pollutants that may cause death or illness, or those that are defined as carcinogenic (cancer causing) or mutagenic (related to genetic mutations). Under NESHAP, the EPA is directed to create rules protecting air quality and health that generate an "ample margin of safety" from exposure to toxic pollutants in outdoor air.

<u>New Federal Motor Vehicle Emission Limitations</u> (NFMVEL; Title II, CAA, 1970, Amended 1990). NFMVEL allows the EPA to regulate tailpipe emissions of hydrocarbons (HC), carbon monoxide (CO), and nitrogen oxides. This regulation also allows the EPA to establish deadlines for automakers to comply with emissions regulations related to these air pollutants for new vehicles. Fines of up to $10,000 per noncomplying vehicle sold may be levied on new vehicle manufacturers. Provisions include emission control regulations, the vehicle fleet program, and fuel regulation programs such as CAFE (corporate average fuel economy).

<u>Acid Rain Precursors and Ozone Protection Statutes</u> (Title VI, CAA, 1990). This legislation restricts source emissions of pollutants (see NAAQS standards) linked to acid rain especially at coal and oil powered electric generation stations. This regulation phases in emission reduction standards and includes an allowance trading provision. The ozone protection provisions specifically address the release and phase

out of hydrochloroflurocarbons (HCFCs) and chlorofluorocarbons (CFCs).

State Implementation Plan (SIP). In order to achieve standards set out under NAAQS, individual states are required to submit a SIP to the EPA. This plan details how a state will enforce rules promulgated under NAAQS, and meet air pollution attainment goals. Each state is required to model air pollution outputs within each AQCR within its boundaries, and specify plans for monitoring and maintaining air quality in the AQCR. This includes specifying an enforcement plan.

The Federal Water Pollution Control Act (FWPCA, 1972) and Clean Water Act (CWA, 1977)

Primary goals

The 1972, FWPCA sought to prevent and eliminate pollution discharges into waterways over which the federal government has constitutional authority (i.e., navigable waterways) by 1985. It sought to establish fishable and swimmable water quality that protects marine and wildlife by 1983. This Act also specifies states' duties aimed at achieving these goals (Section 101(b)). The FWPCA attempts to accomplish its goals through a permit system and the designation of water quality standards.

Description, Select Subsections, and Related Statutes

FWPCA. The FWPCA focuses on, and sets limits for point source water pollutants that include Publicly Owned Treatment Work (POTW, i.e., municipal sewage treatment plants) and industrial sources of water pollution (Section 301). Three point source pollutant categories are regulated: (1) toxic (Section 307), (2) conventional (Section 304), and (3) nontoxic, nonconventional.

National Pollutant Discharge Elimination System (NPDES; Title VI FWPCA). The NPDES regulates the amount and concentration of pollutants discharged to waterways. Section 402 of the NPDES allows certified discharges (defined in Section 401) to obtain a permit to discharge pollutants to waterways. Discharges must be monitored and reported to federal and state authorities (40 C.F.R. Section 122.41(j) and l(4)). Federal or state governments may amend NPDES permits to meet the standards of the FWPCA or CWA (40 C.F.R. Sections 122.41 (b) and 122.62(a)). This regulation also requires that states submit a State Implementation Plan.

Effluent Guidelines and Standards (FWPCA; Section 307(a)). Requires the EPA to establish a list of, and set limits for toxic pollutants.

Best Practicable Control Technology (BPT; 33 U.S.C. Section 1311(b)(1)). Establishes the minimum standard for classes of industrial pollutants reflecting the best existing performance by an individual facility within an industrial group. In setting these standards, the EPA is required to weigh potential pollution reductions against expected costs to industry. Individual dischargers that fail to meet BPT standards must cease operation.

Best Conventional Pollution Control Technology (BCT; 33 U.S.C. Section 1314(a) (4) (1996)). More stringent than BPT, BCT sets standards for conventional pollutants balancing costs of control against benefits derived from a control measure.

Best Available Control Technology (BACT; 33 U.S.C. Section 1317 (a) (2)). The most stringent water pollution control standards, BACTs are set for a class of point source dischargers of toxic and nonconventional pollutants. BACTs are established by the EPA from the performance of best-performing facilities. BACTs must consist of already available technology, and must also be feasible. BACTs for toxins are health based, however, and do not require cost-benefit considerations (see Ferrey, 1997, pp. 206–207). Nevertheless, BACT standards must be economically achievable.

Pollution Permit and State Control of Permitting Processes (402 CWA). This section of the CWA enables the EPA to issue permits to individual polluters for point source emissions. This section also allows the EPA to authorize state plans for water permitting rules, regulations, and enforcement procedures. Any state wishing to control CWA-permitting processes must apply to the EPA and obtain authorization for its plan. Individual point source emission permits must meet BPT, BCT, and BAT requirements. Rules for point source emissions are established on an industrywide basis, though individual variances are allowable.

New Pollution Sources (NSPS; 306 CWA). New sources of pollution, or facilities that come on line after implementation of the CWA, must meet a separate set of pollution standards that require compliance with BAT. Following the 1977 revision of the CWA, these standards became known as "new source performance standards" (NSPS). As noted, NSPS require new facilities discharging waste to water to meet BAT standards when the facility opens. Over time, the EPA is allowed to tighten these restrictions if water quality indicators suggest that water quality is not being maintained (see 303 CWA).

Nonpoint Sources (319 CWA). Created by the 1987 Water Quality Act, this section targets non-point source polluters (e.g., storm water run-off) for waterways that have failed to meet water quality standards. States with waterways that fail to meet specified water quality standards must submit a non-point source pollution control implementation plan to the EPA for approval.

Water Quality Standards (302, 303, and 304 CWA). When a body of water fails to meet water quality standards by complying with section 301 of the CWA, the EPA is required to implement water quality criteria that place further limits on effluent discharges, NPDES permits, and water pretreatment programs, facilities, and criteria. Under these provisions, water quality standards are determined individually by state according to the primary use of the body of water (agricultural use, industrial use, fishing, recreation, and water supply; 304 CWA). The adopted standards must protect the minimal conditions for the existing use for the designated body of water. The EPA may override a state's body of water designation (302 CWA). To facilitate the maintenance of water quality for a designated use, 303 CWA requires states to establish "total maximum daily loads" (TMDL) which are subject to EPA approval and review. If required, TMDL are met through altering permit requirements for individual facilities. A state may not escape water quality standards under these sections of the CWA by altering the body of water use designation (302 CWA). Further, under these sections, water quality standards have specific scientifically derived water quality measures that states may amend only through the addition of narrative or descriptive standards. Cost is not to be considered in meeting these standards.

Publicly Owned Water Treatment Facilities (POWTs; Title IV, 33 U.S.C. Sections 1381–1387 and 406 CWA). 33 U.S.C., 1381–1387 established a loan program to facilitate building POWTs in an effort to reduce waterway pollution in the United States. Individual dischargers can avoid obtaining a NPDES if they discharge effluents to a POWT. To employ this option, however, the discharger must meet pretreatment requirements.

Fundamentally Different Factor (FDF; 33 U.S.C., Section 1311). Individual facilities within an industry may petition the EPA for an exception to industry-specific standards for effluent emission and pretreatment criteria if it can demonstrate that it is fundamentally different from other facilities in its industry class.

The Safe Drinking Water Act (SDWA; 42 U.S.C., Section 300f–300j). The SDWA supplements the CWA, which targets lakes and rivers, by focusing on surface and groundwater drinking supplies. It charges the EPA with the responsibility to create health-based standards for public drinking water supplies. Public drinking water is defined as a system that supplies water for either 25 people, or has 15 connections that operate on a regular basis. Water supplies must employ BAT to meet these standards. State water supply regulations may exceed the requirements of the SDWA. States must provide the monitoring mechanisms to ensure that health-based drinking water standards are met.

Ocean Dumping Act (ODA). The ODA was designed to ensure that the standards imposed in the CWA did not lead to ocean dumping of effluent pollutants in an effort to meet CWA pollution concentration requirements. Under the provisions of this Act, the EPA may issue permits for ocean dumping.

The Superfund Act or the Comprehensive Environmental Response Compensation Liability Act (CERCLA), and the Superfund Reauthorization Act of 1986 (SARA)

Primary Goal

Using the provisions of CERCLA, the EPA's primary objective is to determine who is responsible for creating a hazardous waste site in order to facilitate its cleanup or remediation. The CERCLA accomplishes this goal through provisions that established an information-gathering network, liability provisions, the Superfund trust account that pays for a portion of site remediation, and federal authority to respond to and cleanup hazardous waste sites. The CERCLA's provisions apply to a hazardous substance once it is released into the environment, and applies retroactively, that is to actions that have already occurred. CERCLA hazardous substances include all hazardous substances and chemicals listed under the Resource Conservation and Recovery Act (RCRA), the Clean Water Act (CWA), the Clean Air Act (CAA), and the Toxic Substances Control Act (TSCA), and specifically excludes petroleum, nuclear waste, workplace releases, and federally permitted pesticide contamination (each of which is regulated by agencies other than the EPA).

Description, Select Subsections and Related Statutes

Hazardous Substance Release Notification (42 U.S.C., Section 9603). This section of the CERCLA requires that the person in charge of a facility: (1) who has knowledge of a hazardous chemical release (42 U.S.C., Section 9602(22)) immediately report that release to the EPA's

National Response Center; and (2) notify the EPA if they operate a treatment, storage, and disposal facility (TSDF).

Facility (42 U.S.C., Section 9601(9)). Under the CERCLA, a facility is any site or area where a hazardous substance has been deposited, stored, placed, or disposed, excluding in-use consumer products and vessels.

EPA Response Responsibilities (42 U.S.C., Sections 9640, 96405). The EPA is authorized to undertake both short-term and long-term responses to known hazardous waste sites. Short-term responses may also be emergency responses. The EPA employs money from the Hazardous Substance Response Trust Fund (the Superfund; 42 U.S.C., Section 9611, 9612) to address short-term and emergency responses, and is limited to expenditures not exceeding $2 million in a remediation effort. In the event that an environmental emergency threatens public health, the President of the United States is authorized to take immediate action (Section 9604(a)(4)). Sites posing serious and persistent threats to public health that require long-term remediation (as determined by employing the Hazard Ranking System, 40 C.F.R., Section 300, Appendix A) will be added to the National Priorities List following procedures specified in the National Contingency Plan (42 U.S.C., Section 9605). Using these provisions, the EPA may recover costs from potentially responsible parties (PRPs; 42 U.S.C., Section 9607). Finalizing this process, the EPA issues a Record of Decision. States may request authority to take over the EPA's role as lead remediator.

Superfund Reauthorization Act of 1986 (SARA; 42 U.S.C., Section 9621). This Act strengthened the requirements of the original Superfund Act, enhanced state responsibilities, provided for voluntary settlements between PRPs and the government, and included additional mechanisms for replenishing the Superfund. One of the most important changes was to cleanup requirements, which must now be implemented in ways that protect environmental and public health using cost-effective solutions.

Enforcement Tools (42 U.S.C., Sections 9604, 9606, 9607). CERCLA provides the EPA with several different mechanisms for enforcing its rules and regulations. The least formal is a voluntary cleanup request (U.S.C. 9604), which may occur under threat of a formal order (U.S.C. 9606, 9607). Section 9606 details EPA order and injunction capabilities under "imminent hazard" threats posed by an actual or threatened hazardous release. Imminent hazard responses are taken to protect public health. Section 9606 provides for civil injunctions and judicially non-reviewable unilateral administrative orders. Violations of injunctions and orders issued under 9606 are punishable by fines of up to $25,000 per day, and punitive damages to PRPs up to three times the government's remediation costs. Section 9607 is a strict liability statute. It also defines potentially responsible parties, criteria for remediation, investigation, monitoring, testing, response planning, staff, litigation and attorney cost recovery. This litigation tool is a powerful, sometimes costly, enforcement mechanism.

    Civil and Criminal Penalties. CERCLA rules include a variety of civil and criminal penalties. Penalties may be incurred from violations of notifications requirements (9603(a)(b)), destruction of records (9603(d)(2)), financial responsibility (9608), and orders and settlements (9620; 9622). Individual criminal liability may be imposed (9607(a)) without proximate cause or actual knowledge of the violation. Criminal penalties are pursued by the Department of Justice.

Resource Conservation and Recovery Act (RCRA), or Law Pertaining to the Management of Solid and Hazardous Wastes

Primary Goal
The RCRA's primary goal is to create a "cradle to grave" tracking system for hazardous solid waste that regulates the transportation, handling, storage, and disposal of hazardous waste. Through its provisions, the RCRA encourages reductions in solid waste via recycling and improvement in manufacturing technology, alternatives to land disposal, safe land disposal when such disposal is required, and increased state responsibility for managing solid waste disposal. The wastes that are subject to RCRA requirements include solid wastes as identified in 1003(27) of the RCRA, or as defined in 1004 as a hazardous waste (see 40 C.F.R., Section 261(D)).

Description, Select Subsections, and Related Statutes
Regulation of Waste Generators. Waste Generators are defined as any person or site that produces hazardous wastes as defined under 40 C.F.R., Part 261. Record-keeping and hazardous waste labeling requirements are addressed under RCRA 3002, and are included to promote "cradle to grave" hazardous waste tracking. This procedure relies on the use of a manifest system (RCRA Section 3003). The manifest contains information about the waste such as contents, place of origin, shipping container identifiers, dates of transfer and receipt, and identification of intended handlers and final destination. The

manifest follows the hazardous waste from generators, to handlers and shippers, to storage and disposal.

Regulation of Waste Handlers (RCRA Section 3004, 3005). These sections of RCRA establish a permitting system for the handling of hazardous waste. Persons wishing to do business as owners/operators of a hazardous treatment, storage and disposal facility (TSDF) must receive a permit from the EPA. TSDFs are required to notify the EPA of all hazardous wastes treated, shipped, stored, or disposed (Section 3010). A TSDF must have an EPA identification number, analyze accepted wastes, inspect and monitor the facility, maintain emergency equipment, have an emergency release plan, train facility operators, and provide records of these endeavors to the EPA. In the event that a TSDF experiences a hazardous waste accident or leak, cleanup procedures are implemented pursuant to RCRA Section 3004. Improper treatment, storage, and disposal is addressed by remedies available to the EPA under RCRA 3008.

Inspections, Sampling, and Information Gathering (RCRA Section 3007). RCRA Section 3007 provides any agent of the EPA with the authority to formally request information from regulated hazardous waste facilities. The EPA may not, however, require former owners or owners of inactive hazardous waste facilities to produce requested information (compliance with such a request is voluntary). Remedies for noncompliance with such a request are addressed under RCRA Section 3008. At the request of the regulated facility, the requested information may be treated as confidential. If this request is granted, government agents are barred from disclosing the information to anyone. Section 3007 also authorizes EPA sampling and inspections of active and inactive hazardous waste facilities without the need for a warrant. The EPA must, however, provide a receipt for samples, make samples available to facility operators upon request, and provide sampling test results. Inspections, unlike sampling, require a warrant demonstrating probable cause. Information gathered under 3007 may be used to compel a hazardous waste handler to engage in monitoring and testing as defined in RCRA Section 3013.

Land Disposal Requirements. Legally, land disposal methods for hazardous waste were banned under the RCRA. This is true unless the EPA grants an exemption to a facility under RCRA Section 3004(d)-(f).

Endangerment. RCRA Section 7003 allows the EPA to sue any person who has contributed or is contributing to imminent and substantial endangerment of the public health or environment through the unsafe disposal of hazardous waste. Case law defines the evidence needed for establishing these criteria as consisting of evidence of exposure, including a minimal showing that hazardous chemicals are present at a particular location. In effect, these requirements include a showing of potential or suspected harm, not necessarily actual harm.

Underground Storage Tanks. Supplemental RCRA regulations (Subtitle I, Sections 9001–9010) provide for the regulation of oil/gas or other included hazardous waste (Subtitle C) in underground storage tanks (USTs). This Subtitle includes its own enforcement and remediation program that relies on the use of operator insurance, and the existence of state trust funds for remediation purposes.

Medical Waste. As part of continuing efforts to curb environment harm and threats to public health, the EPA authorized a limited area (New York, New Jersey, Connecticut, Illinois, Indiana, Michigan, Wisconsin, Pennsylvania, Ohio, and Minnesota) as a demonstration project to control medical waste. This effort was expressed in RCRA Subtitle J, which established a separate mechanism for the tracking of medical wastes in these states. Following the usefulness of this project, the majority of states have instituted medical waste tracking systems based on Subtitle J.

Citizen Initiated Actions. RCRA Section 7002 allows citizens to invoke provisions of the RCRA through civil suits. These actions may be directed toward facilities/handlers/owners or the EPA for failure to enforce RCRA, and must demonstrate potential harm. Prior notice of intent to litigate is required. Such suits are banned where the EPA can provide evidence of planned enforcement actions, or ongoing actions.

Criminal Enforcement. Known violations of RCRA regulations may result in criminal actions (RCRA Section 3008). Criminal sanctions are pursued by the Department of Justice. Criminal penalties of up to $50,000 per day, and/or up to 5 years in prison are provided.

UNDERSTANDING LAWS

Put simply, laws are designed to address societal concern and protect the general public from harm. Legislators serve the important role of recognizing public interest and determining whether an issue is significant and/or substantial enough to proceed with the passage of legislation. Public recognition of social problems, and legislator identification of issues as "law-worthy" stem from knowledge and understanding of pertinent issues surrounding the problem. Absent knowledge, particularly in the form of research, ill-defined legislation is quite possible.

Understanding environmental law can be burdensome. The inter-disciplinary nature of environmental crime dictates that environmental legislation account for various issues, which often involve competing interests. Effective legislation should be based on due consideration of numerous factors (e.g., legal and social concerns), with a particular concern that the legislation will be enforced by those charged with doing so. To date, much of the burden of enforcing environmental laws has fallen upon the EPA, although other regulatory agencies and law enforcement groups have played less substantial roles in enforcing environmental law. The following two chapters address the EPA's role in environmental protection and examine current and historical enforcement efforts in relation to environmental protection laws.

CHAPTER 5

The Environmental Protection Agency

The federal government made several notable attempts to manage the environment from the mid-1950s through the late 1960s. A series of environmental acts, including the Water Pollution Control Act of 1956, the Clean Air Act of 1963, the Water Quality Act of 1965, and the Air Quality Act of 1967 symbolized this effort. These attempts were unsuccessful in defining a clear regulatory role for the federal government in environmental protection, however, as they delegated too much authority to the states (Waterman, 1989; Davies, 1970). Although the federal government was unable to assume primary control of environmental protection via this legislation, all was not lost. The government's efforts to regulate environmental pollution spurred environmental groups to lobby Congress for the necessary legislation (Waterman, 1989). Greater environmental concern among politicians and society in general eventually contributed to the expansion of the federal government's role in environmental protection (Waterman, 1989), leading up to the 1970 creation of the EPA.

This chapter highlights the development and practices of the EPA, the agency most responsible for preventing and detecting environmental crime. The EPA is also charged with making environmental enforcement information available to the public. We begin with an overview of the EPA, its origins, objectives, and cooperative efforts. This review is followed by a description of major EPA events by presidential administrations as a means for organizing significant incidents, and assessment of the potential impact of presidential administrations on the EPA. This information helps place environmental crime enforcement efforts into perspective, and facilitates understanding the current state of information made available by the agency.

ORIGIN OF THE EPA

In 1970, President Nixon created the EPA through executive order. On one hand, Nixon's actions were monumental, since he created the EPA through direct presidential action after Congress failed to implement the necessary legislation. Nixon understood that the American people were very concerned with environmental issues at the time, and that it was incumbent upon political leaders to recognize and give power to this voice. On the other hand, Nixon fully understood the political implications of creating the EPA. When he undertook this action, he was also attempting to solidify his presidential reelection bid. His challenger, Democratic nominee Edwin Muskie, had a strong environmental record in a climate of increased public concern with environmental pollution. Nixon was positioned to gain an advantage if he could have a hand in the creation of a federal pollution regulatory agency.

As an independent executive branch agency, the EPA was charged with regulating a wide array of environmental protection issues, although its responsibilities would become increasingly focused. The EPA is headed by an administrator who is nominated by the president and confirmed by the Senate (Table 5-3, at the end of this chapter, lists EPA administrators according to presidential administration). The White House, along with the EPA administrator, sets the primary focus of the EPA.

Creation of the EPA brought about the consolidation of environmental enforcement practices within one agency (Hyatt, 1998; Train, 1996). Train (1996, p. 188) suggests that this organizational change

> provided the capability for integrated management of different pollution sources accompanied by a comprehensive research and development arm. It established in the federal government a highly visible focal point for environmental concerns and provided a governmental institution to reflect and match the widespread and still growing public concern over environmental problems.

This reorganization, based largely on popular perceptions of an environmental crisis, arguably led to the stringent enforcement approach taken by the agency on its inception. For instance, "During its first sixty days, EPA brought five times as many enforcement actions as the agencies it inherited had brought during any similar period"

(Landy, Robert, & Thomas, 1990, p. 36). Mintz (1995, p. 21) notes that upon its creation, the newly appointed EPA leadership sensed the importance of enforcing the few environmental standards in existence, and adopted a "fair but firm" enforcement approach. Mintz adds that the agency focused its initial efforts on large corporations and cities in attempts to control pollution from industrial and municipal sources.

Balancing the interests of the environment and industry was/is a recurring issue for the EPA. For instance, the initially aggressive EPA enforcement approach led conservatives and industry members to view the agency as an anti-business environmental advocate, which in turn initiated a series of White House attempts to more directly influence EPA practices (Landy et al., 1990). The new agency soon became overwhelmed by its rapidly expanding regulatory responsibilities, a lack of direction from the Nixon and Ford administrations regarding the aggressiveness of enforcement efforts, and creative industry tactics to hamper the establishment and enforcement of environmental standards (Gottlieb, 1993).

EPA RESPONSIBILITIES

Given its primary role as the watchdog for environmental regulation, the EPA is tasked with many duties. Although agency objectives change over time, the EPA has consistently focused on regulating air and water pollution, hazardous waste, and hazardous chemicals. At any given time, more or less emphasis may be placed on specific issues, and under different administrators and presidents, the EPA has adopted different areas of focus.

In discussing the EPA's role in administering a broad array of environmental legislation, Switzer and Bryner (1998, p. 46) note that "In one sense, it (the EPA) is a regulatory agency, issuing permits, setting and monitoring standards, and enforcing federal laws, but it also gives grants to states to build waste water treatment and other facilities." These vast powers are difficult to coordinate, and political processes sometimes impact how they are carried out, even across EPA regions. With so many varied responsibilities, it was difficult to determine an organizational mission at the EPA as Landy, Roberts, and Thomas (1990, p. 33) note:

> The president and his allies expected the leader of EPA to be a balancer and integrator, to pursue environmental protection in ways that were compatible with industrial expansion and resource development. The advocacy community, in contrast,

wanted EPA to champion environmental values against counterpressures from elsewhere in government.

The EPA also faces pressure from industrial lobbyists. Confronted with these conflicting demands, EPA administrators often find themselves in a no-win situation. Regardless of the mission they select or the tactics they employ, one of these groups usually will not be pleased.

Rosenbaum (2003, p. 179) is among those who discuss the historical lack of focus in the EPA's mission statement, arguing that absent "an orderly mission statement, the EPA must create priorities according to the programs with the largest budgets, the most demanding deadlines, the most politically potent constituencies, or the greatest amount of congressional attention." The current EPA Agency Mission Statement, found on the EPA Web site (www.epa.gov/history/org/origins/mission.htm), states: "The mission of the U.S. Environmental Protection Agency is to protect human health and to safeguard the natural environment—air, water, and land—upon which life depends." The EPA identifies the following additional goals and purposes:

- Protecting human health and the environment;
- Reducing environmental risks using the best available scientific information;
- Enforcing federal laws protecting human health fairly and effectively;
- Establishing environmental policies that protect the environment while considering natural resources, human health, economic growth, energy, transportation, agriculture, industry, and international trade requirements;
- Providing accurate information to all parts of society so that they may effectively participate in managing human health and environmental risks;
- Contributing to community and ecosystems diversity, sustainability, and economic productivity; and
- Taking a leading role in protecting the global environment.

As the list demonstrates, safeguarding the natural environment is an enormous responsibility, subject to change at any time.

Rosenbaum (2003) cites the difficulties faced with such a charge, including enforcing numerous major environmental statutes, addressing large and technically complex environmental programs and issues, confronting a load of regulatory programs continuously delivered from

Congress without much guidance, and competing for scarce resources and administrative attention. He (2003, p. 177) argues that the "staggering range of responsibility is one major reason why the EPA has been chronically overworked and repeatedly targeted for sweeping organizational reform since 1980," adding that the difficulties faced by the EPA result in "an incoherent regulatory agenda, a massive pile of legislative mandates for different regulatory actions, many armed with unachievable deadlines, leaving the agency without any firm and consistent sense of direction" (p. 179).

EPA ORGANIZATION

With roughly 17,500 staff members and an annual budget in fiscal year 2002 of $7.9 billion, the EPA is the largest regulatory agency in the federal government (Rosenbaum, 2003). In view of the large number of scientists, attorneys, and related professionals working for the EPA, Waterman (1989, p. 100) believes the EPA "has distinguished itself for acquiring an impressive cadre of experts on environmental affairs, and many of them have been strong advocates of environmental protection." Despite such professionalism and concern for the environment, EPA employees are by no means in complete agreement regarding a specific environmental approach for the agency (Waterman, 1989). In part, these disagreements have something to do with the organization of the EPA.

The EPA is organized into thirteen primary offices, although the present work is most concerned with the responsibilities of three particular offices: The Office of Enforcement and Compliance Assurance, the Office of Environmental Justice (located within the Office of Enforcement and Compliance Assurance), and the Office of Environmental Information. The Office of Enforcement and Compliance Assurance (OECA) addresses compliance with U.S. environmental laws and encourages pollution prevention. Within the OECA is the Office of Environmental Justice (OEJ), which attempts to ensure that low income and/or minority communities receive protection under environmental laws. The Office of Environmental Information (OEI) is responsible for the creation, management, and use of environmental information. These three offices provide a wealth of information for researchers examining environmental crime and justice issues.

In addition to a national office in Washington, DC, the EPA maintains 10 regional offices (see Table 5-1), each responsible within its region for the execution of EPA programs. Most EPA employees are located in regional offices, while most scholarship on the EPA is directed toward environmental issues and policies originating from the national office in Washington, DC (Waterman, 1989). Waterman (1989, p. 189) observed that the decentralization/regionalization of EPA offices "necessitated by EPA's strong intergovernmental component...undercuts the direct authority of the (EPA) administrator."

Table 5-1: EPA Regional Offices and State Coverage

Region 1–Connecticut, Maine, Massachusetts, New Hampshire, Rhode Island, Vermont

Region 2–New Jersey, New York, Puerto Rico, the U.S. Virgin Islands

Region 3–Delaware, Maryland, Pennsylvania, Virginia, West Virginia, the District of Columbia

Region 4–Alabama, Florida, Georgia, Kentucky, Mississippi, North Carolina, South Carolina, Tennessee

Region 5–Illinois, Indiana, Michigan, Minnesota, Ohio, Wisconsin

Region 6–Arkansas, Louisiana, New Mexico, Oklahoma, Texas

Region 7–Iowa, Kansas, Missouri, Nebraska

Region 8–Colorado, Montana, North Dakota, South Dakota, Utah, Wyoming

Region 9–Arizona, California, Hawaii, Nevada, the territories of Guam and American Samoa

Region 10–Alaska, Idaho, Oregon, Washington

The EPA also relies heavily on state environmental agencies for cooperation. As a result, "the EPA is a curious blend of centralized control by the administrator and decentralized authority over its many functional responsibilities, the other federal agencies with which it shares responsibility, and the intergovernmental component of environmental regulation" (Waterman, 1989, p. 100). Despite its decentralized structure and contending with substantial jurisdictional issues, the EPA is recognized by some as the most important of the major regulatory agencies (e.g., McCormick, 1989).

Given these organizational limits, the EPA has nevertheless been responsible for many great achievements and is credited with conducting admirable work in protecting the environment. Flippen (2000, p. 226) recognizes the agency as "a bulwark against pollution," adding that the EPA's importance is symbolized by its large structure (see also, Sale & Foner, 1993; Train, 1996). It is an understatement to suggest that its role in protecting the environment is vital. The agency, however, is not without its critics, as unclear agency objectives, strong political influences, and corrupt leadership are among the problems the agency has faced (Rosenbaum, 2003, p. 180).

EPA AND OTHER AGENCIES

Prior to the creation of the EPA, environmental policy existed in piecemeal fashion and fell under the domain of a variety of federal government agencies. The country's historically limited concern for environmental policy was prevalent in both the executive office and Congress (Switzer & Bryner, 1998). Today, the EPA shares jurisdiction with several other federal agencies on different environmental issues, though it shares primary responsibility over environmental matters with the Department of the Interior (DOI) (Switzer & Bryner, 1998). The DOI has jurisdiction over federal and public lands, including National Parks, and enforces laws on its lands based on policies provided by the EPA (Hyatt, 1998). The creation of the EPA, however, "relegated the Department of the Interior to a backseat status as far as environmental issues were concerned" (Switzer & Bryner, 1998, p. 50).

Other federal agencies that maintain partial jurisdiction over the environment include: the Department of Agriculture (e.g., the Hazardous Materials Management Group) which has authority over the National Forest Service, grasslands and natural resources; the Department of Justice, which is responsible for prosecuting all criminal cases related to the environment; the Department of Defense, which has jurisdiction over military installations, including the disposition of chemical and nuclear weapons; the Department of Energy (e.g., the Office of Environmental Management); and the Nuclear Regulatory Commission, which works closely with the Department of Defense to deal with issues pertaining to nuclear fuel and radioactive materials/waste. Several additional federal agencies have secondary environmental authority: the Department of Health and Human Services; the Department of Labor; the Department of Housing and Urban Development; the Department of Transportation; the National Highway Traffic Safety Administration; the Consumer Product Safety Commission; the Federal Maritime Commission; and the Federal Trade Commission (e.g., Switzer & Bryner, 1998; Hyatt, 1998). The EPA must also work closely with other groups maintaining interest in the environment, including the Council on Environmental Quality (CEQ), state regulatory agencies, and industry. Of particular significance is the CEQ.

CEQ

Established in 1970 as part of the National Environmental Protection Act (NEPA), the CEQ provides policy advice on environmental issues to the president, and coordinates federal environmental efforts, policies, and initiatives (Switzer & Bryner, 1998). It was perhaps most influential during the Nixon administration, primarily because Nixon staffed the council with qualified environmental advocates. The CEQ's impact diminished beginning with Nixon's second term for a variety of reasons (most important perhaps was the Nixon administration's concern with matters other than the environment). Perhaps the greatest damage stemmed from the Reagan administration's almost successful attempt to abolish the CEQ (Flippen, 2000).

State Environmental Agencies

By 1990, each state had adopted a regulatory agency similar to the EPA, and each maintains at least one environmental regulatory agency. State environmental regulatory agencies provide invaluable services for protecting the environment and possess a wealth of information on environmental crimes. Like the EPA, state environmental agencies are charged with protecting the environment, although each must address the unique challenges posed by environmental concerns in their respective state. Given its mission, the EPA must cooperate with the 50 state environmental regulatory agencies (please see Appendix B for contact information for each state agency). This decentralized approach to environmental protection limits the EPA's environmental protection efforts because decision-making authority is spread among multiple levels of government with different focuses, levels of commitment to environmental protection, and financial resources (Bowman, 1984).

Cooperation between the EPA and the states is evidenced in states being required, by the 1970 Clean Air Act, to submit to the EPA a State Implementation Plan (SIPs), which describes the processes by which states will comply with the Act. The EPA, in turn, determines the adequacy of the plans, which provides a sense of regulation by the EPA, although it does not guarantee complete control over the state agencies. The EPA lacks the resources to comprehensively assess each state's environmental protection plans (Waterman, 1989), which ultimately allows a degree of autonomy for the state regulatory agencies. Rosenbaum (2003) cites the strain in the relationship between the EPA and states. On one hand, states believe the EPA is too intrusive concerning issues that should be considered state matters. On the other hand, states also believe the EPA is not aggressive enough in addressing specific issues that adversely affect them.

Industry

Perhaps the most influential group with whom the EPA must interact is the business community or industry; the group with the greatest potential for harming and protecting the environment. Industry is greatly impacted by EPA regulations and enforcement policies. As a result, industries often lobby the White House, legislators, and EPA administrators concerning rule changes and enforcement policy. Industry often laments that EPA regulations cut into profits, and continually seeks to have cost concerns included in legislation and enforcement policy. Recognition of the need to balance environmental concerns with economic considerations are evident throughout EPA history. However, industry often calculates these costs only with respect to financial profits. These calculations do not take into account the costs of pollution to the public, government, or health care and insurance industries.

While industry has expressed concern that the EPA not threaten its profit potentials, those interested in environmental protection expressed concern that industry would attempt to subvert the mission of the EPA. Waterman (1989, p. 108), for instance, notes that policy makers were concerned about the EPA becoming "the pawn of the regulated industry," which would influence the authority and discretion provided to the EPA administrator, and compromise the EPA's mission. As discussed below, EPA practices have been, and continue to be altered by concerns for the economic security of the country.

The EPA is not only affected by its relationship to other organizations, industry, or its organizational structure; it is also influenced by the White House. Thus, it seems logical to discuss the agency in relation to presidential administrations. While the EPA is by no means directly guided by the president, the agency is influenced by the president and there are clear differences in EPA practices across presidential administrations. Such differences can be attributed, in part, to the differing ideologies of Democrats and Republicans. As such, the remainder of this chapter addresses the historical role of the EPA in protecting the environment in relation to each presidential administration since the agency's inception. A discussion of the role of the Executive Office in relation to the EPA and environmental concerns is provided prior to addressing the environmental impact of specific administrations.

THE EXECUTIVE OFFICE AND THE ENVIRONMENT

Although the Executive Office of the federal government does not maintain direct control over EPA practices, its historically persuasive influence over the EPA is well documented. According to Vig (2003, p. 120) "The record of recent presidents demonstrates that the White House has had a significant but hardly singular or consistent role in shaping national environmental policy." Thus, any discussion of EPA practices requires reference to presidential influences, as ideological differences among presidents certainly influence environmental policy and selection of EPA administrator nominees. With vast power tempered by Congressional oversight, the president plays a vital role in determining the direction, extent, and nature of environmental protection. This influence is nowhere more evident than when President Nixon created the EPA by executive order. But, the environment is one of several major issues with which the President must contend (e.g., national security, economic matters, energy policy, etc.). These diverse responsibilities require that the president balance interests across issues and coordinate the actions of many federal agencies (Waterman, 1989). In some cases, balancing interests involves the application of the president's personal beliefs about the value of protecting the environment versus, for instance, economic recovery, inflation, unemployment, or international relations. For instance, the Carter and George H. Bush administrations both expressed interest in environmental issues; both, however, were impeded by external crises when it came to making important environmental decisions (Carter by the oil embargo, Bush by the Gulf War; see: Hyatt, 1998).

As noted, presidential recognition of, and concern for the environment varies, and some presidents choose to emphasize particular presidential roles over others. With limited time, resources, and control, presidents are sometimes constricted in their influence over environmental issues. EPA priorities, for instance, may conflict with more pressing societal concerns, resulting in limited presidential recognition of and attention to environmental issues, and subsequent friction between the Executive Office and environmentalists. Environmental concerns are consistently among the most highlighted issues each president faces. These concerns must be addressed in some manner, regardless of anyone's belief in what the president should or should not do.

It is sometimes difficult to clearly evaluate the impact of presidential administrations on environmental policy, or many other related issues for that matter, as some are apt to look through rose-colored glasses while others are overly pessimistic. For example, the overall merits of the Nixon administration remain under debate decades after he left office. In addition, it is difficult to determine how a president's influence is enhanced or impeded by actions of legislators. To address this issue as it relates to presidential environmental concerns, Vig (2003, p. 105) provides a set of indicators that facilitate evaluation of presidential influence on environmental policy. These indicators include: (1) the president's environmental agenda, (2) key presidential appointments, (3) environmental program budgets, (4) presidential legislative initiatives or vetoes, (5) presidential executive orders, (6) White House oversight of environmental regulation, and (7) presidential response to international environmental agreements. Vig (2003) aptly notes that evaluating presidential practices in relation to these indicators can be difficult.

The remainder of this chapter examines the environmental impact of the presidential administrations that have worked in the Oval Office since the 1970 development of the EPA. Although the following discussion does not directly assess Vig's indicators (although many are addressed), his evaluation of recent presidencies found that the Nixon, Carter, and George H. Bush administrations had the greatest successes in supporting successful environmental legislation (Vig, 2003).

PRESIDENTIAL ADMINISTRATIONS AND THE EPA

Assessments of presidential influence on environmental issues, and more specifically the EPA, highlight the many differences between political groups (Republicans vs. Democrats) and the impact of societal events on public policy. For instance, the pro-business approach of Republican administrations is clearly evident in the Reagan administration, while public support for environmental issues arguably encouraged the Clinton administrations' pro-environmental stances. These assessments also highlight similarities in the relationships between presidents and the EPA, as noted, for instance, in the need for presidents to balance concerns for environmental protection with economic stability.

Below we summarize the relationship between the Nixon, Ford, Carter, Reagan, George H. Bush, Clinton, and George W. Bush administrations and the EPA, address the major issues and challenges faced by each administration, and briefly address each president's influence on the environment. While some differences among the administrations were discussed in Chapter 3 of this work ("History of the Environmental Movement"), this section focuses on presidential practices in relation to the EPA, which subsequently dictates that larger issues pertaining to environmental policy be addressed in the discussion. To be sure, volumes have been written on the EPA (e.g., Landy et al.'s *The Environmental Protection Agency*, 1990), the presidency as it relates to the environment (e.g., Soden's *The Environmental Presidency*, 1999), and particular presidential influences on the environment (e.g., Flippen's *Nixon and the Environment*, 2000). The following overview sheds light on how the EPA has been affected by presidential practices, societal events, and time, with the amount of discussion devoted to each presidential administration varying according to each president's time in office and impact upon the environment.

The Nixon Administration (1969–1974)
Until Nixon's first term in office, the president, with the exception of Theodore Roosevelt, had limited involvement in environmental policy, and even Nixon was initially reluctant to become involved (Switzer & Bryner, 1998). The Nixon administration, however, is credited with many significant accomplishments in terms of environmental protection, including the creation of the EPA, which is, perhaps, the single most influential environmental action occurring under any administration. Seeking to win public support by appearing pro-environment, Nixon supported the National Environmental Policy Act (NEPA) in 1970, declared the 1970s as "the environmental decade," and promoted environmental legislation.

While some suggest that the creation of the EPA via the NEPA was politically motivated, with Nixon appealing to the public's concern in light of an upcoming presidential election, others argue that the agency served a clear purpose other than being a political pawn (Hyatt, 1998). Despite this controversy, it appears that accomplishments during the Nixon era with regard to environmental protection have not been surpassed by any subsequent administration (Train, 1996; Kraft, 1996; Whitaker, 1976; and Hoff, 1994 for further discussion).

Appointment to the Executive Office brings with it an expectation of personal knowledge in numerous areas and/or the selection of a knowledgeable staff. Given the EPA's broad task of protecting the environment, which entails knowledge in a vast array of areas (e.g., hazardous waste, air/water quality, etc.), the EPA relies heavily on the direction of its administrator. Nixon appointed William Ruckelshaus, formerly a member of the U.S. Department of Justice, as the first EPA administrator, despite Ruckelshaus's limited background on environmental issues (Switzer & Bryner, 1998). Ruckelshaus's primary concerns upon appointment included EPA image development, addressing the requirements of the revised Clean Air Act, and controlling the resources associated with regulatory decision making (Marcus, 1980). Ruckelshaus initially attempted to convey the message that the EPA would aggressively enforce the newly created environmental policies (Gottlieb, 1993).

Ruckelshaus's early accomplishments stemmed from his focus on air and water pollution, and included improvement in air quality standards and a shift in agency focus toward health concerns (Cohen, 1986). He is credited with demonstrating to Nixon the significance of the 1972 United Nations Conference on the Human Environment in Stockholm, to which Nixon subsequently persuaded Congress to make notable contributions (McCormick, 1989). Ruckelshaus's task was never easy while at the EPA and his work became an increasing source of frustration. His contributions, however, are recognized as having a tremendous effect on the Nixon administration's impact on the environment (Flippen, 2000).

Ruckelshaus left the EPA in 1973 to become acting director of the FBI (he later became deputy attorney general and played a primary role in the impeachment proceeding against Nixon), and was replaced by acting director, Bob Fri. Fri played a major role in creating automobile pollution standards, which led to the phase out of leaded gasoline. Fri was replaced by Russell Train, whose credentials were more appealing to environmentalists. Prior to assuming the role of EPA administrator, Train offered advice to the president regarding environmental issues through his position as chairman of the Council on Environmental Quality (another Nixon-era creation), and was president of the pro-environmental Conservation Foundation (Waterman, 1989). Train had a sincere interest in environmental protection. His interest, however, would later turn to frustration with the Nixon administration.

Train (1996) argues that current discussions of the overall record of the Nixon administration tend to overlook its substantial contributions to the environment. Among the accomplishments of this period were: (1) increasing U.S. concern for global environmental protection (Switzer & Bryner, 1998); (2) using the Refuse Act of 1899 to reduce pollution (Barkdull, 1998); (3) proactively addressing public concern over the environment (e.g., through initiatives such as land use policy; Train, 1996); (4) forwarding an unprecedented and unmatched amount of environmental legislation; and (5) creation of the EPA through executive order. Legislation in various areas of the environment, including endangered species, pesticide control, ocean dumping, coastal zone management, and marine mammals, was heavily supported by the Nixon administration and an apparently supportive Congress (Flippen, 2002). The Nixon administration is also credited with achieving international cooperation to address a series of environmental concerns (Barkdull, 1998; Train, 1996). Train (1996, p. 185) notes that environmental protection was the "most significant area of domestic policy accomplishment of the Nixon administration," citing the quantity, scope, and innovativeness of Nixon's environmental initiatives as notably impressive.

The above list of accomplishments during the Nixon years is far from comprehensive, as other contributions from this period undoubtedly added to environmental protection (e.g., Barkdull, 1988; Train, 1996; Flippen, 2000). In recognizing these accomplishments, however, one must keep in mind that the executive office does not exist in a vacuum. In particular, not all of the environmental progress of the Nixon administration should be directly attributed to Nixon, and there remains debate regarding whether these advances in environmental protection were sincere or stemmed solely from his political ambitions (e.g., Switzer & Bryner, 1998; Landy et al., 1990; Stine, 1998; Davis, 2002). Stine (1998), for instance, notes Nixon's lukewarm concern for environmental issues while he simultaneously spearheaded pro-environmental policies. Highlighting this Jekyll and Hyde side of his environmental personality, scientist/policy-maker Devra Davis noted that Nixon once told Ruckelshaus to "watch out for these crazy enviros...They're a bunch of commie pinko queers!" (2002, p. 95).

Nixon's personal positions on several issues made it difficult to appease environmentalists while entertaining other pressing problems such as economic growth. These difficulties ultimately led to his occasionally contradictory approach to environmental issues. Such contradiction is perhaps most notable in his support of NEPA and the Clean Air Act amendments, while simultaneously attempting to restrict the efforts of EPA regulators (Landy et al., 1990).

Some question Nixon's direct contributions to the environmental progress experienced during his administration (e.g., Barkdull, 1998), and suggest that other factors were behind the progress (e.g., Genovese, 1990; Flippen, 1995; 1996; 2000). Flippen (2000), for instance, notes that Congress and Nixon's staff played significant roles in environmental progress during Nixon's second-term, when he redirected focus away from environmental issues toward the nation's economic concerns. Flippen (2000, p. 227) adds that Nixon's limited interest in the environment during his second term in office, which included limiting the effectiveness of environmental legislation and attempting to weaken the effectiveness of the EPA, "increasingly antagonized his environmental staff and energized the environmental opposition."

The limited concern for environmental issues displayed by the administration during Nixon's second term (e.g., Waterman, 1989) hampered the effectiveness, and tempered the enthusiasm of EPA Administrator Russell Train. As noted by Waterman (1989, p. 113):

> The Nixon administration attempted to prevent many of the EPA's regulations from taking effect and introduced legislation in Congress that would have greatly weakened the EPA's authority. The reforms would have forced the EPA to become more cost-conscious, rather than environmentally cautious. Train vehemently opposed these White House initiatives. His opposition was so strident that the EPA became an active opponent of White House policy in the area of environmental protection.

Nixon's environmental retreat was impacted by several events. For instance, faced with, among other things, an energy crisis and a political scandal, Nixon had to confront more controversial political demons than the environment. Flippen (2000, p. 228) notes that "To expect a weakened president in the midst of a scandal to press forward with any energy program other than the most politically expedient was, perhaps, to entertain unreasonable hopes," adding that Nixon "could not afford the perspective of a single-minded lobby, however legitimate, but had to consider the broader context, constantly weighing costs, both financial and political" (p. 228).

Despite Nixon's second-term retreat, substantial improvements to environmental regulation are well documented throughout his presidency. Political powers are often required to appease wide interests, and the ability of one individual to affect public policy is limited. Social events of the Nixon administration notably affected his impact on the environment, a trend that is evident throughout the presidencies following Nixon. For instance, Flippen (2000) notes that upon entering office President Ford inherited a troubled economy, which contributed to a continuation of Nixon's second-term retreat on environmental issues.

The Ford Administration (1974–1977)

In completing Nixon's second term, Gerald Ford made few significant contributions to environmental issues, and is not recognized for influencing any environmental initiatives. The only notable environmental legislation to emerge from Ford's time in office was the Federal Lands Policy and Management Act of 1976 (Flippen, 2000). Switzer and Bryner (1998, p. 51) suggest that "The environmental slate for Gerald Ford is a clean, albeit empty, one."

Switzer and Bryner (1998, p. 51) note that Ford's limited environmental record can be explained, in part, by three issues. First, the 1973 Arab oil embargo disrupted legislative concern for pollution. Second, there was growing industrial concern with the costs of complying with EPA regulations during an economic recession. Third, the momentum of the environmental movement, which appeared so strong just a few years earlier, was waning by 1976, and the Ford administration did little to restore the momentum.

Entering the presidency under non-traditional circumstances (Nixon's resignation), Ford made few changes in environmental policy. He retained the services of EPA Administrator Train, who would serve in that role throughout Ford's term. Despite the friction between Train and Ford, the president likely recognized the importance of retaining Train, who was popular with environmentalists that constituted a substantial public interest group wielding notable clout in Washington. Although the Ford presidency is not credited with substantial contributions to environmental issues, Train's tenure as EPA administrator "reinforced the image of the EPA as an aggressive environmental advocate" (Landy et al., 1990, p. 38). Concern for environmental issues would reappear within the Executive Office with the 1977 election of Jimmy Carter.

The Carter Administration (1977–1981)

In contrast to Gerald Ford, Jimmy Carter arrived at the White House with a sincere interest in protecting the environment and was intent to carry out an environmental agenda (e.g., Flippen, 2000). Prior to his election, Carter received recognition from the League of Conservation Voters for his environmental record as governor of Georgia, even though his presidential campaign focused more directly on issues other than the environment (Switzer & Bryner, 1998). Carter recognized the importance of courting environmentalists, benefited from societal concern for the environment, and became the first U.S. presidential candidate to campaign successfully on environmental issues. His administration reflected his environmental concern (Stine, 1998).

Although Carter kept most of Nixon's environmental employees, he replaced Russell Train with Douglas Costle as EPA Administrator (Switzer & Bryner, 1998). Costle's appointment initially offended one of the environmental movement's leaders, Senator Edmund Muskie, who objected due to Costle's limited background in environmental issues (Switzer & Bryner, 1998). Costle, who would remain EPA Administrator throughout the Carter administration, had little connection to Carter, and was also suspect because of his service in Republican administrations at the national and state levels (Landy et al., 1990).

At the time of Costle's appointment, the EPA viewed itself, and was viewed by others as an environmental advocate, and Costle's record as a successful administrator and his role in the creation of the EPA made him attractive to the Carter administration (Landy et al., 1990). Costle would maintain the agency's image of environmental advocacy, form a strong team of EPA administrators, and redefine the mission of the EPA to focus on public health in place of the earlier mission that focused on the maintenance of ecological balance (Landy et al., 1990).

The Carter administration was interested in administrative reform and enhanced efficiency, and Costle immediately took the lead at the EPA. He focused on sending a message to the public that the EPA was a public health agency (Landy et al., 1990), and played a notable role influencing Congress to pass the 1980 Comprehensive Environmental Response, Compensation, and Liability Act (commonly known as Superfund). Superfund, a $1.6 billion trust fund financed primarily by a tax imposed on industrial feedstock chemicals, expanded EPA jurisdiction. It permitted the agency to more forcefully address hazardous waste issues by allowing the EPA to sue offending agencies for cleanup costs associated with illegal hazardous waste disposal (Flippen, 2000). The agency now shifted its focus from pollution to toxins and in doing so increased the presence of the organization such that it received a 25 percent budget increase during a time of financial austerity (Switzer & Bryner, 1998).

Similar to the expectations faced by the Clinton administration years later, the election of Jimmy Carter brought great hope to environmentalists, who believed his administration would emphasize environmental issues. Carter courted environmentalists during his four years in office, hoping the group would carry him through reelection (Switzer & Bryner, 1998). Despite the initial enthusiasm about the administration, Carter made several decisions and faced several crises that detracted from his environmental agenda and ultimately his environmental record. Carter faced runaway inflation, a stagnant economy, and an oil embargo, among other things, which limited his focus on the environment. The inability of Congress to create a comprehensive energy policy under the Carter administration led many to question the president's abilities as a leader and as an environmental advocate (Switzer & Bryner, 1998). Carter's policy differences with the EPA, which included several attempts to reduce regulatory costs to businesses to stimulate the economy (Waterman, 1989), and his institutionalization of cost-benefit analysis to control government regulation also aroused questions of Carter's concern for environmental issues.

Governmental cost-benefit analysis requirements forced the EPA to recognize the costs of regulatory provisions in relation to business and economy. A more intense version of this approach would be evidenced during Reagan's tenure in office (Tolchin & Tolchin, 1983). Carter, however, maintained the hopes of environmentalists while Reagan, as noted below, did not. Carter's employment of cost-benefit analysis lacked consistency, often shifting between pro-environmental and pro-business approaches, leaving his appointees uncertain as to his commitment, and ultimately limiting his control over the EPA (Waterman, 1989).

Several notable environmental accomplishments during his years in office have led some to rank Carter along with Theodore and Franklin Roosevelt as the presidents most concerned with conservation (e.g., Stine, 1998). Stine (1998, p. 196) notes that despite not completely appealing to dogmatic environmental advocates, Carter adopted the goals of the environmental movement and "advanced the cause of environmental policy as has no occupant of the White House since FDR." Carter's decision to balance three goals related to quality of life issues (environmental regulation, jobs, and economic development), and his recognition of global environmental issues led Stine (1998, p. 195) to suggest that "Carter was ahead of his time."

Despite passage of substantial legislation such as Superfund and maintaining environmental issues among its priorities, the Carter administration fell short of meeting the "unrealistically high expectations" of environmentalists (Stine, 1998, p. 179). Stine (1998, p. 195) notes that despite issues such as inflation and deficit control, and energy initiatives and economic recovery that sometimes took precedence over environmental issues, "the environmentalists' criticisms of Carter were overstated, attributed perhaps to the movement's political immaturity and what was then an absolutist approach to deal making." If environmentalists were disappointed with the Carter administration, they were enraged by the Reagan administration.

The Reagan Administration (1981–1989)

The Reagan administration did immense damage to the EPA during the president's two terms in office. In fact, the agency still bears some of the scars. Reagan's 1980 campaign, which centered on improving the American way of life through less government intrusion (Landy et al., 1990), signified impending trouble for the EPA and environmentalists. Cannon (2000, p. 468) notes that in the six-year period beginning with his second term as governor of California and his first term as president "Reagan had no pro-environment advisers and became increasingly dependent on his pro-development friends in business and industry." This "less government, more industry" approach is documented by numerous analyses of the Reagan administration (e.g., Johnson, 1991; Vig & Kraft, 1984; Friedrichs, 1996; Landy et al., 1990; Switzer & Bryner, 1998), and contributed to the administration's "stormy chapter in environmental politics" (Switzer & Bryner, 1998, p. 52).

Reagan's environmental agenda centered on: (1) regulatory reform, (2) heavy reliance on the free market to distribute resources, and (3) encouraging states to accept increasing responsibility for environmental issues (Vig & Kraft, 1984). Landy and colleagues (1990) suggest that the Reagan administration chose to appease its conservative supporters with its environmental policies primarily through regulatory relief and transferring greater discretion to state governments. Further, Landy et al. identify the Reagan administration's efforts to reorganize the EPA through assigning loyalists to significant posts, allowing loyalists to control the EPA, and curtailing EPA budgets as attempts to ensure the EPA's compliance with the administration's wishes. This shift in policy from earlier presidential administrations generated unprecedented turbulence with regard to the EPA administration and practices. Stine (1998) suggests that Reagan was moderately successful in attempts to dismantle the environmental progress of the Carter administration, with some critics suggesting that the Reagan administration was almost solely responsible for destroying the accomplishments made with regard to pollution control (e.g., Switzer & Bryner, 1998).

The EPA experienced strict budget cuts between 1980 and 1982, which were accompanied by substantial personnel reductions (Lash, Gillman, & Sheridan, 1984). The personnel reduction began on Reagan's first day in office when he issued a memorandum to the heads of executive departments and agencies declaring a hiring freeze of federal civilian employees, which in essence prohibited the replacement of EPA staff members who left the agency (Mintz, 1995). Further, over twenty senior EPA officials were removed from office and several others resigned under pressure by the end of Reagan's third year in office (Johnson, 1991).

Personnel turnover was a notable concern during the Reagan years, as were his choices for key environmental agency appointments. For example, James Watt was selected as Secretary of the Interior, a move that ultimately backfired after Watt's anti-environmentalist approach and thoughtless comments (e.g., Cannon, 2000, pp. 530–531; Lash et al., 1984, p. 231) led to his Reagan-coerced resignation. Reagan then assigned William Clark to the post. Clark was as unsuccessful as Watt and was replaced after less than a year and a half later by Donald Hodel (Switzer & Bryner, 1998). As discussed below, Reagan's appointment of Anne (Gorsuch) Burford as the EPA Administrator would also lead to problems, and Burford would resign facing, among other things, congressional and public group accusations of favoritism and mismanagement.

The EPA appeared disoriented upon Reagan's election as president, with infighting and uncertainty taking precedence over environmental protection (Hyatt, 1998). Amidst key agency heads either leaving or being fired from the EPA, bitter political arguments over the administration of the agency, staff and budget cuts, changes in administrative procedures, and confusion about the agency mission (Hyatt, 1998), the EPA would experience a period of limited support and progress.

The limited progress and support is evidenced in, among other things, the Reagan administration's initial approach to regulating environmental issues. The pro-business approach adopted during the Reagan era resulted in decisions to shift EPA regulatory practices from a confrontational approach to voluntary compliance. The administration argued this approach would generate enhanced compliance from the business community (Hyatt, 1998). EPA Administrator, Anne Burford, a conservative who embraced the anti-regulatory approach to government, made voluntary compliance standard operating procedure at the EPA. Hyatt (1998, p. 121) suggests that "Throughout its contentious history, few of the agency's actions were as controversial as its decision...to seek voluntary compliance." The switch to voluntary compliance brought about a reduction in the number of enforcement actions taken against those found guilty of environmental harms (Hyatt, 1998).

Several events would alter the way the EPA addressed environmental crimes. In response to public and congressional pressure following several turbulent years at the agency (during the latter portion of Reagan's terms in office), the EPA shifted its approach toward more enforcement, becoming increasingly vigilant in efforts to control the environment (e.g., Friedrichs, 1996; Hyatt, 1998). This redirected approach provided some positive results. Barnett's (1993) study of EPA actions regarding environmental cleanup under Superfund found that a pro-regulatory approach was notably effective in quantitative and qualitative outcome measures, despite continued industry resistance.

While controversy surrounded EPA enforcement practices, perhaps the greatest controversy faced by the agency concerned allegations targeted toward one of its directors, Anne Burford, and the individual who headed the hazardous waste program during Burford's tenure, Rita Lavelle. Burford was one of the youngest Reagan appointees, and her inexperience became apparent soon after she assumed the EPA Administrator position. Environmentalist groups believed that her appointment represented the Reagan administration's pro-business approach. She began her tenure by restructuring the agency, and eliminated divisions within the EPA that would eventually be reestablished (Switzer & Bryner, 1998). She eliminated the Office of Enforcement and the EPA's regional enforcement offices, transferring their duties to various programs and offices, including the newly created Office of Legal and Enforcement Counsel, which lacked a "clear demarcation of authority" (Landy et al., 1990, p. 249). Burford's efforts resulted in positions being downgraded, professionals being passed over for promotion for political appointees, and EPA careerists generally feeling demoralized (Switzer & Bryner, 1998). Nevertheless, her actions were consistent with the Reagan administration's concern for deregulation. Such "administrative incoherence" (Landy et al., 1990) would eventually catch up to Burford, who would become the unenviable target of several groups.

In the autumn of 1982, Burford became the focus of an investigation initiated by John Dingell, chairman of the House Committee on Energy and Commerce. Dingell was concerned with possible abuses in Superfund enforcement and sought EPA documents as part of the investigation (Landy et al., 1990). It was alleged that the Superfund was being used to reduce the federal deficit as opposed to cleaning up hazardous waste sites, and that the EPA had become overly accommodating to corporations involved in illegal toxic waste disposal procedures (Friedrichs, 1996). Burford was subpoenaed to appear before the Committee to provide requested documents; however, she refused to do so, citing executive privilege. With the support of the

Justice Department, Burford was able to avoid appearing before the Committee, despite a vote by the House to declare her in contempt of court (Switzer & Bryner, 1998).

Protection from the Justice Department did not last, however, following the discovery of dioxin in the roadways of Times Beach, Missouri, which drew substantial press coverage and additional charges of EPA mismanagement of cleanup operations (Switzer & Bryner, 1998). The director of the project, Rita Lavelle would be convicted on perjury and obstructing a congressional investigation, and was sentenced to six months in prison and a $10,000 fine, and ultimately fired by Reagan (Switzer & Bryner, 1998). It was found that Lavelle and several other EPA associates were "more concerned with accommodating the administration's corporate supporters and maintaining positive ties with potential future employers in regulated industries than with fulfilling the EPA's mandate" (Friedrichs, 1996, p. 290). Because it was initiating its own investigation of the EPA following the Times Beach affair, the Justice Department withdrew its protection of Burford from congressional charges of contempt (Landy et al., 1990).

The incident, and the continuous White House disinterest in her well-being (Lash et al., 1984), would lead to Burford's resignation on March 9, 1983, amidst increased concerns about her ability to manage the agency. In August 1984, a House Energy and Commerce Oversight Committee noted ethical concerns in the EPA, and suggested that between 1981 and 1983 "top level officials of the EPA violated their public trust by disregarding the public health and environment, manipulating the Superfund program for political purposes, engaging in unethical conduct, and participating in other abuses" (Johnson, 1991, p. 171). Following the Burford/Lavelle fiasco, a sense of stability would once again appear at the EPA upon the return of William Ruckelshaus.

Ruckelshaus, the first ever EPA Administrator, reluctantly returned to the EPA from industry and quickly restored some stability and credibility to the agency, which was in desperate need of image enhancement. He addressed the demoralized EPA workforce by stressing his commitment to the agency's mission and removing or transferring unqualified officials (Cannon, 2000). Among other things, the preceding, turbulent years brought about a loss of public confidence in agency objectives (Hyatt, 1998). Landy and colleagues (1990) suggest that Ruckelshaus's upstanding reputation and the need for the Reagan administration to restore some environmental credibility provided the administrator with substantial leverage, adding that perhaps Ruckelshaus's greatest contribution was agreeing to return to the agency.

Under Ruckelshaus, the EPA made notable progress in substantially reducing lead in gasoline and removing ethylene-dibromide, a major pesticide, from the market (Hyatt, 1998). Yet, despite such progress, Reagan and his staff refused to commit to environmental issues once the scandals were no longer prominent in news coverage (Cannon, 2000). The insignificance of Ruckelshaus's role became evident during a key 1984 meeting in which Ruckelshaus stressed the need for resources to reduce acid rain. During the meeting, Reagan confused Ruckelshaus with Middle East special envoy Donald Rumsfeld, twice referring to his EPA Administrator as "Don" instead of "Bill" (Cannon, 2000).

Ruckelshaus would become increasingly frustrated with the Reagan administration, particularly with its uncooperative approach to addressing acid rain. His frustration would lead to his resignation after one and a half years as administrator (in November 1984) following Reagan's second term election (Cannon, 2000). Lee Thomas, Assistant Administrator for Solid Waste and Emergency Response, replaced Ruckelshaus as EPA Administrator. Among other things, Thomas would redirect the EPA's focus toward ecology, which had become less of a concern for the agency following Costle's public health strategy during the Carter administration. The result would be increased public and scientific awareness of the dangers posed by ecological threats (Landy et al., 1990). Thomas, recognized as a career EPA employee, drew increasing attention to global concerns, engaged the United States in international forums, reestablished the environment as a major policy issue (Landy et al., 1990), and returned the agency's reputation for strong enforcement with the intent to discourage abusers of environmental policies (Hyatt, 1998; Switzer & Bryner, 1998).

Not all was lost with regard to the environment during the Reagan administration. Reagan supporters highlight the achievements during Reagan's tenure in office, including legislative accomplishments that strengthened the Superfund Act and the Clean Water Act (Lash et al., 1984). Critics, however, argue that any legislative accomplishments should be attributed to congressional initiatives and not Reagan's influence (Switzer & Bryner, 1998), and that the agency devoted disproportionate attention to low-impact, high-profile cases such as the discovery of toxic waste in Love Canal, as opposed to more substantial issues such as global warming (e.g., "William Reilly's Green...," 1991).

The EPA budget and personnel reductions during Reagan's first term in office precluded any opportunity for significant second-term accomplishments on the environmental front. Ruckelshaus and Thomas restored some credibility and funding to the agency, while Reagan, who had underestimated public support for the environment (Flippen, 2000) and lost "the battle of public opinion on the environment" (Vig, 2003, p. 109), tried to recover. Recognizing the situation, he curtailed the assault on the EPA. Perhaps his most significant accomplishment was stimulating increased support for, and membership in, environmental organizations as a response to his anti-environmental policies (Vig, 2003). Vig (2003) suggests that it was not surprising that Reagan's successor in the Executive Office, George H. Bush, distanced himself from the Reagan administration with regard to concern for the environment.

The George H. Bush Administration (1989–1993)

George H. Bush's election provided some hope to environmentalists. If nothing else, it meant the departure of Reagan. Bush, who declared himself "the environmental president" during his campaign, recognized the political importance of the environment. Bush supported his declaration by appointing William Reilly as EPA Administrator. Reilly, previously of the World Wildlife Fund, was the first environmental professional to serve as EPA Administrator (Switzer & Bryner, 1998).

Bush "learned to master the rhetoric of environmentalism but to steer a middle course in an attempt to pacify all powerful interests" (Flippen, 2000, p. 230). The result was an inconsistent environmental record that sometimes favored industry, and at other times favored the environment. Such wavering resulted in the Bush administration facing criticism from both environmentalists and conservatives (Switzer & Bryner, 1998).

Reilly and Bush are credited with breaking the legislative gridlock on clean air legislation that hadn't been revised in 13 years (Switzer & Bryner, 1998). This move seemed to signal the beginning of a productive environmental administration. The Bush administration, however, soon undermined its environmental record by helping open "wetlands to real estate development, allowing strip-mining to continue, encouraging logging in national forests, and refusing to comply with the global warming treaty" (Daynes, 1999, p. 259). Similarly, the reluctance of the Bush administration to address global environmental concerns left the United States "isolated and embarrassed in international environmental diplomacy" (Vig, 2003, p. 110).

The productive approach to environmental issues initially taken by the Bush administration evolved into defensive disarray during Bush's final year in office (Vig, 2003), and emphasized an anti-regulatory tone reminiscent of the early Reagan administration. His failure to win re-election once again brought a sense of optimism to environmentalists who believed democrat Bill Clinton would restore credibility and support to the EPA.

The Clinton Administration (1993–2001)

The 1992 election of William Jefferson Clinton provided environmentalists with a level of optimism unseen during the twelve years of the Reagan and Bush administrations. While Bush's campaign focused on protecting jobs and the Endangered Species Act, Clinton provided an appetizing platform for environmentalists which included efforts to prevent global warming, an issue Bush failed to take seriously (Switzer & Bryner, 1998). Despite Clinton's unimpressive environmental record as Governor of Arkansas, environmentalists were frustrated with the Reagan and Bush administrations and had high expectations for Clinton and his "green" vice president, Al Gore (Daynes, 1999). Such anticipation and optimism resulted in environmentalists providing extensive political support for Bill Clinton ("How Green is the …," 1994). Clinton entered office with the intent to balance jobs, stimulate the economy, and enhance environmental protection (Daynes, 1999), although he found devoting ample attention to these tasks difficult, often frustrating optimistic environmentalists.

The Clinton administration had few major environmental victories. Of significance, the administration helped establish the Office of Environmental Justice to address alleged inequities in environmental protection. Clinton's first two years in office witnessed a detrimental impact on the EPA, which resulted in substantial research staff reductions (Switzer & Bryner, 1998). The Clinton administration would, however, reestablish some environmental credibility by opposing Republican initiatives and, during the latter part of his presidency, taking a more proactive environmental approach.

The Democratic majority of the House was surrendered to the Republicans in 1994. The new Republican congress proposed using their influence to roll back environmental regulations and curtail EPA activities through budget cuts (Hyatt, 1998; Switzer & Bryner, 1998). Clinton saw opposing these Republican efforts as an opportunity to regain public support for his environmental stance. This was the beginning of the Clinton administration's renewed recognition of the benefits of supporting environmental issues, and Clinton rallied against

Newt Gingrich and his Republican supporters, along the way gaining public support and limiting harms to the environment.

Environmental concerns were again in the political spotlight during the 1996 presidential election, won by Clinton. In Clinton's second term, the administration expanded its involvement with the environment beyond simply opposing Republican initiatives, although it never met the expectations of environmentalists. As suggested by McCarthy, Thompson, and Thornburgh (2000, p. 65):

> Clinton's environmental record, like his overall place in presidential history, is muddled. It can be argued that he has done more for nature than any other President since Theodore Roosevelt, but he has also missed opportunities that may never present themselves again, given the irreversibility of much of the damage being done to the planet.

Like most presidents, Clinton faced distractions that interfered with the implementation of his environmental agenda; some of which were self-inflicted (e.g., the Monica Lewinsky/impeachment fiasco) and others that were beyond his control (e.g., Republican resistance regarding the reduction of U.S. pollution emissions level).

Clinton appointed Carol Browner as EPA Administrator, and she would proceed to become the longest-serving head in the agency's history. Following work as an environmental official in Florida, Browner adopted a pro-regulatory stance that infuriated industry and Republicans in Congress (Nash, 2000). The EPA, under Browner, would encounter turbulence in 1998 when over a dozen career EPA employees claimed the agency engaged in "egregious misconduct," arguing, among other things, that employees were harassed by superiors, and whistleblowers were retaliated against by every level of management (B. Cohen, 1998). Bonner Cohen (1998, p. 38), in a scathing assessment of the EPA under Browner, suggested the agency became "an instrument of environmental zealotry that knows no legal or ethical bounds." Cohen cites a host of agency shortcomings including the neglect of scientific research, an argument stemming from an article in the journal *Nature* offered by EPA research microbiologist David Lewis. Lewis chastised the director for disproportionately focusing on issuing regulations rather than developing the necessary science. Accusations of illegalities and unethical practices at the EPA seem to fit the bill for the Clinton administration. Regardless of such claims and a slow start with regard to environmental regulation, the administration's environmental record would finish strong.

The administration strengthened the EPA and took notable steps to protect public lands and endangered species during the latter part of Clinton's terms in office (Vig, 2003). EPA Administrator Browner is credited with strengthening and enforcing existing regulations, and issuing new regulations, particularly tighter air quality standards (Vig, 2003). Most of the Clinton administration's significant contributions to the environment (outlined in Daynes, 1999, p. 301) came late in his second term, including several new regulations addressing various forms of pollution.

Environmentalists, however, believe that Clinton waited too long to address serious environmental issues, which provided the unattractive result of leaving them to the incoming Republican administration (McCarthy et al., 2000). McCarthy and colleagues (2000, p. 64) note, "Clinton tried to be the new Teddy Roosevelt, but his efforts to help preserve nature may have been too little too late." Further, although he is recognized as the first president to become immersed in the international arena as an environmental president (Hunter & Noonan, 1993), Clinton was criticized for his failure to properly address "the greatest challenge of the new century, climate change" (Vig, 2003, p. 114). Despite its shortcomings, Clinton's administration provided greater hope to environmentalists than did the election of George W. Bush.

The George W. Bush Administration (2001–Present)

George W. Bush entered the Oval Office amidst political controversy and environmentalist pessimism. Touting himself as environmentally friendly, Bush made his *real* environmental stance clear soon after taking office when his administration made several policy decisions. First, Bush placed a sixty-day moratorium on Clinton administration rules, which had yet to take effect and impacted several very important environmental policies. Next, Bush reversed a campaign pledge to control carbon dioxide emissions from power plants. The Bush administration also: announced that the U.S. would withdraw from the Kyoto Protocol on climate change; sought to open the Arctic National Wildlife Refuge to oil exploration; withdrew the EPA's new arsenic-in-drinking water standards; and had the boundaries of 19 National Parks redrawn to encourage oil exploration (e.g., Vig, 2003). In perhaps the most egregious act of anti-environmentalism, the Bush administration joined with DaimlerChrysler to present an *Amici Curiae* brief seeking to overturn the state of California's self-selected, zero-emission vehicle law, while, at the same time, claiming that states would be given more control over environmental issues.

With these acts—and hundreds more like them (see Bush's environmental record at the National Resource Council Defense Fund Web site, www.nrdc.org)—Bush has set into motion what is sure to become *the worst record* on environmental issues achieved by any modern president. White (2003, p. A31) notes that after two and a half years in office, "the Bush administration's overall record on the environment has been regressive and harmful."

Bush's environmental record as president should come as no surprise given the record of environmental degradation he achieved while governor of Texas. For example, one of Bush's first actions as Governor of Texas was to cut the state's environmental protection agency's (the Texas Natural Resource Conservation Commission, TNRCC; now called the Texas Commission on Environmental Quality, TCEQ) budget by 20 percent. Bush then appointed Ralph Marquez, formerly with Monsanto Chemicals and the Texas Chemical Council, as the first appointee to the TNRCC. Marquez responded by helping Houston businessmen suppress smog advisories and smog data from public view. Bush also appointed Barry McBee, an opponent of the Right-To-Know legislation. Having been turned into a voice for industry rather than public health, TNRCC opposed new EPA air quality regulations on several occasions over the next few years, and refused to meet federal standards.

While he was stocking TNRCC with pro-industry representatives, Bush was also busy gutting other environmental legislation that protected public health, such as the vehicle emission inspection program. The governor was sued for this action because it violated a contract with a private business entity (not because it violated Clean Air Act requirements for designated non-containment areas). The private contractor won the suit, which lead to a $140 million settlement against the state of Texas. To make the settlement payment, Bush cut the TNRCC's budget by an additional 18 percent ($125 million).

Further, the Bush administration's record on environmental issues should come as no surprise given that Bush's largest campaign contributors have been oil/gas, chemical, and automobile companies, including the now-defunct Enron. For instance, companies that took advantage of his controversial plan to lower penalties against polluters contributed more than $116,000 to his reelection campaign between 1996 and 1998 (Public Employees for Environmental Responsibility; www.txpeer.org/bush/quietlittlewar3.html). Overall, large polluters contributed more than $1 million to Bush's election. His appointments to key policy positions that influence the president's environmental position have also been staffed with industry representatives (see Table 5-2).

Table 5-2: Names, Position, and Former Employment of Key Political Appointees of the Bush Administration

Spencer Abraham, Energy Secretary. The former, one term, Michigan Senator has taken a clear anti-fuel economy standards position. He received more money from the automobile industry than any other politician.

Andrew Card, White House Chief of Staff. Formerly chief lobbyist for General Motors, and CEO of the American Automobile Manufacturers Association, Card opposes fuel-economy standards.

Vicky Bailey, Assistant Energy Secretary, International Affairs and Domestic Policy. Bailey is the former President of PSI, a subsidiary of Cinergy Gas.

Francis Blake, Deputy Energy Secretary. Former Senior Vice President and General Counsel at General Electric.

Kathleen Cooper, Under-Secretary of Commerce, Economic Affairs. Former chief economist at ExxonMobil.

Don Evans, Commerce Secretary. Former Chairman and CEO of the oil/gas company, Tom Brown.

Cam Toohey, Interior Specialist, Alaska. Former Director of Arctic Power, a lobbying group solely designed to obtain the rights to drill for oil and gas in the Arctic National Wildlife Refuge.

Gale Norton, Interior Secretary. An understudy to James Watt, Norton has served as legal counsel to mining industries and other anti-environmental groups.

Lawrence Lindsay, Presidential Economic Advisor. Before his appointment, Lindsay was a consultant on natural gas issues to Enron.

Clay Johnson, Director, Presidential Personnel. Johnson's role involves appointing members of the Federal Energy Regulatory Commission. He was a major stockholder ($250,000) in El Paso Energy Partners, a Texas gas/oil company.

Lewis Libby, Vice President Cheney's Chief of Staff. Large stockholder in ExxonMobil, Texaco, Chesapeake Energy, and Enron.

Karl Rove, Senior Presidential Political Advisor. Large shareholder in Amoco, Royal Dutch/Shell, and Enron.

Condoleeza Rice, National Security Advisor. Former board member at Chevron. An oil tanker was named after her.

The Bush administration demonstrated its anti-environmental policies from the moment it entered the White House, calling for increased fossil fuel exploration, minimizing rules against strip mining, and encouraging the Justice Department to drop EPA-initiated lawsuits against coal-fired power plants. This pro-fossil fuel stance was itself fueled by campaign contributions that total more than $25 million to Republicans during the 2000 elections.

The administration's lack of concern for environmental issues is further evident in its 2001 proposed energy plan, which requested substantial increases in future energy supplies, particularly domestic oil and gas production. The plan called for streamlining environmental regulations with the intent to accelerate the production of new energy (Vig, 2003; Sanger & Kahn, 2001). Bush's first budget proposal also demonstrated a lack of concern for environmental issues as it "called for a modest 4 percent increase in overall domestic discretionary spending but an 8 percent reduction in funding for natural resource and environmental programs. The EPA's budget was to be cut by nearly $500 million, or 6.4 percent" (Vig, 2003, p. 118). At $7.3 billion, the EPA's fiscal year 2002 budget would be lower than the budgets of all preceding years dating back to 1998, and greater authority would be transferred to the states (Hess, 2001).

Republican Christine Todd Whitman, former Governor of New Jersey, and President Bush's appointee as EPA Administrator, brought to the position "political skills, experience and the ability to strike a balance between conflicting interest groups" (Nash, 2001, p. 29). She was recognized by some as a moderate; for instance the Sierra Club suggested they "could work with her" (Nash, 2001, p. 29), although others failed to see the moderation with regard to her impact on the environment. Ireland (2001, p. 18), for example, argues that "Whitman has been an unmitigated disaster for New Jersey's environmental protection," adding that "...she decapitated the state Department of Environmental Protection staff by 738 employees in her first three years in office, cut the remaining staff's workweek by five hours, eliminated fines of polluters as a source of DEP revenue and made large cuts in the DEP's budgets" (p. 18).

Stating she wished to spend more time with her family, Whitman resigned from her position on June 27, 2003, after approximately two and half years serving as EPA Administrator. Despite the optimism she brought to the position, her tenure in office is categorized by passivity and bowing to industry; her actions arguably inspired by her role within an anti-environment Bush administration. In a critical assessment of Whitman's EPA, environmental attorney Michael White (2003, p. A31) notes:

> Under Christie Todd Whitman's watch at the (EPA), the Bush White House introduced a slew of anti-environmental rules and regulations, making it one of the most anti-environmental administrations ever. But some would argue that she was a bulwark preventing considerably worse offenses from taking place.

As EPA Administrator, Whitman was recognized "as sympathetic to environmental causes but also as someone who lacked the will or the influence within the administration to aid many of those concerns" (Greene, 2003, p. 1A). She faced a difficult challenge in balancing the interests of the environment with a pro-industry Bush administration. Perhaps the challenge is best exemplified in her attempts to persuade President Bush to have the United States participate in the Kyoto Protocol on global warming, only to have the president dismiss the idea. Whitman's final day as EPA Administrator was preceded by the resignation of the second-ranking EPA official, Deputy Administrator Linda Fisher, who announced her resignation the day before Whitman left her job. Fisher's position was temporarily filled by Stephen Johnson, who was in charge of the EPA pesticides program, while Whitman's position was filled, on an interim basis, by Marianne Lamont Horinko who was previously in charge of the Superfund program.

In August 2003, President Bush nominated Utah Governor Michael O. Leavitt to assume the role of EPA Administrator. Leavitt, who at the time of this writing is awaiting Senate confirmation, brings to the agency a pledge to find a balance between environmental concerns and business interests. In nominating Leavitt, Bush pledged that the governor would help shift environmental regulation out of Washington, DC and into the states. In accordance with many Bush nominees, Leavitt's nomination was hailed by Republican lawmakers and industry, and criticized by Democrats and environmentalists. Leavitt was recognized by Bush for his environmental record as governor and his respect for the abilities of state and local governments. The Bush administration believes that Leavitt's "low-key, competent demeanor makes him the ideal choice to head an agency that Bush would like to have a low profile" (Allen and Milbank, 2003, p. A1).

Critics of Leavitt include Senator Joseph Lieberman (D-CT) who, suggested the Senate not confirm the governor, and stated that Leavitt "shares the same disregard for clean air, clean water, land conservation and global warming" as the Bush administration (Allen and Milbank, 2003, p. A1). Philip Clapp, president of the National Environmental Trust suggested that Leavitt's philosophy centers on "less regulation, no matter what the cost to public health and the environment" (Allen and Milbank, 2003, p. A1). Spangler and Dougherty (2003) note that, if confirmed, Leavitt would regulate many of the same companies that strongly supported his political campaigns. They note that from 1997 to 2002, "Leavitt raised more than a half million dollars (one-eighth of his contributions) from companies that are regulated to a greater or lesser degree by the EPA, or regulated under authority granted by the EPA to the state" (p. A1).

Virtually all of Bush's other appointees were considered anti-environment (Vig, 2003), leading some to recognize the administration as more conservative than the Reagan administration (Milbank & Nakashima, 2001). In a scathing, public resignation from his position as director of the EPA's Office of Regulatory Enforcement, Eric Schaeffer, who had been at the EPA for 12 years, cited the Bush administration's disregard for environmental issues, particularly pollution control. Schaeffer (2002) also cited the administration's failure to fill key vacancies in the agency, its practice of slashing enforcement budgets, and its overall destruction of years of environmental progress. Schaeffer's comments are evidenced, in part, by accusations that the White House deliberately nominated unqualified and "soft" candidates to fill the vacant position of director of the EPA's Office of Regulatory Enforcement (Franz, 2002). Some call Schaeffer an attention-seeking martyr (e.g., Levine, 2002), although his claims at the very least confirm the Bush administration's lack of concern for environmental control.

Following pressure resulting from his decision to revisit the numerous environmental regulations put forth by Clinton during his last few weeks in office, President Bush apparently took heed of his developing reputation as one who disregards environmental issues. In response, he attempted to improve his image by offering several environmental regulations of his own, including extensive paperwork for small users of lead and an efficiency standard for new washing machines ("Green Bush," 2001). Bush also agreed to tighten the standards for arsenic in water, although not to the extent proposed by Clinton ("Green Bush," 2001), and further showed support for environmental regulation by deciding to maintain the cabinet rank of the EPA administrator (Nash, 2001). Some suggest that Bush's largest mistake since assuming office is his lack of communication, particularly with regard to his decision to repeal, yet not fully discuss why, many of the proposed Clinton regulations ("Green Bush," 2001).

Based on early practices of the current Bush administration, it appears environmentalists have much work ahead of them, and the EPA is in for a struggle. As noted by Vig's (2003, p. 120) assessment of Bush's first year in office:

> Although there were no major domestic policy rollbacks comparable to those of the early Reagan years, [because] Congress appeared ready to block many of the president's environmental cutbacks, Bush used his administrative powers to weaken many regulations and has appointed subordinates who are largely unsympathetic to environmental needs.

The Bush administration's early anti-regulatory approach to environmental protection conjures images of the Reagan administration, although shifts in focus and approach are always possible.

SUMMARY OF EPA HISTORY

The short history of the EPA demonstrates an agency with an incredibly large mandate, fluctuating support, and limited direction. Rosenbaum (2003) suggests that, despite the EPA accomplishing more than its critics concede, dissatisfaction with the agency's accomplishments exists with both EPA proponents and opponents. The EPA, similar to the presidential administrations that have largely shaped the agency, often faces a no-win situation. For instance, environmentalists may believe that particular pro-regulatory practices are not enough, despite industry's claims that such pro-regulation hampers their abilities to survive financially.

One could argue that presidential influence on the EPA contributes to its unstable nature. Oval Office directives that change agency focus, impact its direction through the selection of an administrator, and affect budgetary support issues can severely alter the tasks the EPA undertakes. The need to battle Congress, which consists of individuals maintaining their own agendas, results in further difficulties for an agency dependent on governmental/political support.

Despite the notable efforts of many career EPA employees who maintain sincere concerns for environmental protection, the level of disorganization and inconsistency characterizing the history of the EPA led to piecemeal progress and limited efficiency with regard to environmental regulation. The EPA remains, however, the primary agency charged with regulating the environment and historical inconsistencies do not necessarily imply future problems. In fact, despite the current Bush administration's apparent disregard for environmental issues, the EPA makes available to the public a wealth of information, which speaks to the partial autonomy of the agency.

From a researcher's standpoint, the increased availability of environmental crime–related information, for instance, suggests a positive step forward for the agency. In fact, one could argue that the agency encourages researchers to identify problems by making its data so freely available. With limited resources, the EPA has little time to closely analyze much of the data it collects. The increased availability of EPA data in conjunction with the increased availability of environmental crime data provided by state regulatory agencies limits the opportunities for environmental crime researchers to argue that they have limited access to environmental crime data. A large sample of this wealth of information available to researchers is addressed in later chapters in this work.

Table 5-3: EPA Administrators

Administrator	Years	President
William D. Ruckelshaus	1970-1973	Nixon
Bob Fri*	1973	Nixon
Russell E. Train	1973–1977	Nixon/Ford
John Quarles*	1977	Ford
Douglas M. Costle	1977–1981	Carter
Steve Jellinek*	1981	Carter
Walter Barber Jr.*	1981	Carter
Anne M. (Gorsuch) Burford	1981–1983	Reagan
Lee Verstandig *	1983	Reagan
William D. Ruckelshaus	1983–1985	Reagan
Lee M. Thomas	1985–1989	Reagan
John Moore*	1989	Reagan
William K. Reilly	1989–1993	G.H. Bush
Carol M. Browner	1993–2001	Clinton
W. Michael McCabe*	2001	G.W. Bush
Christine T. Whitman	2001–2003	G.W. Bush
Marianne Lamont Horinko*	2003	G.W. Bush
Michael O. Leavitt	2003	G.W. Bush

* = Acting Director

CHAPTER 6

Enforcing Environmental Laws

This chapter discusses some issues involved in enforcing environmental regulations. Particular issues of concern involve the diverse array of laws the EPA is charged with enforcing; the effect of budgetary restraints on enforcement; variations in enforcement of environmental laws across states; and the ability of the EPA and state environmental enforcement agencies to interface with one another.

ENFORCEMENT EFFORTS: GENERAL BACKGROUND

The extensive and growing body of environmental legislation offers little without consistent monitoring and enforcement practices designed to increase industry compliance. For instance, some suggest that weak and unenforced environmental legislation contributes to continued pollution with relative impunity, despite the notable number of laws passed during the 1970s (Brown, 1979, 1988; Goldman, 1991). What is the purpose of laws if they cannot be properly enforced?

Several years ago, Nader, Brownstein, and Richard (1981) characterized environmental crime as a serious health and safety concern for millions of Americans. One could argue that environmental crime remains problematic, due in part to the relatively limited enforcement response to such acts, and the continual impact of environmental pollution on public health. For example, environmental pollution makes a significant contribution to the rates of many diseases, especially cancers, respiratory problems, and learning disabilities (Colborn, Dumanoski, & Myers, 1997; Wargo, 1998; Steingraber, 1998; Lappe, 1991; Lynch & Stretesky, 2001).

Fully implementing environmental laws has proven difficult for environmental regulators because they face numerous constraints including limited budgets, legal challenges from regulated industries, jurisdictional conflicts, industry's manipulation of administrative procedures (Friedrichs, 1996; Adler & Lord, 1991; Starr, 1991), and public opinion (Lynch & Stretesky, 1999). For these reasons, Cable and

Benson (1993, p. 465) suggest that "The impact and effectiveness of national environmental regulation is a matter of debate."

AN ORIENTATION TO REGULATION

The EPA is certainly a starting point for any discussion of federal environmental enforcement efforts. The EPA is assisted in fighting environmental crime by, among others, state and local environmental regulatory agencies and law enforcement groups. Such a fragmented, decentralized approach arguably results in uncoordinated enforcement that makes environmental law enforcement efforts resemble a "jigsaw puzzle" (Hyatt, 1998, p. 117). A few of the many challenges faced by EPA enforcement officials follow.

Limited Resources
One primary weakness regarding current EPA regulatory practices is limited resources, which ultimately restricts the agency's ability to (closely) monitor industry practices. Environmental regulators, in turn, rely on self-monitoring by industries, which are encouraged to report their activities to regulators; a practice that contrasts government approaches to traditional crime. Imagine for a moment a system of criminal law enforcement in which the police relied on criminals to voluntarily report when they have violated the law. One can only speculate that such an effort by police would be met with great suspicion and, perhaps, laughter.

Unclear Legislation
Another problem facing environmental regulators includes broadly defined legislation that creates too much discretion for EPA officials. Mintz (1995) argues that broadly drafted legislation results in federal environmental regulatory administrations being granted vast discretion in establishing rules consistent with regulatory statutes and enforcing new and existing laws. Ross (1996) echoes this statement in noting that the EPA has broad discretion in taking actions to ensure industry compliance with federal environmental legislation.

No Comprehensive Strategy
The EPA has also been criticized for failing to adopt and retain a comprehensive strategy consistent with environmental regulation and protection. For instance, Hyatt (1998) notes the historical absence of a comprehensive congressional environmental protection strategy, adding that Congress chooses to pass separate laws as perceived needs or

threats arise, a practice seemingly followed by the EPA, which traditionally and continually creates a separate enforcement division within the agency to administer each new law.

EPA enforcement managers, often the target of critique, are tasked with the heavy burden of ensuring that environmental legislation is enforced, and particular interests are recognized. In doing so, these individuals assume a wide array of duties ranging from (Mintz, 1995, p. 14):

> ...hiring, training, overseeing, evaluating, and retaining their staffs to preparing and justifying budget requests, relating to other managers at a peer level, responding to inquiries from investigative entities (such as the EPA Office of Inspector General and the GAO), and keeping abreast of the frequent changes in law, science, and policy that may have an impact on their enforcement work.

STATE AGENCIES

As noted, the EPA works with other agencies to enforce environmental law. For instance, the EPA regularly works with state environmental regulatory agencies, primarily through its regional offices (Hyatt, 1998). State environmental regulatory agencies must adopt federal environmental protection standards, although they may impose more stringent regulations than those offered at the federal level (Hyatt, 1998). As a result, much variation exists among the enforcement practices of the 50 state regulatory bodies, arguably attributable to societal views of particular environmental issues, state fiscal issues, the influence of various interest groups (Hunter & Waterman, 1996), and the geographic distribution of certain industries and natural resources across the country.

Despite variation among the states, Epstein (1998) notes similarities in the structure of state environmental enforcement agencies and the enforcement model established at the federal level, adding that the state has played an increasingly significant role in the regulation of environmental crime. However, state and federal regulatory agencies are not the only groups charged with protecting the environment. Law enforcement agencies at all levels are also charged with enforcing environmental crime legislation, although historically their role in enforcement efforts has been limited.

PUBLIC ATTITUDES TOWARD ENFORCING
ENVIRONMENTAL LAW

Public attitudes toward environmental crime in the 1980s shifted away from viewing environmental crimes as costs of doing business toward viewing crimes against the environment in a manner similar to the way traditional crimes are viewed (Humphreys, 1990). Carter (1998) suggests this change in public attitude is attributable, in part, to law enforcement agencies becoming increasingly aggressive in pursuing environmental crime offenders.

Clifford (1998) echoes Carter's suggestion that law enforcement is taking a more aggressive approach to environmental crimes, adding that law enforcement agencies believe enforcement actions can improve public health. Clifford (1998) notes that increased emphasis on environmental crime by law enforcement encouraged local prosecutors to develop and implement strategies and techniques to successfully prosecute environmental crime offenders.

Despite advances in environmental law, protection, and prosecution, surveys indicate that many Americans (48%) believe that laws implemented to protect the environment have not gone far enough, and that preserving nature is more important than preserving economic growth (53%) (ag.arizona.edu/arec/wemc/papers/DealingConsumer). A typical response to public opinion on this matter is to question how much the public really knows about environmental law and pollution. While the public's knowledge on specific issues may be wanting, its overall opinion reflects some current trends in pollution, such as rising levels of pollution in recent years, and weakened enforcement of environment laws under the Bush administration. Still, efforts to assess the validity of public opinion require some basis for comparison. One mechanism for establishing a basis for comparison is to measure the extent of environmental crime.

MEASURING ENVIRONMENTAL CRIME

There is no easy way to measure the level of environmental crime. Although there are numerous data sources on environmental crime and pollution, none provide a single, comprehensive measure of this phenomenon. The data presented throughout the chapters in this book illustrate this problem.

Similar to difficulties experienced when measuring traditional crime, attempts to measure environmental crime seem futile. Epstein (1998, p. 153) argues that "Estimating the extent of environmental crime is both practically and conceptually very difficult" adding that "At the present time, little or no national research has been conducted to discover the numbers and types of environmental crime." Such limitations in measurement do not, however, extend to data concerning government environmental crime enforcement efforts. Recent numbers suggest a decline in EPA enforcement efforts coinciding with the beginning of the Bush administration in 2000. This is not surprising, since Bush froze many new directives that impacted environmental regulations, and weakened the EPA through budgetary and personnel cuts (see the discussion on the Bush administration in Chapter 5). Table 6-1 depicts select enforcement findings from 2000 to 2002.

Table 6-1: EPA Enforcement Actions FY 2000–2002			
	2002	2001	2000
EPA Inspections	17,668	17,560	20,417
Civil Referrals to DOJ	342	327	368
Civil Judicial Settlements	216	221	219
Judicial Penalties (millions)	$55.8	$101.7	$54.9
Criminal Referrals to DOJ	250	256	236
Criminal Sentences (years)	215.9	256	236
Criminal Penalties (millions)	$62.3	$94.7	$122.0

(Source: U.S. Environmental Protection Agency, Enforcement and Compliance Program, available online at: http://cfpub.epa.gov/compliance/newsroom/index.cfm)

As Table 6-1 indicates, the number of civil and criminal cases referred to the U.S. Department of Justice (DOJ) decreased since the record-setting 644 referrals during 1999, although these numbers still suggest an EPA emphasis on referrals. In light of Ringquist's (1993) finding that aggressive enforcement efforts impact preservation of the environment, at least with regard to air pollution regulations, recent EPA efforts compromise environmental protection. In May 2003, this issue became more apparent when then-EPA Director, Christie Todd Whitman, who disagreed with the president on environmental policy over the past two years (most importantly, the president's public rebuttal of Whitman's favorable opinion of the Kyoto Protocol on global warming), resigned from her position.

EARLY ENFORCEMENT EFFORTS

Harms to the environment went virtually unregulated for most of American history. Prior to the 1970s, private civil suits brought by concerned parties were basically the only threats faced by offending parties (Friedrichs, 1996). Starr (1991) notes that despite passage of the 1899 Rivers and Harbors Act (a.k.a., "the Refuse Act"), which is recognized as the first piece of environmental pollution legislation (Friedrichs, 1996), it was not until the late 1970s that law enforcement began to apply criminal sanctions to harms against the environment. Prosecuting environmental crimes was rare until the 1970s when government officials recognized the utility of the strict liability provisions located in the Refuse Act (Cohen, 1992). By reintroducing provisions of the Refuse Act, the federal government was able to prosecute a small number of environmental cases during the 1970s (Cohen, 1992). Some suggest the emergence of an environmental movement in the late 1960s and early 1970s brought about increased societal concern for environmental issues and less concern for industrial profitability at the expense of the reckless destruction of natural resources (e.g., Hedman, 1991).

Certainly, harms against the environment occurred before the 1970s, yet the government appeared disinterested in penalizing such practices. Beginning in the 1970s, a series of new laws and the creation of the EPA resulted from a shift in public opinion about environmental pollution. Despite these new laws, there was little interest in actually prosecuting environmental criminals. Offering an explanation for the limited enforcement of environmental crime legislation, Friedrichs (1996, p. 259) states that, despite the existence of environmental protection laws, the interest in protecting economic development and the interests of economic elites dominates environmental protectionism.

The EPA adopted an enforcement orientation upon its inception. This early enforcement approach stemmed from the passage of a series of environmental protection laws during this time, although criminal prosecution of environmental offenders did not occur until the late 1970s during the Carter administration (Hedman, 1991). Perceiving the need to enforce criminal sanctions under the Clean Air Act, the EPA issued guidelines in June 1976 for bringing criminal charges and recognized the need to engage in such prosecution (McMurry & Ramsey, 1986). Over 30 major pieces of environmental legislation were passed by the federal government during the 1970s. Civil sanctions, penalties, and injunctive relief generally constituted the government's approach to judicial enforcement of environmental regulations and statutes prior to 1981, and filing criminal charges was of low priority (McMurry & Ramsey, 1986).

The initial enforcement-oriented approach adopted by the EPA slowed following the oil embargo of the early 1970s, a time when society became increasingly concerned about economic security and less concerned with environmental issues (Hyatt, 1998). However, as McMurry and Ramsey (1986) note, several factors generated increased emphasis on enforcement at the EPA in 1977. First, a change in EPA leadership brought a more active administration to the agency. Second, statutory compliance deadlines in the Clean Air Act and the Clean Water Act arrived, resulting in numerous violations of air and water pollution statutory requirements. Finally, the EPA budgeted more resources toward the enforcement of environmental crimes.

Faced with an increased focus on enforcement, the EPA implemented its Major Source Enforcement Effort (MSEE), a program designed to bring violators into compliance with the Clean Air Act and the Clean Water Act (McMurry & Ramsey, 1986). The MSEE program sought to share enforcement activities with the states, while using civil judicial enforcement actions to deter potential violators and bring about expeditious compliance (McMurry & Ramsey, 1986). The civil penalties, among other things, served as a form of punishment and helped eliminate the competitive advantage gained by those who disregarded environmental statutes (McMurry & Ramsey, 1986). The program sought quick compliance from a large number of violators.

Existing EPA investigators and inspectors, "...were technically oriented persons whose focus was to bring violators into compliance through cooperation and negotiation. They were not trained criminal investigators and were not comfortable with the notion that air and water pollution could be another type of white-collar crime" (McMurry & Ramsey, 1986, p. 1138). Nevertheless, the message had been sent that filing criminal charges would become part of the EPA's enforcement repertoire.

RECENT ENFORCEMENT EFFORTS

Only 25 federal criminal cases were referred to the Department of Justice for criminal prosecution during the 1970s (DiMento, 1993), reflecting the conservative practices of the Nixon and Ford administrations. The small number of criminal case referrals pales in comparison to the 250 cases referred in 2002. The number of enforcement actions would increase under the Carter and Reagan administrations, with the increase during the Reagan administration largely attributable to societal concern for environmental harms and extensive coverage of corrupt EPA practices (Friedrichs, 1996).

Cohen (1992) notes the significant changes that evolved with regard to the criminal enforcement of environmental crimes during the 1980s, including the EPA's development of its Office of Criminal Enforcement, and the Department of Justice's newly formed Environmental Crimes Unit of the Lands Division (Cohen, 1992). Also during the 1980s, Congress offered input to the increased enforcement of environmental crime by redefining particular environmental offenses from misdemeanors to felonies (Starr, 1991). While some government officials claimed an enhanced commitment to addressing environmental crime cases (e.g., Thornburgh, 1991; Strock, 1991), others suggest that prosecutions of environmental crime cases leveled off and that sanctions were considerably light when compared with other crimes, and compliance with environmental statutes was poor (e.g., Friedrichs, 1996; Adler & Lord, 1991).

In their analysis of environmental crime enforcement, Adler and Lord (1991) discovered limited evidence of environmental crime enforcement. They found that although nearly two-thirds of Fortune 500 companies violated federal environmental laws between 1984 and 1990, only 6 percent were prosecuted. To further illustrate their point, Adler and Lord added that it wasn't until 1984 that a large corporation was prosecuted under federal environmental laws.

Friedrichs (1996, p. 309) best describes the situation regarding enforcement of environmental crimes in suggesting that:

> Despite some modest increases in prosecutions, fines and prison sentences for individual corporate executives, there has been a systematic reluctance to imprison environmental offenders or to fine corporate environmental offenders more than a fraction (1-5 percent) of the statutory maximum for these offenses. There has in fact been a historical reluctance to prosecute corporate environmental crime cases in the first place.

SANCTIONING OPTIONS

The EPA seeks primarily to achieve voluntary compliance from federal agencies, state and local agencies, and the general public (Hyatt, 1998). The agency, and state environmental regulatory agencies, are authorized to enforce compliance through imposing the sanctions identified in major environmental laws should requests for voluntary compliance go unheeded (Hyatt, 1998). Cases in which voluntary compliance is not obtained become the responsibility of the EPA's Office of Enforcement and Compliance Assurance (OECA), which organizes evidence of noncompliance, engages in civil enforcement proceedings, and assists the Department of Justice in criminal enforcement cases when necessary (Hyatt, 1998). Many infractions brought to the attention of EPA enforcement officials are routine and promptly resolved. More serious violations, however, present greater difficulty for enforcement officials and require extensive resources, particularly in the form of time, causing delays in case settlements, or avoidance of prosecution (Landy et al., 1990).

In general, the OECA "... seeks to ensure full compliance with laws intended to protect human health and the environment. OECA staff work to identify and reduce noncompliance, maintain a strong enforcement presence, and increase the use of compliance assistance tools and incentives policies" (EPA, 1999, p. 7). In identifying its priorities, the EPA claims to provide a strong enforcement effort while attempting to deter regulated groups into seeking assistance, and using "incentive policies and providing fairness in the marketplace to ensure that noncomplying facilities do not gain an unfair competitive advantage over facilities that have dedicated resources to compliance" (EPA, 1999, p. 7).

In noncriminal cases, the EPA uses several sources of information gathering including "self-monitoring, record keeping and reporting by individual sources of pollution, inspections by government personnel, and the specific complaints of concerned citizens" (Mintz, 1995, p. 11). Most EPA inspections are announced prior to a site visit with the intent to ensure that vital personnel will be present (Mintz, 1995). Kraft (2001, p. 136) notes that "Despite the public impression to the contrary, visits and inspections of industrial facilities by regulatory officials are infrequent."

The EPA generally uses a three-prong approach to confront environmental violators: administrative enforcement (also known as regulatory enforcement), civil enforcement, and criminal enforcement (Ross, 1996; Hyatt, 1998). The enforcement process generally begins with the EPA gathering information and, if warranted, notifying an alleged violator and requesting a stop to the alleged violative behavior. Compliance on behalf of the accused results in no further action. If offenders fail to comply, however, the next step involves informal negotiations between the EPA and the accused with the intent to reach agreement concerning a course of action designed to remedy the problem. Failure to reach agreement in this informal manner leads to formal processing, beginning with the issuance of Notices of Violations.

An administrative enforcement action is pursued should the informal negotiations stall, at which point an Administrative Order is issued and an administrative hearing is scheduled with an administrative law judge hearing the case and rendering a decision. The court's decision can be appealed to the EPA administrator and to the federal court with the possibility of reaching the U.S. Supreme Court. Failure to reach agreement under administrative law may lead to EPA officials taking more punitive steps, such as adding names to a list of companies ineligible for federal contracts, loans, and grants. After exhausting all efforts to reach an agreement, the case will then be turned over to the Department of Justice (DOJ) for civil or criminal processing.

The case will be referred to the DOJ for civil or criminal prosecution should the EPA enforcement agents feel that a resolution is unattainable (e.g., the violator fails to participate in the administrative process). Representatives from the DOJ review the case and determine a course of action. Minor infractions or cases involving first-time offenders are generally addressed through the civil enforcement process, in which offenders are required to rectify the problem and may have to pay a fine. More serious cases, or cases involving offenders with a long history of violations are primary targets of criminal enforcement actions (see Discussion Box 6-1). Offenders in these cases are prosecuted in criminal courts and may be fined and/or incarcerated (for a detailed account of this process, please see Hyatt, 1998, p. 128; Mintz, 1995, p. 11). Much like those prosecuting traditional crimes such as rape, robbery, and murder, prosecutors must consider a variety of issues in determining whether or not to proceed with each case. Among the considerations for those prosecuting environmental harms are (Hyatt, 1998, p. 130; Rebovich, 1996):

- The degree of harm to the environment
- The degree of provable criminal intent
- The offending company's prior record
- The offending company's cooperation during the investigation and its willingness to pay to fix the problem
- Media interest in the case
- The possibility of organized crime connections
- The cost of the prosecution and the available investigative resources

Discussion Box 6-1

The Case of Gary Benkovitz and Tampa Drum and Steel: What Happens to "Serious" Polluters?

Gary Benkovitz (a.k.a. Gary Blake), owner of Tampa Bay Drum and Steel, a facility that buys refurbished and recycled 55-gallon steel drums, was charged with various violations of the federal Clean Water Act and the Resource and Conservation Recovery Act for the years 1990 to 1998. Benkovitz had also previously been charged with conspiring to violate the CWA and RCRA. Benkovitz received a 13-year prison sentence, believed to be the longest sentence ever received in a pollution case. The case was unusual in several ways, which may be one reason for the long sentence received by Benkovitz.

As noted, Benkovitz was previously charged with conspiracy to violate CWA and RCRA. He settled that case by agreeing to serve as a state witness, and to help law enforcement officials gather evidence on co-conspirators. Benkovitz, however, broke the agreement when he telephoned his co-conspirators and told them about the plan to capture their conversations on tape. Unfortunately for Benkovitz, that conversation was also taped.

At trial, Tampa Drum and Steel employees testified that Benkovitz had personally ordered them to violate RCRA and CWA regulations. Employees were ordered to run garden hoses into the Tampa Bay sewer system, and to dump the toxic waste from recycled 55-gallon drums directly into the sewer system. Employees also described the fake evaporation tank Benkovitz constructed on site. (Evaporation tanks are used to reduce liquid toxins into sludge form for disposal by a licensed contractor.) Benkovitz, however, had a hidden valve built into the evaporation unit so that its contents could be discharged directly into the Tampa sewer system. This saved Benkovitz the expense of having to hire a licensed hazardous waste disposer. Benkovitz also had federal tracking numbers on waste barrels and EPA-required paperwork altered. Further, he engaged in hiring unlicensed haulers to dispose of toxic waste, and bribed Tampa sanitation workers to haul toxic waste barrels to the Tampa landfill and incinerator.

As suggested, the EPA anticipates and encourages voluntary compliance and formally sanctions upon failure to reach agreement. In discussing this informal approach to environmental regulation at both the state and federal levels, Kraft (2001, p. 137) argues that "Even where the laws appear to be coercive in nature and invite adversarial relations between government and industry, the reality is that the enforcement process is fundamentally one of self-compliance and negotiation." Kraft adds that, due to their visibility and symbolism, civil and criminal actions are sometimes used to signify the EPA's pro-enforcement efforts in attempts to encourage voluntary compliance.

CRIMINAL PENALTIES

Investigators and prosecutors seeking criminal prosecution of environmental violators must compete for resources with those involved with imposing civil sanctions. In turn, "the number and complexity of criminal cases that can be handled is severely constrained" (McMurry & Ramsey, 1986, p. 1144). Adding to the difficulties faced in seeking criminal charges are "overlapping, sometimes confusing statutory provisions," including criminal sanctions noted in environmental laws and general criminal statutes that pertain to environmental violators (McMurry & Ramsey, 1986, 1145).

As noted, the criminal prosecution of environmental offenders is a somewhat recent development, beginning in the late 1970s. Increased enforcement efforts at that time coincided with Department of Justice and EPA attempts to address issues pertaining to hazardous waste disposal, which, in 1978 lead to the newly formed Hazardous Waste Task Force identifying 52 civil actions using nuisance theories and portions of the RCRA (McMurry & Ramsey, 1986). Even without budgeted resources, the government began to increase the number of criminal prosecutions (McMurry & Ramsey, 1986).

Department of Justice attorney Peter Beeson was named director of the EPA Office of Criminal Enforcement created in January 1981. The office was charged with actively pursuing criminal sanctions and generally enhancing the effectiveness of the enforcement program. It was not until October 1982 that criminal investigators were hired by the EPA, with most investigators having law enforcement experience yet no background with regard to environmental issues (McMurry & Ramsey, 1986).

The Department of Justice's Land and Natural Resources Division established a special unit within its Environmental Enforcement Division to investigate and enforce environmental crimes at about the same time as the creation of the EPA's Office of Criminal Enforcement (McMurry & Ramsey, 1986). The newly developed Environmental Crimes Unit received referrals from the EPA and oversaw prosecution of criminal environmental cases (McMurry & Ramsey, 1986). Criminal enforcement became an established part of EPA enforcement practices, particularly with regard to blatantly egregious and/or harmful violations (McMurry & Ramsey, 1986). Criminal enforcement had clearly become institutionalized at the EPA, which had and continues to have well-defined "criteria and procedures for case selection and prosecution," although compliance and cooperation through civil enforcement remained the objectives for the EPA (McMurry & Ramsey, 1986, p. 1143). The EPA's enforcement efforts would soon take a different approach as congressional pressure and the EPA's recognition of the potential of seeking voluntary compliance "led to a more active and broad-based criminal program" (McMurry & Ramsey, 1986, p. 1141).

The mid-1980s brought about a change in federal prosecution practices regarding environmental offenses. It has been suggested that the federal government increased efforts to prosecute environmental offenders instead of filing civil charges (e.g., Habicht, 1984; DiMento, 1990). Friedrichs (1996) cites the uncharacteristic increase in criminal prosecutions of environmental offenders during the 1980s, given the conservative Reagan administration's hands-off approach to private enterprise. Upon entering office, the Reagan administration discouraged enforcement efforts. However, a widely publicized scandal involving corrupt EPA officials in 1983 forced a change in enforcement approach (Friedrichs, 1996). The increased emphasis on enforcing environmental laws is recognized as a reaction to, in part, widespread coverage of the scandal and increased citizen concern regarding environmental protection.

Regardless of increased enforcement efforts, some suggest that compliance with environmental statutes was lagging and greater enforcement was needed (Adler & Lord, 1991; Hedman, 1991). Federal sentencing guidelines implemented in the late 1980s attempted to provide consistency in sentencing, while increasing the penalties for environmental offenders (see Cohen, 1992, for a discussion of sentencing guidelines and environmental crimes), however, it appears that much work remains in properly sanctioning and deterring harms against the environment (Friedrichs, 1996).

OVERCRIMINALIZATION?

The significance of criminal sanctions is noted in Szasz's (1986) suggestion that incarceration is one business cost that cannot be forwarded to consumers. However, as criminalizing environmental violations continues, such efforts remain highly controversial. It is understood that those charged with addressing environmental concerns must balance their enforcement efforts with the rights of businesses to conduct business. As noted by Friedrichs (1996, p. 260), "...there is and always will be a tension between the objective of providing a safe, clean environment and the economic concerns about the costs (in terms of jobs, prices, and the like) of tough environmental law enforcement." Some (e.g., Cohen, 1992) cite the difficulties associated with overcriminalizing environmental harms, particularly in cases involving crimes by companies or their employees through negligence, strict liability, or vicarious liability.

Accordingly, it is argued that recent aggressive enforcement efforts could be considered unnecessarily harmful to businesses. For instance, some suggest that U.S. businesses suffer on an international basis by having to contend with numerous and complex environmental regulations (Tucker, 1982; Weidenbaum, 1986). The concern is that overcriminalization of environmental crime could produce "overdeterrence" and result in a decrease in operations necessary for businesses to provide consumer goods and services (M. Cohen, 1998, p. 232).

Finding an appropriate level of enforcement is a difficult, yet necessary condition for stable production and markets. The term "appropriate level," however, is highly subjective and is typically interpreted differently by regulators, society, and industry. The perils of underenforcement are well documented in the environmental crime literature, although one must also consider the consequences involved with overenforcement. Understandably, the costs associated with producing goods and services increase as businesses are required to meet increased regulation and enforcement.

Overcriminalization could also result in reducing the stigma attached to the label "criminal" (M. Cohen, 1998). Cohen notes that by "criminalizing minor infractions, criminal law risks becoming trivialized. If every action that harms society is a crime, criminal law loses its one distinguishing characteristic—the moral stigma attached to being labeled a criminal. Without that moral stigma, people might have much less respect for environmental laws and might be less apt to care about violations that are truly egregious" (1998, p. 245). The morality aspect of criminal sanctions is noted by Hyatt (1998, p. 139), who suggests that "Despite the small numbers, felony prosecutions of environmental crimes stand out as the major change in environmental enforcement over the past 20 years. Civil judgments carry little public stigma, but, in contrast, criminal sanctions can serve as effective deterrents."

Proposed solutions to address the problem of overcriminalization and overdeterrence include greater cooperative efforts among involved parties, and greater reliance on sentencing guidelines. The latter, however, have apparently done little to address the issue. In his study of legal responses to environmental crime, Cohen (1992) found that the Sentencing Reform Act of 1984, which instituted sentencing guidelines at the federal level, did little to address the problem of overcriminalization and overdeterrence. Cohen (1992, p. 1106) argues that sentencing considerations should be based on harms caused by offenders, and the offender's probability of getting caught, arguing that "...criminal sanctions for environmental crimes should be inversely related to the probability of detection."

Recognizing the potential for negotiation among involved parties, Mintz (1995, p. 14) notes the integral role of bargaining in the ongoing activities of EPA enforcement managers, adding that most of the time "bargaining serves the interests and goals of both the agency itself and the . . . enterprises . . . subject to enforcement action." Kraft (2001) agrees, explaining that many in state and local governments, and those in industry have complained that environmental regulations are expensive, burdensome, and too rigid. Critics argue that environmental policy could be more effective through cooperation, financial incentives for industry, and negotiation between involved parties (Sexton, Marcus, Easter, & Burkhardt, 1999). Kraft (2001) notes that even as the EPA imposes larger penalties, it encourages compliance through interactive compliance assistance Web sites.

THE NEED FOR STUDY

Enforcement of environmental laws generally began with the introduction of the EPA. The use of criminal sanctions emerged in the 1970s and is currently institutionalized within the agency. The EPA is assisted by other groups, most notably law enforcement agencies, in attempts to regulate environmental harm. Charged with the broad task of environmental regulation, the EPA faces a difficult challenge in balancing the interests of environmentalists and industry. The growing body of research in this area will hopefully provide greater insight into the extent and nature of environmental crime and result in more effective regulation.

Research on environmental crime dates back to the mid-1980s and early 1990s (Rebovich, 1998). Rebovich (1998, p. 351) suggests that:

> Research in this area is in its infancy, and much work remains to be done. Thus far, attention has mainly been focused on characterizing typical offenders, delineating the methods for committing criminal acts, and determining how alleged offenders are handled in the criminal justice system. While this research provides a notable preliminary step, more specific attention is needed.

It is suggested that the increased research focus on environmental crime, including responses to these actions will likely result in more effective environmental regulation. The EPA and others have taken steps toward facilitating enforcement research, particularly by offering grants and other avenues of support for empirical evaluations. This growing body of research must be accessible to those in government and the general public to enable proper consideration of the future direction of environmental regulation. Similar to current efforts to seek proper remedial efforts for violators of more traditional laws, it is argued that we continue to seek the proper means to ensure that the environment is protected from those who seek to harm it, and we find the most effective means to address those who violate environmental laws.

CHAPTER 7

Environmental Crime Data: Databases, Aggregate Reports, and Information Resources

In discussing the availability of environmental crime data, Lynch and colleagues (2002, p. 114) argue that "Numerous qualitative and quantitative data sources on environmental harms exist. Local information on environmental hazards may, for instance, be obtained from city or regional planning commissions and newspapers, as well as state agencies charged with protecting the environment." They add that "...the EPA maintains the most comprehensive database on environmental hazards" (p. 114).

Corporate crime researchers, however, often lament the lack of data available. What they are really complaining about when they make these kinds of statements is the lack of a centralized system of data collection comparable to the one most states and the FBI maintain for street crimes. However, much has changed with regard to access to corporate crime data, especially with respect to data on environmental crime. Although access to data maintained by the EPA has expanded with the growth of the Internet, EPA data are restricted to legal violations enforced by the EPA. Accordingly, much of the information provided in this book is available from the EPA. It should be noted, however, that an equally rich source of data on environmental crime is maintained by each individual state's environmental protection agency.

While providing more extensive access to environmental crime data in this book would be of great value to environmental crime researchers (and one could argue that such a book would make a publication like the *Sourcebook of Criminal Justice Statistics* look small), the wealth of available information and the space required to present such materials dictate that we take an alternative route by providing examples of available data (and reports generated from these data) from select databases, present locations for researchers to access information, and general descriptions of available data for researcher consumption. These resources are presented in the following chapters and appendices. These chapters also provide overviews of aggregated environmental crime data, which can be used to examine environmental crime, and the types of data previously used by researchers examining environmental crime and justice. Chapters 7 and 8 examine particular databases and related information sources of use to environmental crime researchers (most of which are available from the EPA), Chapter 9 specifically examines available Sector Facility Indexing Project (SFIP) data, while Chapters 10 and 11 demonstrate the wealth of information available from sources other than the EPA. Chapter 12 uses fuel economy data to demonstrate how to study environmental crime and justice issues. It is hoped that this approach, among other things, directs researchers to available data.

Web sites for the EPA, state environmental regulatory agencies, and select special interest groups were visited in our attempts to compile a wide range of environmental crime data (Appendix B lists contact information for the EPA, EPA regional offices, and state environmental regulatory agencies). The next step involved culling Web sites for environmental crime data. It should be noted, at this point, that each state agency operates in a different manner. In other words, the information provided on each state Web site varies, making it impossible to describe all of these variations in detail. Identifying appropriate data was very simple in some cases, for instance, as several states had links titled something along the lines of "Enforcement Information" placed on their Web site home page. In other cases, it was necessary to visit a state's annual report to examine environmental enforcement data. The quantity and quality of data presented by each state varies greatly. Florida's Department of Environmental Protection Web page, for example, allows users to download data that is already in Geographic Information System (GIS) format. Other states provide little, if any enforcement-related information on their Web pages.

Those interested in obtaining data from the EPA national office, EPA regional branches, or state environmental regulatory agencies are encouraged to do so. Researchers should, however, be aware that they may encounter difficulties obtaining data of choice from state agencies. Our personal requests for data were welcomed by most agencies, yet challenged by others. Others chose to ignore our requests, while some merely directed us to the national database maintained by the EPA (the latter directive frequently occurred in response to requests for data from the EPA regional branches). We will refrain from identifying particular agencies or individuals who were uncooperative. In general, state representatives were extremely helpful. They sometimes asked for clarification concerning our requests. One individual, for example, mentioned the need for us to more clearly define our request, as the information we sought would need to be delivered in a tractor trailer! Through our experience requesting data we encountered numerous courteous, professional individuals willing to assist us.

Researchers interested in collecting environmental crime data from the EPA national office, EPA regional branches, or state regulatory agencies are encouraged to first visit agency Web sites. While some of these sites could be more user-friendly, most are easily navigated. Web sites for states with a decentralized structural design are generally more difficult to navigate than sites for states maintaining a centralized environmental protection department. Researchers unable to locate the information they seek online should directly contact the agency. Contact numbers or e-mail addresses are typically accessible from agency home pages. Depending on the nature of the request, those seeking data may have to file a Freedom of Information Act (FOIA) request. The FOIA request should be used as a last resort and only applies to agencies of the federal government.

Filing a FOIA request permits an individual to inspect or obtain copies of public records. There are exceptions to what information is available (as noted on the EPA—FOIA Web site www.epa.gov/foia). Our personal experience filing FOIA requests, however, suggests that these requests are taken seriously and can be of significant assistance to those interested in gathering data. Filing a request is easily done through the EPA Web site, which guides the user through the necessary steps.

Those filing a FOIA request may be charged a fee depending on the information requested and the effort required to furnish the requested information. Should a fee be required, requestors will be notified (an invoice for the information will be sent) prior to receiving the information. Be aware that those filing a FOIA request have a right to appeal should their request be denied. Requestors generally have a right to a decision within 20 days of their appeal.

THE DATA

Lynch and colleagues (2002, p. 114) note that "Criminologists have largely neglected EPA data in their study of corporate crime," adding that the criminological literature on toxic crimes is "practically non-existent" (p. 109). Though the lack of a centralized source of data may mean fewer studies of environmental crime compared with street crime, there is a wealth of information available to generate studies of environmental crime. If, for example, a researcher wants to know the number of homicides that occur in each state, they can acquire this information from one table in the *Sourcebook of Criminal Justice Statistics*. Collecting comparable information on environmental crimes is more difficult. First, the researcher may have to contact each state to acquire information about those crimes prosecuted at the state level. Next, the researcher may need to access EPA data to include federal investigations and prosecutions. The process is cumbersome and appears to discourage researchers. In this section, we describe sources of data on environmental crime, which, among other things, facilitate environmental crime research. This is not necessarily an easy task, and may require that users possess some knowledge of various computer programs to download the data into useable formats.

DATABASES

The following databases are available for environmental crime researchers to use via the Internet. Those interested in these databases should be aware that although extensive information is generally located in these resources, learning how to access the data is often required. Specifically, researchers should be prepared to read and follow the downloading/accessing/help-related information often provided with these databases. While some databases are easier than others to access and navigate, they all require some knowledge of database management. Those who have read the help manuals and exhausted online assistance yet still experience difficulties accessing/using data through these resources are encouraged to directly contact the agency providing the information. Contact information is often provided on the Web site.

The following databases are presented according to agency affiliation. To demonstrate the wealth of information within these databases, particular emphasis is placed on a discussion of the EPA's "Envirofacts Warehouse," "IDEA," and "ECHO" databases. Keep in mind that some of the databases noted below provide actual datasets, while others respond to user queries and only provide user-requested reports pertaining to specific information. Some provide links to online clearinghouses. Experimentation and exploration are essential to identifying the necessary information. At the very least, each resource provides information that could be considered data.

EPA MULTIMEDIA DATABASES: ENVIROFACTS, IDEA, AND ECHO

The following sections provide Web addresses and brief discussion of various EPA multimedia data systems and databases. Three particularly helpful data sources found on the EPA Web site are "Envirofacts Warehouse," the "Integrated Data for Enforcement Analysis" (IDEA) and the "Enforcement and Compliance History Online" (ECHO). These resources contain numerous searchable databases available to researchers interested in analyzing almost any aspect of environmental regulation.

Envirofacts (www.epa.gov/enviro/index_java.html)

As noted on the EPA Web site, the Envirofacts Warehouse provides access to databases containing information about facilities or environmental activities anywhere in the country, on issues related to air, waste, water, toxics, radiation, and land. These data sources permit the retrieval of information from multiple databases at one time, or one database at a time. Mapping applications incorporated within the databases enable researchers to create maps/diagrams depicting the data. Location-related information provided in Envirofacts databases includes all of the longitudinal and latitudinal coordinates for EPA facilities. Lynch and colleagues (2002, p. 118) cite the importance of this feature, suggesting that location information accompanying EPA data facilitates and enhances examinations of "environmental justice as it allows for the testing of the distributive justice hypothesis that minorities and the lower classes are more likely to reside near environmental hazards than affluent whites" and subsequently more likely to be harmed by corporate crime.

IDEA
(www.epa.gov/compliance/planning/data/multimedia/idea/index.html)

As noted on the Web page, IDEA pulls data from various individual media systems and integrates the data into multimedia reports for particular facilities or types of activities. Implemented in early 1991, IDEA retrieves data across program office databases to study problems pertaining to air, water, hazardous waste, toxics, enforcement, spills, demographics, federal facilities, and other areas. While the Envirofacts Warehouse provides a wealth of information related to environmental issues, the databases found within IDEA are more directly related to environmental crime and its control.

IDEA databases include:

- Aerometric Information and Retrieval System (AIRS)/AIRS Facility Subsystem (AFS)
- Biennial Reporting System (BRS)
- Comprehensive Environmental Response, Compensation and Liability Act (CERCLA) Information System (CERCLIS)
- Census Demographic Data by ZIP Code (ZIP)
- Criminal Enforcement Docket (CRM)
- Civil Enforcement Docket (DOCKET)
- Emergency Response Notification System (ERNS)
- Federal Facility Information System (FFIS)
- Facility Identification Initiative (FII)
- National Compliance Data Base (NCDB)
- Integrated Management Information System (IMIS)/Occupational Safety and Health Administration (OSHA)
- Permit Compliance System (PCS)
- Resource Conservation and Recovery Act (RCRA) Information System (RCRIS)
- Site Enforcement Tracking System (SETS)
- Toxic Release Inventory System (TRIS)

Enforcement and Compliance History Online (ECHO) (www.epa.gov/echo)
The EPA was experimenting with a new online, public access information retrieval system called ECHO at the time we were compiling this work. ECHO (Enforcement and Compliance History Online) is designed to allow users to search geographic locations for violations of the Resource Conservation and Recovery Act (RCRA), Clean Water Act (CWA), and Clean Air Act (CAA). Violations of these regulations are listed within ECHO by facility. These data are further explained in the following sections. Before doing so, we present a word of caution about our description of ECHO. As noted, ECHO was available for public use and comment while we were writing this book. It is likely that ECHO, or some revised version of it based on public comment, will become part of the EPA Web site. The permanent version of ECHO (if it becomes permanent) is likely to differ from the experimental version. Consequently, our description may not be entirely accurate when applied to the permanent version. For this reason, we review the major aspects of ECHO and forego a complete discussion of all of its features.

Theoretically, ECHO provides access to specific environmental information for all major (and, if requested, minor) facilities that are required to report under provisions of the RCRA, CWA, and CAA to local, state, or federal authorities. ECHO, in other words, provides access to the same kinds of data found in the SFIP discussed in Chapter 9. The difference is that SFIP provides access to only a select sample of RCRA, CWA, and CAA violations, while it would be theoretically possible to construct a complete list of all RCRA, CWA, and CAA violations using ECHO. Because ECHO and SFIP cover similar databases and have similar structures, readers are directed to read the description of SFIP in Chapter 9 if they desire a more complete understanding of ECHO.

The ECHO home page allows several different types of searches to be performed. Because the primary purpose of ECHO is to provide the public with access to EPA data on environmental hazards regulated under the RCRA, CWA, and CAA, the most prominent search option is the geographic search located near the top of the ECHO home page. Users may enter a zip code, city and state name, or county and state name in this box. Pressing the "go" button generates an area report by facility across the RCRA, CWA, and CAA.

The ECHO geographic facility report has five columns. The first column contains the name and address of the facility. Users may click on the facility name to review a detailed facility report. The detailed report includes facility permits and identifiers (statute and permit, street address, city, state, zip code); facility characteristics (including operating status, latitude and longitude identifiers, primary and secondary SIC codes); inspection and enforcement summary (for two years, including dates of inspection, formal actions and penalty amounts); inspection history by regulation and responsible agency; compliance summary (quarters in noncompliance over past two years by regulation); two-year compliance status by quarter; CWA/NPDES status (by NPDES effluent violation); RCRA compliance; EPA formal enforcement actions; environmental conditions (e.g., watershed involved); and demographic profile of surrounding area by one-, three-, or five-mile radius, with radius longitude and latitude. Following the facility report, a link is provided that allows the user to map the facility's location and select community characteristics the user wishes to map (e.g., school locations, hospitals, roads, etc.). Columns 2 through 5 indicate whether the facility has been inspected, and whether it had violations, current significant violations, and enforcement actions over the past two years.

To test the capacity of the ECHO search engine, we performed a geographic search. In the search box provided, we entered "New York, NY" to generate ECHO's response for a search of all RCRA, CWA, and CAA monitored facilities in New York City. ECHO identified 555 major facilities, but noted that the number of facilities located exceeded the report limit of 500. Because we exceeded the ECHO search engine limits, no results were displayed and we were instructed to revise our search parameters using the "advanced search" option. Instead of restricting our search to produce fewer cases, we asked for a report on "minor" facilities. ECHO identified 124,000 minor facilities in New York City, and again indicated that the results of the requested search could not be displayed because we had exceeded the search limit of 500 facilities.

This limitation means that anyone wishing to use ECHO to create a large database would need to carefully plan their search procedures. While ECHO might be used to determine the total number of cases in an area quite easily, obtaining facility-specific information for these cases might be more difficult. For example, we used the advanced search engine to request data on all facilities in the United States. The search returned 83,647 major facilities, which could not be listed because we had exceeded the search limit of 500. We extended this search by checking the "include minor facilities" box and found 833,589 major and minor facilities, as there were 749,942 minor facilities in the United States. While it was simple enough to determine the universe of facilities reporting under the RCRA, CWA, and CAA using ECHO (and while this search could easily be broken down into facilities required to report under each of these Acts), extracting information for each of these facilities was much more difficult. To ensure that an accurate dataset is constructed employing ECHO, individual zip codes for the United States would have to be entered individually. Each output can be downloaded as a comma delimited data file for each zip code. This procedure would, however, be quite time consuming.

Prospects for constructing a city-level dataset for which the number of cases exceeds 500 would appear more feasible. For New York City, for example, the names of the smaller geographic units comprising New York City could be entered (e.g., Brooklyn, NY; Bronx, NY, etc.). For smaller cities, no such additional steps would be necessary.

As noted, our initial experiments with ECHO did not generate data that could be displayed by the system. In order to examine an ECHO output for a smaller city, we entered "Tampa, FL" into the geographic search engine. ECHO reported locating 119 major facilities for Tampa that had reported under requirements of the RCRA, CWA, and CAA. A listing of these facilities along with aggregated facility data was displayed on the computer screen. Performing a count of these data indicated that 83 of reporting facilities in Tampa (69.8%) had been inspected in the previous two years. Further, 44 of the inspected facilities (53%) had a violation in the previous two-years. Current significant violations were reported at seven (8.4% of inspected facilities, 15.9% of facilities with reported violations) Tampa facilities over the previous two years. We also discovered that 23 facilities had enforcement actions taken against them in the previous two years (27.7% of inspected facilities, or 52.3% of facilities with violations).

It should be noted that ECHO data may be searched in several other ways using the advanced search engine. The advanced search engine is divided into seven parts. Each may be used separately or in combinations to produce customized searches. The "facility characteristics" search allows users to search for an individual facility (by entering the facility name) by SIC classification (using the drop-down SIC code menu or by entering the SIC code manually). This search may also be limited to federal facilities by checking the appropriate box.

The advanced "geographic location" search allows users to search by EPA region, city, state, zip code, county, and to restrict the search to Indian lands. The "inspection/enforcement history" advanced search allows the user to select the time since last enforcement, formal enforcement action limits, or penalty limits. Under the "compliance information" search, users may select no search restrictions, any violation, significant violation/violator, or multiple significant violations/violator. The "demographic profile" search allows users to select a one-, three-, or five-mile radius surrounding the facility for reporting of demographic data. Users may also select to limit their searches by "media" (where media indicates the medium of exposure: air, water, etc.). The "by media" advanced search can be used to identify either all facilities, or only those with an "Air ID," (CAA/NPDES), water permit (CWA), or RCRA ID.

In sum, ECHO has some limited uses for researchers interested in collecting environmental violation, penalty, and inspection data from the EPA. This, however, is not the primary use for which ECHO was designed. ECHO is primarily designed to enhance public access to EPA data. On this account, ECHO performs well. For example, ECHO is easy to use, and members of the general public would face little difficulty entering specific zip codes or cities into the ECHO search engine in order to discover localized environmental hazards that may exist in their communities.

OTHER EPA RESOURCES

Many additional data resources are available on the EPA's Information Sources (located online at: www.epa.gov/epahome/resource.htm). The following is not a comprehensive list of data resources available from the EPA, but rather a listing of those most useful to environmental crime researchers. Descriptions of these resources were largely taken directly from the EPA Web site.

Biennial Reporting System (BRS)
www.epa.gov/epaoswer/hazwaste/data/index.htm
The BRS is a repository of information collected under the Resource Conservation and Recovery Act (RCRA) of 1976 as amended by the Hazardous and Solid Waste Amendments of 1984. The majority of BRS data is collected by States and/or EPA Regions using the Hazardous Waste Report, Instructions, and Forms (commonly called the Biennial Report) produced by the EPA. The BRS database contains data reported by Large Quantity Generators (LQGs), and Treatment, Storage, and Disposal (TSDs) sites.

Emissions Tracking System (ETS)
www.epa.gov/ceisWeb1/ceishome/ceisdocs/ets/ets-exec.htm
The ETS stores data collected under the auspices of the Acid Rain Program and the Clean Air Act. Title IV of the Clean Air Act requires fossil-fueled utility plants and other sulfur dioxide emitters to monitor and report their emissions of sulfur dioxide, nitrogen oxides, carbon dioxide, and the volume and opacity of their emissions flow. The overall goal of the Acid Rain Program is to achieve significant environmental and public health benefits through reductions in the emissions of sulfur dioxide and nitrogen oxides, the primary causes of acid rain.

Environmental Data Registry (EDR)
www.epa.gov/airmarkets/reporting/edr21/index.html
The EDR is a comprehensive, authoritative source of reference information about the definition, source, and uses of environmental data. The EDR catalogs the EPA's major data collections and helps locate environmental information of interest. As the major tool supporting the EPA's data standards program, the EDR records and

disseminates information about EPA data standards and the standard-setting process. The EDR does not contain the environmental data itself, but rather information that describes the data to make it more meaningful.

Integrated Risk Information System (IRIS)
www.epa.gov/iris/index.html
The IRIS is an electronic database containing information on human health effects that may result from exposure to various chemicals in the environment. It was initially developed for EPA staff in response to a growing demand for consistent information on chemical substances for use in risk assessments, decision-making, and regulatory activities. The information in IRIS is intended for those without extensive training in toxicology, but with some knowledge of health sciences.

National Hydrography Dataset (NHD)
www.epa.gov/ceisWeb1/ceishome/ceisdocs/nhd/nhd.htm
The NHD, a joint effort of the EPA and the U.S. Geological Survey, is the latest in a series of hydrological databases pertaining to the surface waters of the continental United States and Hawaii that provides a consistent national framework for managing watershed data. The NHD provides comprehensive coverage of hydrographic data for the United States.

Safe Drinking Water Information System/Federal Version (SDWIS)
www.epa.gov/ceisWeb1/ceishome/ceisdocs/sdwis/sdwis-ex.htm
The SDWIS is an EPA national database of information on the nation's drinking water. Designed to replace the Federal Reporting Data System, the SDWIS stores the information the EPA needs to monitor public water systems. The database covered over 172,000 public water systems in 1996, the most recent year for which annual figures were compiled. The SDWIS tracks information on drinking water contamination levels as required by the 1974 Safe Drinking Water Act and its 1986 and 1996 amendments.

STOrage and RETrieval System for Water and Biological Monitoring Data (STORET)
www.epa.gov/storet
The updated STORET is the EPA's principal repository for marine and freshwater ambient water quality and biological monitoring information. It combines the functions of the original STORET with that of the Biological Information System, and the Ocean Data

Evaluation System (ODES). These systems served as the EPA's primary sources of point and non-point source ambient water quality and biological monitoring data. Their analytical tools supported a wide range of EPA water quality and ecosystem health assessment activities. Together, these systems contain over 250 million parametric observations collected primarily by state agencies from over 700,000 sampling stations nationwide.

NON-EPA DATABASES

Although the EPA provides a wealth of information pertaining to environmental crime, it is not the sole provider of such information. The following sections provide a brief description of other databases, with some discussed in greater detail in Chapters 10 and 11. Although non-EPA agencies do not always contain information related to crime, violations, or unethical behavior, these data sources can be used with other data to facilitate observations of illegal or unethical practices that, for example, pertain to issues such as environmental justice. Creativity is a primary tool for further development of these crime/justice-related issues.

 · Researchers must bear in mind that many of these public agencies are not bound by the Freedom of Information Act, and thus, obtaining data may be a bit more difficult. Nevertheless, as noted below, it appears that many of these non-EPA sources make their data openly available. Descriptions of these data sources were, for the most part, taken directly from their respective Web sites.

Environmental Council of the States (ECOS)
www.sso.org/ecos
ECOS is the national non-profit, non-partisan association of state and territorial environmental commissioners. One of ECOS's missions is to describe the contributions that states make to environmental protection. During the past few years, ECOS has conducted research on federal environmental programs that have been delegated to the states; state contributions to federal environmental databases; state environmental and natural resource funding; and state contributions to enforcement and compliance.

FedStats
www.fedstats.gov
FedStats provides researchers access to statistics from over 70 U.S. federal agencies; those agencies reporting expenditures of at least

$500,000 per year in various statistical activities. Researchers could use FedStats, for example, to track economic and population trends, health care costs, aviation safety, foreign trade, energy use, and farm production.

National Aeronautics and Space Administration (NASA)
www.nasa.gov

NASA collects remote-sensed data to support climate research and to describe and measure the energy and environmental phenomena that may contribute to climate variation and change.

National Environmental Data Index (NEDI)
www.nedi.gov

NEDI provides direct access to environmental data and information descriptions, and thereby, improves awareness of and facilitates access to data and information holdings. The overall goal of NEDI is to facilitate the use of the widest possible range of environmental data and information to support the betterment of society. NEDI currently provides a full-text search of the environmental information compiled by several agencies of the federal government, including the EPA and the Department of the Interior. The objective of the project is to facilitate access to multiple agencies' databases from one site.

National Geophysical Data Center (NGDC)
www.ngdc.noaa.gov

NGDC is part of the U.S. Department of Commerce, National Oceanic and Atmospheric Administration (NOAA), National Environmental Satellite, Data and Information Service (NESDIS). It is one of three NOAA National Data Centers. The NOAA NESDIS mission is to provide and ensure timely access to global environmental data from satellites and other sources to promote, protect, and enhance the Nation's economy, security, environment, and quality of life. To fulfill its responsibilities NESDIS acquires and manages the United States' operational environmental satellites, provides data and information services, and conducts related research. The Center works closely with contributors of scientific data to prepare documented, reliable data sets. The NGDC's data holdings currently contain more than 300 digital and analog databases.

National Oceanic and Atmospheric Administration (NOAA)
www.noaa.gov

NOAA gathers worldwide environmental data about the ocean, earth, air, space, and sun and their interactions to describe and predict the state of the physical environment. The NOAA Server System links more than a dozen environmental databases in many organizations in NOAA, including the National Weather Service and the National Marine Fisheries Service.

United Nations Environment Programme (UNEP)
www.unep.org

UNEP works to encourage sustainable development through sound environmental practices throughout the world. UNEP's present priorities include environmental information, assessment, and research, including environmental emergency response capacity and the strengthening of early warning and assessment functions. Information networks and monitoring systems established by UNEP include (1) the Global Resource Information Database (GRID), (2) the International Register of Potentially Toxic Chemicals (IRPTC) and, (3) the recent UNEP.Net, a Web-based interactive catalogue and multifaceted portal that offers access to environmentally relevant geographic, textual, and pictorial information.

United States Geological Survey (USGS)
www.usgs.gov

Through its Water Resources Division, USGS collects and maintains data on the quality, availability, and use of the nation's water, including streamflow data for hydropower plants, groundwater subsistence, erosion, backwater, flooding, water contamination, and sedimentation.

These databases provide ample opportunity for research, particularly in relation to crime and justice. Readers are encouraged to visit these databases and explore the research possibilities. The following section examines various environmental crime-based research projects/reports utilizing these and other data sources.

AGGREGATED ENVIRONMENTAL CRIME DATA

Researchers are strongly encouraged to utilize available databases to generate their own reports. In some cases, however, the raw data have already been compiled and statistical reports prepared. Information culled from a series of these reports could be used to further analyze various environmental issues. Data displays gathered from the EPA national office, EPA regional branches, ECOS, and various state environmental regulatory agencies are provided below. While not comprehensive, these displays are representative of the material researchers can easily access via the Internet or through a simple request. Some of the following tables consist of entire reports, while others depict a portion of the information. The information is **not** provided for the reader's use. It is, instead, provided to demonstrate the types of available information and hopefully spur thoughts on how this information can be used to further our knowledge in this area.

The section is divided into seven parts, which are by no means exhaustive. The areas examined include available data sets (actual data sets/information not compiled into a report), data/reports presented according to EPA region; reports assembled by ECOS (which, among other things, facilitates state comparisons); reports concerning citizen complaints, regulatory investigations, and the training of personnel to address environmental crime; enforcement information; and a list of tables representing the type of information currently available to researchers.

Researchers are encouraged to consider whether these reports/data sets can be analyzed in their "report-like" format, or if the actual body of data used to compile the reports would be more useful. Information found in these reports is sometimes available for multiple years. While data may not be available for earlier decades, researchers are encouraged to investigate whether the reporting agency could generate particular information for a select number of years.

Data Sets

Tables 7-1 through 7-6 offer examples of data sets available from the EPA national office, EPA regional offices, and various state regulatory agencies that are easily accessible via the Internet. Data provided in tables 7-1 through 7-5 can be used to quantitatively analyze violation penalty amounts within the context of offense, offender, and location. Researchers could also consider using such information in conjunction with other data. They could, for instance, compare this information among states as such state-level data are often readily available. Data found in Table 7-6 could be used for qualitative research purposes, or in the manner suggested for tables 7-1 through 7-5.

Table 7-1: Penalty Summary First-Quarter Penalties, January–March 2001					
Date	Company /Individual	City of Violation	County of Violation	Description of Violation	Penalty Amount
2/20	John Carman	Prosser	Benton	Constructing wells w/out a drilling license	$62,500
3/26	U.S. Dept. of Justice	Richland	Benton	Failure to identify and manage reactive chemical waste	$57,800
1/ 4	Port of Port Angeles	Port Angeles	Clallam	Allowing shipyard activities w/out permits to protect water quality	$14,000
2/1	Steve Schultheis	Port Angeles	Clallam	Unlawfully discharging oil into water at Port Angeles Marina	$2,000

Source: *Washington State Department of Ecology*

Table 7-2: Historical Data: Ground-Level Ozone, 8-Hour Exceedances*		
Date	Site Name	Concentration
6/1/00	Ancora St. Hospital	.099
6/1/00	Clarksboro	.089
6/1/00	Colliers Mills	.090
6/1/00	Flemington	.086
6/1/00	Rider University	.091
6/1/00	Rutgers University	.091
6/1/00	Ancora St. Hospital	.110

*Exceedings of the 8-hour Ozone Standard in New Jersey, 1998-2000; June 2000 Ozone Exceedances (8-hour averages, per million)

Source: *New Jersey Department of Environmental Protection*

Table 7-3: Quality Enforcement Summary, January–March 2001				
Date	**Company or Individual**	**Facility site location**	**Nature of Violation(s)**	**Penalty type**
1/9	Smilin Rog Development	Pine City	Construction without permit, storm water controls	APO–$3,500 forgivable, $1,200 nonforgivable
1/16	Potlatch Corp.	Cloquet	Test failure for sulphur dioxide and carbon monoxide	STIP–$12,500
1/17	Hutchinson Utilities	Hutchinson	Spill permit violations	APO–$2,200 forgivable $5,500 nonforgivable

Source: *Minnesota Pollution Control Agency*

Table 7-4: Executed Orders Under Authority of the Asbestos Safety Act	
Facility:	Kroger Distribution Center; order issued to Schultz Design, LLC
Location:	Fulton County
Order Number:	EPD-ASB-1641
Date of Issue:	June 12, 2001
Cause of Order:	Violations of Rules for Air Quality Control, Solid Waste Management
Requirement(s) of Order:	Attend proper Asbestos Inspector's Course and Supervisor Course, submitting proof of attendance; comply with Act and Rules at all times
Settlement Amount:	$1000

Source: *Georgia Environmental Protection Division*

Table 7-5: U.S. EPA Region 5, Office of Regional Counsel, Draft 3/3/00

Respondent/ Defendant	City/ State/ County	Statute Violated	Order Date	Cost of Compliance Actions	Cost Recovery
R Adams County/ Quincy Landfills	Quincy, IL 62301 – Adams	CERCLA 107	5/99	$16,000,000	$224,104
D Akzo Coatings of America	Davisburg, MI 48350 – Oakland	CERCLA 106, 107	12/98	$7,000,000	$7,905,398
D Allied Signal	South Point, OH 45680 - Lawrence	CERCLA 106(a) & 107(a)	11/98	$4,000,000	$50,000

Source: *US EPA - Region 5*

Table 7-6: Massachusetts DEP Enforcement Actions Examples

• 6/5/2001: DEP entered into an ACO with Chudy Oil Co. to resolve the company's failure to complete required response actions at a site where several releases of heating oil took place. A penalty of $7,000 will be suspended if Chudy satisfactorily completes all work within the agreed upon timelines.

• 6/4/2001: DEP finalized an ACOP with Graziano Redi-Mix Inc., under which the Bridgewater concrete processing company will pay a penalty of $2,500 for hazardous waste management and water pollution control violations. Graziano will discontinue all industrial wastewater discharges by installing an on-site holding tank and also will improve its hazardous waste and used oil storage practices.

Source: *Massachusetts Department of Environmental Protection*

Regional Data

EPA regional data are easily accessible and offer various avenues of analysis for researchers. The following tables represent the extensive body of information available from EPA regional offices. These statistics/data offer researchers opportunities to, among other things, compare enforcement, prevention, inspection, and other activities between various EPA regions as well as regions of the United States. Depending on the report, interstate comparisons may also be an option. Data for all ten regions are available for each of these tables, however, only regions 1 through 3 and totals are presented as examples. "..." denotes excluded data.

Table 7-7: FY 2000 Inspections at Regulated Facilities: EPA and State

Region	EPCRA Total EPA Inspections at Section 313	Total EPA Inspections at Section Non-313	TSCA Total EPA Inspections	Total State Inspections
1	12	29	22	184
2	87	98	220	146
3	92	93	113	102
...	...	...	...	...
Total	472	1,366	1,400	1,210

Source: *US Environmental Protection Agency*

Table 7-8: Dollar Value of FY 2000 EPA Enforcement Actions (by Region)

	Criminal Penalties Assessed	Civil Judicial Penalties Assessed	Administrative Penalties Assessed	$ Value of Injunctive Relief
Reg I	$5,938,574	$165,000	$1,141,903	$393,027,188
Reg II	$7,363,469	$9,170,500	$1,995,799	$152,614,114
Reg III	$4,618,730	$4,003,493	$2,019,148	$187,624,663
...	...	...	...	...
HQ	$0	$0	$769,801	$140,578
Totals	$121,974,488	$54,851,765	$25,509,879	$1,562,824,364

Source: *US Environmental Protection Agency*

Table 7-9: Civil Referrals to DOJ, FY 1998–2000 (by Region)							
	CAA	CERCLA	CWA	EPCRA	FIFRA	...	TOTAL
Region I							
1998	6	7	1	0	0	...	18
1999	6	14	12	0	0	...	33
2000	4	13	12	0	0	...	30
Region II							
1998	9	17	7	0	0	...	41
1999	8	17	8	0	0	...	37
2000	7	16	5	0	0	...	32
Region III							
1998	15	23	8	1	0	...	50
1999	9	35	10	1	0	...	58
2000	11	23	10	0	0	...	46
...							
...	...	...	...	...	...	...	...
Totals							
1997	113	138	81	11	4	...	411
1998	109	148	87	12	0	...	403
2000	125	121	73	8	0	...	368

Source: *US Environmental Protection Agency*

Table 7-10: Significant Noncompliance Two-Year Recidivism Rates*				
Region	State	CAA		
		Facilities RTC from SNC FY98	Facilities SNC again in 2 Yrs	Rate of Recidivism
1	CT	1	1	100%
	MA	3		0%
	ME	2	1	50%
	NH	1		0%
	RI	1		0%
	VT			
Region 1 Total		**8**	**2**	**25%**
2	NJ	5		0%
	NY	16	· 1	6%
	PR	2		0%
	VI			
Region 2 Total		**23**	**1**	**4%**
3	DC	3		0%
	DE	6		0%
	MD	20	1	5%
	PA	67	6	9%
	VA	63	4	6%
	WV	30	2	7%
Region 3 Total		**189**	**13**	**7%**
...	...	...	...	...
...	...	...	...	...
Total		1072	224	21%

*Significant Noncompliance Two-Year Recidivism Rates By State For Facilities (a) Returning From SNC During FY 1998, and (b) Either Inspected Within Two Years of Their Return, or Whose SNC Status Was Found By Some Other Method

Source: *US Environmental Protection Agency*

Table 7-11: FY 2000 Concluded EPA Enforcement Actions: Types of Compliance Activity (Does not include SEP Impacts)

Type of Impact from FY 2000 Cases	Reg I	Reg II	Reg III	...	HQ	Total
Use Reduction	3	6	7	...	0	157
Industrial Process Change	4	4	3	...	1	166
Emissions/ Discharge Change	8	26	88	...	0	336
Storage/ Disposal Change	10	16	9	...	0	223
Remediation/ Restoration	11	11	129	...	6	424
Removal	15	13	19	...	1	299
Remedial Design/ Remedial Action	3	5	7	...	0	44
Testing	19	51	18	...	5	412
Auditing	6	2	22	...	17	258
Monitoring/ Sampling Only	0	6	3	...	0	78
Total Monitoring/ Sampling Only	28	70	32	...	6	714
Recordkeeping Only	1	11	1	...	1	52
Total Recordkeeping	24	133	115	...	12	897
Labeling/ Manifesting	7	16	12	...	4	223
Reporting Only	92	447	179	...	0	1562
Total Reporting	113	590	204	...	16	2541
Information Letter Response	5	28	6	...	1	202
Permit Application	4	16	81	...	2	244
Training	9	28	93	...	13	390
Provide Site Access	7	11	14	...	1	214
Site Assessment	3	6	4	...	1	174
Remedial Investigation/ Feasibility Study	3	5	2	...	0	24
Other Result/ Impact Only	22	85	34	...	1	761
Total Other Result/ Impact	38	110	120	...	7	1375
Total # Case Settlements/ Conclusions	237	920	526	...	141	5609
# Settlements w/ Actions Reported	189	786	424	...	35	4455
Total # of Impact Types	354	1179	1030	...	98	9818
Cases were for Penalty Only	34	32	45	...	5	501
Average Actions per Case Reported	1.9	1.5	2.4	...	2.8	2.2

Source: *US Environmental Protection Agency*

Environmental Council of the States (ECOS)

As noted earlier, a primary mission of ECOS is to evaluate state contributions to environmental crime enforcement. Accordingly, ECOS is a credible resource for information regarding state involvement in the prevention, investigation, enforcement, and sanctioning of environmental crime. As with any secondary data source, however, one must consider its limitations. One concern is the challenge faced in compiling data from decentralized, independent state agencies. ECOS information, however, provides researchers with an attractive avenue for analyses of state level environmental crime and enforcement actions. Tables 7-12 through 7-14 depict some of the information provided by ECOS. Data from all states are available for most reports. The tables below are limited to a few states as examples.

Table 7-12: Citizen Complaints, 1997–1999				
State	Number of Programs Reporting	1997	1998	1999
Alabama	12	2,284	2,958	3,136
Alaska	1	580	544	383
Arkansas	2	450	431	470
California	1	958	649	616
…	…	…	…	…
TOTALS	119	81,220	83,719	88,417

Source: *ECOS*

Table 7-13: State and EPA Significant Violations, 1997–1999						
State	1997		1998		1999	
	EPA Count	State Count	EPA Count	State Count	EPA Count	State Count
Alabama	18	522	38	681	31	439
Arkansas	13	148	39	157	32	156
California	37	145	30	83	34	108
…	…	…	…	…	…	…
TOTALS	12,466	26,402	12,979	28,089	15,577	25,738
GRAND TOTAL	EPA Count: 60,786 State Count: 112, 631					

Source: *ECOS*

Table 7-14: Compliance Assistance Activities and Counts, 1999						
State	On-site Visits	Seminars	Seminar Attendees	Toll-Free No.	Web Access	Newsletter Recipients
Ala	Y	108		Y	Y	
Ark	Y	Y		Y	Y	
Cal	5	37	634		119,513	Y
...	...	...	...	...	...	...
TOT	31,170	3,638	13,741	N/A	6,196,466	17,606

Source: *ECOS*

Complaints

An interesting, yet neglected area of environmental crime research involves citizen complaints. Little research has examined the effectiveness, resolutions, or distributions of complaints, although data concerning complaints are freely available from many state environmental regulatory agencies. Tables 7-15 and 7-16 demonstrate the types of available information concerning environmental crime complaints. Such data are generally presented along with complaint resolution actions, if any.

Table 7-15: ECLS Complaint Resolution (by Quarter)				
	QTR1	QTR 2	...	TOTAL
Total Spills/ Complaints Received	1,644	1,371	...	6,198
Spill/ Complaints Referred to Other Agencies	130	81	...	383
Spills Referred	28	28	...	114
Complaints Referred	102	53	...	269
Total DEQ Spills/ Complaints	1,507	1,214	...	5,674
Spills Received	98	92	...	355
Complaints Received	1,409	1,122	...	5,319
Public Water Supply Complaints	156	55	...	316
Publicly Owned Wastewater Complaints	227	199	...	872
Industrial Wastewater Treatment Complaints	7	9	...	34
Stormwater Complaints	52	21	...	199
Fugitive Dust Complaints	66	83	...	224
Unpermitted Emissions Complaints	4	2	...	29
Excess Emissions Complaints	42	27	...	120
Landfill Complaints	10	11	...	37
Hazardous Waste Complaints	16	14	...	63
Unpermitted Disposal Complaints	268	178	...	958
Private Sewage Complaints	320	261	...	1,441
Private Water Complaints	12	10	...	48
Open Burning Complaints	83	79	...	310
Tire Disposal Complaints	19	21	...	69
Complaints from Other Sources	127	152	...	599
Chronic Complaints	0	0	...	0
High Profile Complaints	0	0	...	1
Target Complaints	12	11	...	35
Number of Complaints Resolved	1,409	1,122	...	4,764
Number Resolved within 90 Days	1,409	1,122	...	3,917
% Resolved in 90 Days	100	100	...	82.2
Complaint Responsiveness			...	
Complaints Requiring Response	723	568	...	2,861
Met 2 Working Day Response	575	450	...	2,386
Mediation Referrals	0	1	...	1
Successful Mediations	0	1	...	2

Source: *Oklahoma Department of Environmental Quality*

Table 7-16: Summary of Citizen Complaints, December 1, 1999 to November 30, 2000				
PROGRAMS	Total Rec'd: 1998	Closed: No Violation	Closed: Voluntary Correction	Closed: Enf. Action Taken	Total Closed: 1998
Act 250:					
Permit violations	29	6	6	3	23
Unpermitted activity	69	30	5	8	67
Air Pollution:					
Air toxics	7	2	1	1	6
Direct/ indirect sources	29	10	0	0	15
Odors	39	18	0	0	28
Open burning	111	32	26	8	84
Water Quality (WQ):					
Aquatic Nuisance	1	0	0	0	1
Lakes & ponds	6	6	2	1	11
Standards violations	32	11	5	1	21
Stream alterations	28	18	3	4	28
Wetlands	133	51	25	15	116
WQ Discharges:					
Agricultural	15	6	5	1	18
Erosion	31	13	7	3	30
Logging	24	7	10	1	22
Permit violations	5	2	1	1	7
Unpermitted	202	93	39	11	182
TOTALS	**1560**	**513**	**491**	**89**	**1404**

Source: *Vermont Agency of Natural Resources*

Investigations

Tables 7-17 through 7-20 depict examples of the available data concerning investigations. Investigations data can be used in conjunction with information concerning complaints, enforcement actions, and sanctions. Researchers can aggregate these data in various ways (e.g., year, type of process, environmental program).

Table 7-17: Summary of Criminal Investigation Information

	Fiscal Year		
	1998	1999	2000
Number of Search Warrants	15	11	19
Number of Cases Resulting in Convictions	8	13	11
Number of Convictions Against Individuals	10	14	16
Number of Convictions Against Corporations	1	3	2
Total Number of Convictions	11	17	18
Number of Felony Counts	7	13	30
Number of Misdemeanor Counts	36	8	8

Source: *Texas Natural Resources Conservation Commission*

Table 7-18: Environmental Crimes Unit Investigations Statistics

	1998	1999	2000	Average
Actions Opened	43	66	67	53.6
Resolution of Reported Actions				
Administrative	2	14	27	14.2
Civil	3	1	2	1.2
Criminal	6	15	15	12.6
Unfounded	6	5	3	4.6
Unresolved	1	1	1	1.8
Other	25	30	19	19.2

Source: *Alaska Department of Environmental Conservation*

Table 7-19: Environmental Crimes Unit Investigations Conducted During CY 2000

Source of Complaints	Complaints Reviewed	Investigations Opened
Division of Air & Water Quality	16	12
Division of Environmental Health	5	4
Division of Spill Prevention & Response	13	10
Total Referred From ADEC Programs	34	26
Actions Initiated by ECU	14	2
Referred From Other Sources	19	9
TOTAL	67	37

Source: *Alaska Department of Environmental Conservation*

Table 7-20: Department of Environmental Conservation Complaints Investigated By Programs

Code	Program	1998	1999	2000
AQI	Air Quality Improvement Program	36	48	189
AQM	Air Quality Maintenance Program	160	126	171
CS	Contaminated Sites Program	3	1	1
DOD	Contaminated Sites (DOD) Program	1	0	0
DW	Drinking Water / Wastewater Program	158	55	52
ECU	Environmental Crimes Unit	43	66	67
IPP	Industry Preparedness Program	0	0	11
IPPT	IPP-Terminal and Tank Farms Program	4	7	3
PERP	Preparedness Emergency Response Program	84	40	67
SAN	Sanitation Program	1	3	0
SEA	Seafood Program	4	1	0
SPS	Statewide Public Service (All Offices)	3	2	5
SW	Solid Waste Program	27	21	22
UST	Underground Storage Tank Program	5	2	2
WS	Water Shed Management Program	15	11	13
	TOTAL	544	383	603

Source: *Alaska Department of Environmental Conservation*

Training

The law enforcement research literature is filled with studies/analyses of police officer training. A large void exists, however, in the environmental crime literature with regard to the training provided to those responsible for enforcing laws pertaining to harms against the environment. Researchers, in an attempt to fulfill this void, are encouraged to consider training-related data as they apply to environmental crime. This concern should be considered in light of Rebovich's (1998, p. 351) suggestion that those currently enforcing environmental crime laws are "hampered by a lack of training." Table 7-21 depicts the type of information sometimes available via state regulatory Web sites.

Table 7-21: Environmental Crimes Unit Enforcement Training Classes

Course Title	Students	Dates	Type Students
Environmental Enforcement Pitfalls	45	Mar 2000	ADEC Regulatory
Basic Environmental Investigations	73	Apr 2000	ADEC Regulatory, Attorneys, & Law Enforcement
Environmental Crimes Awareness Training for Law Enforcement	12	Sept 2000	Law Enforcement
Complaint Automated Tracking System & Court Room Testimony	57	Oct & Nov 2000	ADEC Regulatory

Source: *Alaska Department of Environmental Conservation*

Enforcement

The following enforcement information concerning environmental crime is likely to be of interest to criminal justice researchers. As this section demonstrates, much of the same information used to analyze conventional crime is available for environmental crime. Keep in mind that we have provided only a small sample of the information currently available. Although a single year of information is provided below in many cases, researchers are encouraged to ask publishers for previous years of data as needed. Tables 7-22 through 7-33 depict the type of enforcement information available to researchers.

It should be obvious from inspecting these tables that there are few criminal cases, strictly speaking. Consider Table 7-24, which shows the number of civil, administrative, and criminal cases for Montana for 1999 through 2000. During this period, Montana handled 394 environmental cases. Only one of these cases involved criminal charges. As seen in Tables 7-28 and 7-29, criminal environmental cases are likely to result in a fine. Nationally, criminal fines constitute nearly 60 percent of environmental fines collected by the EPA (Table 7-27), while comprising only 30 percent of environmental fines collected by states (Table 7-28).

Table 7-22: New York State Department of Environmental Conservation Environmental Enforcement Statistics by Calendar Year			
	1998	**1999**	**2000**
Consent Orders	800	2477	3066
Payable Penalties Imposed thru Consent Orders	$3,972,016	$7,382,180	$7,276,775
Commissioner's Orders	15	13	42
Payable Penalties Imposed through Commissioner's Orders	$4,079,649	$195,250	$1,579,050
Total Value of EBP's	$4,436,500	$3,109,350	$934,965
Total Payable Penalties & EBP's	$12,488,165	$11,152,140	$10,873,100
Vol. Cleanup Agreements	29	31	52
AG Referrals- Oil Spill	93	223	224
AG Referrals- Civil	149	47	50
AG Referrals- Criminal	149	74	77
Superfund Orders	56	63	52
Total Value of Superfund Orders	$87,700,000	$158,500,000	$59,269,250

Source: *New York State Department of Environmental Conservation*

Table 7-23: Supplemental Environmental Projects (SEPs)

Program	Number	Value	Confirmed Performance
Act 250	1	$25,000	N/A
Air Pollution	1	$2,300	$2,000
Forests, Parks & Recreation Dept.	1	$6,000	$6,000
Hazardous Materials	6	$185,000	$35,000
Solid Waste	2	$16,000	$1,500
Water Quality	3	$8,500	$8,500
TOTALS	14	$242,300	$53,000

Source: *Vermont Agency of Natural Resources*

Table 7-24: Analysis of Enforcement Actions by Enforcement Action Type

Statute	1999-2000 Case Load	Enforcement Action Type		
		Administrative	Civil	Criminal
Air Quality Act	49	42	7	
Asbestos Control Act	11	5	6	
Strip and Underground Mine Reclamation Act	39	38		
Hazardous Waste Act	17	15	2	
Metal Mine Reclamation Act	14	14		
Motor Vehicle Recycling & Disposal Act	13	6	7	
Opencut Mining Act	22	22		
Public Water Supply Act	103	94	9	
Solid Waste Act	18	11	7	
Sanitation & Subdivision Law	1	1		
Underground Storage Tank Act	58	54	2	
Water Quality Act	49	41	6	1
Total	394	343	46	1

Source: *Montana Department of Environmental Quality*

Table 7-25: MPCA Enforcement and Penalty Summary		
State FY	Total Enforcement Actions	Penalties Assessed
1975	2	$27,000
1976	3	$13,250
1977	8	$193,750
...	...	...
1999	243	$867,984
2000	347	$1,449,497

Source: *Minnesota Pollution Control Agency*

Table 7-26: Massachusetts: Numerical Summary of Statewide Activity				
FY Totals	1998	1999	2000	+/- Change (FY99–FY00)
Higher Level Enforcement Cases (Admin. Only)	390	453	547	+ 21%
Admin. Penalty Cases	195	216	256	+ 18.5%
Admin. Penalty Dollars Assessed	$2.561 million	$1.571 million	$1.613 million	+ 2.7%
Referrals to Attorney General	40	17	23	+ 35%
Notices of Non-Compliance	2148	2686	2649	- 1.4%
Compliance Inspections Performed	7608	7046	7073	+ 0.4%
Higher- Level Enforcement as a Percentage of Inspections	5.7%	6.8%	8.1%	+ 19%

Source: *Massachusetts Department of Environmental Protection*

Table 7-27: FY '99 Prosecutions Case Disposition Statistics				
Case Type	# of cases concluded in court	Fines, restitution, environmental project costs		Jail time	
		Imposed	To be paid	Imposed	To Be Served
AIR	1	$2,000	$1,000	0	0
WASTE	17	$213,500	$184,000	14 mos.	0
WATER	13	$30,930	$12,175	0	0
TOTAL	31	$246,430	$197,175	14 mos.	0

Source: *Maryland Department of the Environment*

Table 7-28: Dollar Value of FY 2000 EPA Enforcement Actions (by Statute)			
	Criminal Penalties Assessed	Civil Judicial Penalties Assessed	Administrative Penalties Assessed
CAA	$5,714,318	$21,827,013	$3,629,256
CERCLA	$70,400	$426,000	$0
CWA	$39,730,733	$21,579,394	$5,403,201
EPCRA	$0	$52,297	$4,578,602
FIFRA	$583,745	$0	$2,078,506
RCRA	$38,509,153	$10,863,061	$9,401,878
SDWA	$29,840,156	$104,000	$821,515
TSCA	$1,492,084	$0	$3,345,544
Title 18/ Other	$6,033,899	$0	$0
Totals	$121,974,488	$54,851,765	$29,258,502

Source: *US Environmental Protection Agency*

Table 7-29: Penalties Collected by States 1997–1999			
	1997	**1998**	**1999**
Administrative	$34,788,102	$37,262,038	$45,310,647
Civil	$20,031,175	$33,760,856	$17,434,094
SEPs	$29,758,939	$38,624,785	$21,949,216
Criminal	$5,290,847	$8,028,956	$275,003
Combined	$5,608,445	$17,668,168	$7,001,742
TOTALS	$95,477,508	$135,344,803	$91,970,702

Source: *ECOS*

Table 7-30: Environmental Crimes Unit Penalty Statistics				
Criminal Fines & Civil Penalties	**1998**	**1999**	**2000**	**TOTAL**
Criminal	$517,800	$94,861	$101,500	$932,711
Civil	$150,000	$2,500	$20,000	$226,318
Suspended	$274,500	$550	$45,000	$415,200
Jail Time (days)				
Imposed	0	325	0	980
Suspended	0	220	0	602
Probation (years)	15	3	10	71.5

Source: *Alaska Department of Environmental Conservation*

Table 7-31: FY 2000 Concluded EPA Enforcement Actions: Types of Compliance Activity (by law, does not include SEP Impacts)					
Type of Impact from FY 2000 Cases	CAA	CERCLA	CWA	EPCRA	Total
Use Reduction	12	0	123	4	157
Industrial Process Change	12	2	128	4	166
Emissions/ Discharge Change	38	5	273	2	336
Storage/ Disposal Change	7	2	145	1	223
Remediation/ Restoration	17	29	326	1	424
Removal	6	59	186	0	299
Testing	40	15	145	0	412
Auditing	16	1	125	90	258
Total Monitoring/ Sampling Only	64	40	272	2	714
Recordkeeping Only	13	0	0	2	52
Total Recordkeeping	88	18	362	35	897
Labeling/ Manifesting	10	5	120	1	223
Reporting Only	118	4	68	97	1,562
Total Reporting	188	22	298	203	2,541
Information Letter Response	18	8	148	2	202
Permit Application	7	0	232	1	244
Training	33	2	287	3	390
Provide Site Access	0	56	138	1	214
Site Assessment	0	11	138	0	174
Other Result/ Impact Only	28	119	193	16	761
Total Other Result/ Impact	64	146	335	36	1,375
Penalty Only	72	17	204	40	501
Total # of Cases	534	381	1,264	382	5,609
Total # of Impact Types	692	480	4,004	426	9,818
# of Settlements w/ Action Listed	338	286	926	235	4,455

Source: *US Environmental Protection Agency*

Table 7-32: Use of "Informal" Enforcement Mechanisms by State Environmental Agencies, 1997–1999				
State	# of States Reporting	1997	1998	1999
Oral Warnings	38	3,825	4,523	6,714
Warning Letters	38	22,618	28,057	30,456
Notices of Violation	50	38,646	37,159	36,798
Consent Agreements	31	4,145	5,063	7,347
TOTAL		69,234	74,802	81,315

Source: *ECOS*

Table 7-33: Trends in State Enforcement and Compliance, 1998–1999				
Trend	# of States Included	1998	1999	+/- Change (1995 - 1999)
Determining Compliance				
Sites/ Facilities/ Incidences	33	959,049	969,673	+4.6%
Inspections	49	287,979	296,807	+18.0%
Evaluations/ Assessments	33	179,002	178,858	+4.4%
Citizens' Complaints	26	54,845	58,841	+16.2%
Issuing Violations				
Significant Violations	27	11,468	11,535	-0.8%
Initial Enforcement Steps				
Oral Warnings	31	3,953	4,073	+9.3%
Warning Letters	36	12,057	12,886	+5.1%
Notices of Violation	41	29,771	29,012	+8.1%
Consent Agreements	27	4,185	5,011	+55.3%

Source: *ECOS*

List of Tables
The following table from an EPA Office of Enforcement and Compliance Assurance report includes an account of the information provided in their Fiscal Year (FY) 2000 RECAP *Measures of Success Management Report*. To illustrate the breadth of this data, only the names of the tables and graphs are reported here. Again, data for multiple years are available upon request.

Table 7-34: FY 2000 Measures of Success Management Report— List of Tables and Graphs

Section A: Projected Environmental and Compliance Benefits

1. Results of EPA Enforcement Actions Concluded in FY 2000
2. Number of Actions Requiring a Physical Compliance Action since FY 1996
3. FY 2000 Concluded Actions: Types of Compliance Activity by Region
4. Frequency Distribution of Complying Actions by Region
5. FY 2000 Concluded Actions: Types of Compliance Activity by Law
6. Frequency Distribution of Complying Actions by Statute
7. Pollutants Most Frequently Identified as Required Reductions
8. 20 Pollutants with the Largest Expected Reductions Reported, FY 2000

Section B: Enforcement Activity Counts

9. National Totals - FY 2000 Enforcement Activity
10. FY New Formal Enforcement Actions (by Region and Type)
11. FY 2000 Enforcement Action Conclusions/ Settlements
12. FY 2000 EPA Case Initiations and Conclusion by Statute
13. EPA Criminal Enforcement: Major Outputs FY 1998 to FY 2000
14. FY 2000 Civil Referrals to DOJ Compared to FY 1998 and 2000
15. FY 2000 APO Complaints Compared to FY 1998 and FY 1999
16. Regional Enforcement of Consent Decree Violations
17. EPA Civil Referral and Settlements During FY 1998 to FY 2000
18. Regional Civil Judicial Outputs FY 1998 to 2000 Compared to FTE
19. Regional APO Outputs FY 1998 to FY 2000 Compared to FTE
20. Regional Proportions of Significant FY 2000 Enforcement Outputs
21. EPA Civil Referrals to DOJ Since FY 1973
22. Various Historical APO Data Charts
23. EPA Criminal Program Shows Sustained Growth in Key Outputs
24. FY 2000 State Enforcement Activity by Region
25. FY 2000 Notices of Violation (by Region and Statute)

Section C: Dollar Values and Penalty Amounts

26. Dollar Value of EPA Actions Concluded in FY 2000
27. Enforcement Case Values Beyond Penalty Assessments
28. Dollar Value of FY 2000 EPA Enforcement Actions by Region
29. Dollar Value of FY 2000 Enforcement Actions (% by Office)
30. FY 2000 EPA Civil Penalties by Region
31. Dollar Value of FY 2000 EPA Enforcement Actions by Statute

32. Dollar Value of FY 2000 Enforcement Actions (% by Statute)
33. FY 2000 EPA Civil Penalties by Statute (Number and Averages)
34. Dollar Value of FY 2000 CAA EPA Enforcement Actions
35. FY 2000 EPA CAA Penalties (Number and Averages)
36. Dollar Value of FY 2000 CERCLA EPA Enforcement Actions
37. Dollar Value of FY 2000 CWA EPA Enforcement Actions
38. FY 2000 EPA CWA Penalties (Number and Averages)
39. Dollar Value of FY 2000 EPCRA EPA Enforcement Actions
40. FY 2000 EPA EPCRA Penalties (Number and Averages)
41. Dollar Value of FY 2000 FIFRA EPA Enforcement Actions
42. FY 2000 EPA FIFRA Penalties (Number and Averages)
43. Dollar Value of FY 2000 RCRA EPA Enforcement Actions
44. FY 2000 EPA RCRA Penalties (Number and Averages)
45. Dollar Value of FY 2000 SDWA EPA Enforcement Actions
46. FY 2000 EPA SDWA Penalties (Number and Averages)
47. Dollar Value of FY 2000 TSCA EPA Enforcement Actions
48. FY 2000 EPA TSCA Penalties (Number and Averages)
49. EPA Enforcement Penalties Since its Creation

Section D: Supplemental Environmental Projects

50. EPA Supplemental Environmental Projects in FY 2000
51. Use of SEPs in FY 2000 Enforcement Actions
52. Percent of FY 2000 Settlements that Included a SEP
53. SEP Categories Reported for FY 2000 EPA SEPs (by Region)
54. SEP Categories Reported for FY 2000 EPA SEPs (by Law)
55. Use of SEPs in Judicial & Adm. Penalty Actions: FY 1998–2000
56. Use of SEPs in Judicial & Adm. Penalty Actions: FY 1998–2000
57. EPA's Use of SEPs in Formal Actions: FY 1995 to FY 2000

Section E: SNC, Inspections, Investigations, and Citizen Complaints

58. Addressed/Resolved Significant Noncompliance FY 2000
59. NPMS SNC Duration (by Region for CWA and RCRA)
60. NPMS SNC Duration (by State for CWA and RCRA)
61. NPMS SNC Recidivism for CAA, CWA and RCRA
62. NPMS SNC Recidivism for CAA, CWA and RCRA (by State)
63. FY 2000 Inspections at Regulated Facilities: EPA & State for CAA
64. FY 2000 Inspections at Regulated Facilities: EPA & State for CWA & RCRA
65. FY 2000 Inspections: EPA & State for EPCRA, FIFRA, SDWA & TSCA
66. FY 2000 Inspection Coverage at Regulated Facilities: CAA & CWA

67. FY 2000 Inspection Coverage at Regulated Facilities: RCRA
68. EPA Regional Inspection Trend: FY 1994 to FY 2000
69. NPMS – Civil Investigations and Citizen Complaints by Statute

Section F: Compliance Incentives/Assistance/Capacity Building

70. Disclosing/Correcting Violations Under Audit Policy Since FY 1997
71. FY 2000 Compliance Assistance for Sector & Statute Compliance
72. FY 2000 Compliance Assistance: How Entities Were Reached
73. FY 2000 Compliance Assistance for Sectors by Industry/Business
74. FY 2000 Compliance Assistance for Statutory Compliance by Statute
75. Regional Proportions of Selected Compliance
76. Region I Compliance Assistance Summary
77. Region II Compliance Assistance Summary
78. Region III Compliance Assistance Summary
79. Region IV Compliance Assistance Summary
80. Region V Compliance Assistance Summary
81. Region VI Compliance Assistance Summary
82. Region VII Compliance Assistance Summary
83. Region VIII Compliance Assistance Summary
84. Region IX Compliance Assistance Summary
85. Region X Compliance Assistance Summary
86. NPMS—Capacity Building Activities (by Region)

Section G: Completeness of EPA Enforcement Data

87. Regional Consent Decree Tracking and Follow-up Status
88. % of Active Decrees with Status Maintained in Docket
89. Completeness of CCDS Cases Attributes in Docket
90. Pollutant Data Reported for FY 2000 EPA Civil Settlements

Section H: MOA Priority Activity

91. FY 2000 Regional Inspections in MOA Priority Areas
92. NPMS—Number of Investigations at Refineries
93. Selected FY 2000 Outputs for MOA Priority Areas—Wet Weather
94. Selected FY 2000 Outputs for MOA Priority Areas—Petroleum Refining
95. Selected FY 2000 Outputs for MOA Priority Areas—SDWA Microbial
96. Selected FY 2000 Outputs for MOA Priority Areas—Metals Services
97. Selected FY 2000 Outputs for MOA Priority Areas—RCRA Permit Evaders
98. Selected FY 2000 Outputs for MOA Priority Areas—Air Toxics/NSR/PSD

DATA USED IN PREVIOUS STUDIES

Environmental crime researchers should consider all environmental-based data sources along with other, relevant information, including census data accessible through the EPA and some state regulatory agency Web sites. Lynch and colleagues (2002, p. 118), for instance, note that through combining data sets "Criminologists can study the distribution of environmental hazards across diverse populations." Creativity, theoretical soundness, and solid research skills are required to effectively combine data sets. A closer examination of previous research projects and the data involved in these studies sheds additional light on avenues for environmental crime research.

Clifford (1998, p. 254) argues that "To date, few studies and larger works have exclusively dealt with the topic of environmental crime." However, several environmental crime (and related) studies have certainly advanced our knowledge in this area. Discussion of these research projects is separated into two primary areas: "Enforcement Efforts" and "Environmental Justice."

It should be noted that these two areas are not exhaustive of the research regarding environmental crime. Lynch, Stretesky, and Hammond (2000), for instance, used a media outlet to examine the frequency and content of newspaper reports concerning accidental chemical releases brought to the EPA's attention through the Emergency Response Notification System (ERNS), while Lynch, Nalla, and Miller (1989) compared American and Indian media accounts of an international environmental crime. Burby and Strong (1997) conducted a telephone survey to examine the association between race and perceptions of pollution, while Edwards (1996) mailed surveys to state police agencies and state attorneys general regarding various aspects of environmental crime (enforcement issues, threats, frequency of environmental crimes, etc.). Stretesky and Lynch (2001) used census data and information from the EPA's Cumulative Exposure Project (which provides estimated concentrations of various air pollutants covered under the Clean Air Act) to support findings that there is an association between lead exposure and violent behavior. The following studies, however, are identifiable as related to either enforcement efforts or environmental justice.

Enforcement Efforts

Earlier studies from Cohen (1989; 1992), McMurry and Ramsey (1986), and Ross (1996) provide examples of what can be done with environmental crime enforcement data. McMurry and Ramsey used internal data collected from the U.S. Department of Justice to, among other things, demonstrate the federal government's increased use of criminal sanctions in the enforcement of environmental laws. Ross (1996) reviewed EPA criminal, civil, and administrative enforcement data to measure the EPA's ability to effectively deter environmental crime. Ross used several EPA data sources, including the Civil Enforcement Docket, the EPA's "Enforcement Accomplishments Report," and the EPA's "Summary of Criminal Prosecutions Resulting from Environmental Investigations." Ross noted that more effective and timely EPA enforcement efforts are needed to deter environmental crime, calling for an integrated data system.

Cohen's 1989 study "Corporate Crime and Punishment: A Study of Social Harm and Sentencing Practice in the Federal Courts, 1984-1987," analyzed 288 corporate offenders sentenced between 1984 and 1987. The original sources of his data were the "Administrative Office of the United States Courts' Master File" and the "Federal Probation Sentencing and Supervision Information System." He supplemented these data with detailed information found in presentence investigation reports. In some cases the "Judgment and Probation/Commitment Orders" was used. His 1989 research involved summarizing criminal fines and known monetary sanctions for environmental crimes, the size of fines received for environmental crimes, and the damage resultant from these crimes.

Cohen's (1992) later work updated these data and expanded this research agenda. He used enforcement-related data to examine sanctions for environmental crimes, including the distribution of offenses and offenders, criminal sanctions for convicted organizations and individual co-defendants guilty of environmental crimes, and noncriminal sanctions for corporate environmental crimes. Cohen also observed the impact of sentencing guidelines on environmental sanctions. The data used by Cohen, McMurry and Ramsey, and Ross in these studies are more accessible today than they were when these studies were published. Follow-up, supplementary, and/or related studies are certainly possible given the increasing availability of environmental crime data.

Several studies funded through National Institute of Justice (NIJ) grants during the mid-1990s shed light on environmental crime enforcement and offer alternative methods of data collection. Hammett and Epstein's (1993) study, "Local Prosecution of Environmental Crime," employed site visits to five local prosecutors' offices. Their qualitative approach to analyzing environmental crime fighting was supplemented with a review of relevant literature, statutes, and case law. This study, along with another 1993 NIJ report prepared by the same researchers (titled "Prosecuting Environmental Crime: Los Angeles County") provided a foundation for their 1995 NIJ Report, "Law Enforcement Response to Environmental Crime" (Epstein & Hammett, 1995). This report includes law enforcement training issues and interagency cooperation concerns, and stems primarily from telephone interviews with 21 environmental law enforcement programs and personal visits to three programs; each with a different organizational approach.

Hammett and Epstein were not the only researchers funded by NIJ to investigate environmental crime during this period. Rebovich and Nixon (1994) also studied environmental crime prosecution, surveying prosecutors across the United States in jurisdictions with populations over 250,000. These results were supplemented with interviews of regulatory personnel at seven sites regarding prosecution of environmental crime in their jurisdictions.

Environmental Justice

Concern for environmental justice, an umbrella term which encapsulates environmental racism (see Downey, 1998; Clifford, 1998; and Bullard, 1994 for discussions of these terms), emerged from the work of activists intent on addressing disparities in exposure to environmental hazards between majority and minority groups in America. In contrast to studies concerning the enforcement of environmental harms, research in this area has utilized many of the aforementioned databases. Examinations of environmental justice and environmental racism represent the difficulties often found when studying corporate crime issues: Some corporate or government behaviors may be legal (e.g., locating hazardous waste plants in minority neighborhoods), but not ethical, moral, and/or just.

Research in this area sometimes involves U.S. Census data, and as updated, allows for continuous re-evaluation as well as new research. The following provides a brief account of available environmental justice research with a focus on the data used.

Downey (1998) examined Toxic Release Inventory (TRI) data for Michigan to observe emission levels in relation to race (race data were obtained from the U.S. Census). Earlier, Bowen, Salling, Haynes, and Cyran (1995) used TRI data to suggest that income was a better predictor of TRI emissions than race. Ringquist (1997) examined the roughly 30,000 TRI facility locations across the United States and found a relationship between release patterns and racial and income characteristics. Pollock and Vittas (1995) are among the researchers who have examined TRI data in relation to various demographic characteristics.

Anderton, Anderson, Rossi, Oakes, Fraser, Weber, and Calabrese (1994) used TSDF (Treatment, Storage, and Disposal of Hazardous Waste) data with census tract information as their unit of analysis to measure the possibility of racial bias in the distribution of waste facilities. Others used TSDF data to examine the location of hazardous waste facilities in relation to the demographic characteristics of neighboring communities (e.g., Mohai & Bryant, 1992; Boer, Pastor, Sadd, & Snyder, 1997), while Hamilton (1993, 1995) used TSDF data to examine TSDF treatment facility expansion and contraction behaviors in relation to social factors. Hamilton also considered the location of newly constructed treatment facilities.

Other researchers analyzed air quality in relation to demographics within the context of environmental justice. Cutter (1994), for example, analyzed toxic air emissions in South Carolina and found that urban, nonwhite counties were disproportionately subject to poor air quality, while Brajer and Hall (1992) noted a positive association between elevated air pollution levels and a higher proportion of low-income, black, and Hispanic residents. Earlier research by Asch and Seneca (1978), and Earickson and Billick (1988) also examined air quality levels in relation to demographics.

Researchers also examined the location of Superfund sites in relation to various social factors (e.g., Zimmerman, 1993; Hird, 1993; Lynch et al., 2002; Stretesky & Hogan, 1998). Hird (1993), for instance, observed the relationship between residential, political, and economic factors of census tracts in the neighborhoods surrounding the nation's 788 Superfund sites. Lavalle and Coyle (1992) observed enforcement efforts, community characteristics, and the location of U.S. Superfund sites. Finally, Anderton, Oakes, and Egan (1997) found that non-NPL CERCLIS and Superfund sites were less likely to be located in minority census tracts.

Stretesky and Lynch (1999) used 1990 census data to examine the relationship between the racial, ethnic, and economic demographic characteristics of census tracts and serious chemical accidents in Hillsborough County, FL. The data used to map the location of these spills were obtained from the EPA's Accidental Reporting Information Program (ARIP). Their research involved BRS, TRI, and TSDF data available through the EPA Web site.

In one of the largest studies of environmental justice (or, at least the one containing what is likely the largest number of variables), Hird and Reese (1998) provide a multivariate analysis of the relationships between demographic characteristics and 29 measures of environmental quality. Using variables demonstrative of environmental quality in several areas, the authors examined: (1) industrial air emissions (number of smoke stacks, hazardous chemicals, number of hazardous waste incinerators, and number of permit violators); (2) industrial water discharges (number of industrial water discharge facilities, hazardous chemicals, and suspected carcinogens); (3) water quality (percentage of impaired rivers and streams, number of public water supply violations, amount of sewage outflow, and level of public supply risk); (4) air quality (amount of hazardous chemical emissions; level of carbon monoxide concentrations, lead concentrations, nitrogen dioxide concentrations, ozone concentrations, particulate concentrations, and sulfur dioxide concentrations; and number of standards not attained) and; (5) proximity to hazardous wastes (number of hazardous waste generators, estimated amount of waste generated, number of TSDFs, number of land disposal facilities, number of commercial TSDFs, commercial landfill capacity, number of uncontrolled closed sites, number of Superfund NPL sites, number of treatment and storage facilities, and number of groundwater monitoring violators). Hird and Reese gathered socioeconomic data from the census. They purchased the pollution data from Public Data Access, although it appears that much of their pollution-related information can now be accessed online or through requests made to appropriate agencies.

In addition to the various data sources and datasets discussed above, researchers are encouraged to refer to the extensive bibliography used to assemble this work as a tool for their research efforts. Several quality books addressing environmental crime include Rebovich's (1992) *Dangerous Ground: The World of Hazardous Waste Crime* which includes results from an extensive research study; *Environmental Crime and Criminality: Theoretical and Practical Issues*, Edwards, Edwards, & Fields' 1996 edited work with insightful contributions regarding environmental crime; Hammitt & Reuter's (1988) *Measuring and Deterring Illegal Disposal of Hazardous Waste* is also a viable source of information, and Clifford's (1998) *Environmental Crime: Enforcement, Policy, and Social Responsibility* provides helpful contributions from numerous experts in the area of environmental crime. Finally, Bullard's (1996) *Dumping in Dixie: Race, Class and Environmental Quality* highlights issues pertaining to environmental racism and justice.

CHAPTER 8

EPA Web-Based Informational Resources

In this chapter we review some additional online materials that may be accessed through the EPA Web site. Many of these materials may also be requested directly from the EPA. Readers should be aware that the EPA also has other materials available for review that cannot be found on its Web site.

It should be noted that our guide to EPA data and programs excludes resources listed on the EPA Web site that contain descriptions of data, rather than actual data. For example, the EPA home page provides a direct link to its "Compliance and Enforcement" page (as of this writing, in a right-hand navigation bar). Currently, compliance and enforcement data are not available directly through these links. Rather, "Compliance and Enforcement" links simply direct users to a description of data or a specific program. In fact, many links on the Enforcement and Compliance pages have a tendency to direct the user in seemingly endless circles. An exception is the "Enforcement Action Database." Unfortunately, the only available online enforcement data pertain to Region 5 (Illinois, Indiana, Michigan, Minnesota, Ohio, and Wisconsin).

It is unfortunate that the EPA has established barriers to accessing its criminal enforcement data. Reliable public access to criminal enforcement data is necessary for several reasons. First, it is clearly impossible to understand the nature and extent of environmental crime, the distribution of these crimes by place, the types of crimes being committed, prosecuted and punished, and whether corporations or individuals are more likely to be charged with engaging in criminal acts against the environment when access to criminal enforcement data is unavailable. To be sure, the average citizen, and even researchers are discouraged from accessing EPA criminal enforcement data because of its exclusion from Web-based resources. Second, in a democracy, citizens have a right to data concerning crimes being committed against them in order to both protect themselves and to ensure that their elected officials are doing their utmost to protect them from harm. Keeping data from public view is one way to undermine the principles of democracy and citizen oversight of governmental agencies and the elected officials, such as the president, who guide the direction of these agencies.

Gaining access to the EPA's criminal enforcement data is, at this point, not impossible. This can be done by obtaining a user ID and password from the EPA that allows you to access the IDEA database through an EPA Web server. Even after obtaining an ID and password, accessing the server requires following an elaborate set of directions. With these caveats in mind, we proceed to our overview of Web-based, EPA data and documents.

EPA WEB-BASED DATA AND DOCUMENTS

Proposed Rule Changes and Rule Implementation—EDOCKET

EDOCKET contains regulatory and non-regulatory dockets and documents for public review and comments online. A docket is the repository for the collection of information related to a particular agency action or activity. EDOCKET contains Federal Registers, various reports, hearing transcripts; comments written to the EPA on proposed rules and other items used in the rulemaking process can also be accessed. EDOCKET replicates original EPA dockets, with the exclusion of copyrighted, confidential, oversized, audio, and video materials.

EDOCKET was initiated in May 2002 and incorporates materials and supporting decision-making documents related to: (1) The Air and Radiation (OAR) Docket – Clean Air Act; (2) The Superfund Docket (SFUND) – Comprehensive Environmental Response, Compensation, and Liability Act (CERCLA); (3) The Resource Conservation and Recovery Act (RCRA) Docket—RCRA and Office of Solid Waste; and (4) The Underground Storage Tanks (UST) Docket—Underground storage tanks.

Further EDOCKETS to be added include: (1) The Water (OW) Docket—Safe Drinking Water Act (SDWA) and the Clean Water Act; (2) The Pesticides Programs (OPP) Docket—Federal Insecticide Fungicide and Rodenticide Act (FIFRA); (3) The Toxics (OPPTS) Docket—Toxic Substances Control Act (TSCA); (4) The Enforcement and Compliance Assurance (OECA) Docket—EPA enforcement and compliance activities; and (5) The Office of Environmental Information (OEI) Docket—Regulatory and guidance documents supporting the EPA's management of environmental information.

Major Environmental Law

Users may access the text of the following major environmental laws through the EPA Web site.

- National Environmental Policy Act of 1969 (NEPA); 42 U.S.C. 4321–4347.
- Chemical Safety Information, Site Security and Fuels Regulatory Relief Act.
- The Clean Air Act (CAA); 42 U.S.C. s/s 7401 et seq. (1970).
- The Clean Water Act (CWA); 33 U.S.C. ss/1251 et seq. (1977).
- Comprehensive Environmental Response, Compensation, and Liability Act (CERCLA or Superfund); 42 U.S.C. s/s 9601 et seq. (1980).
- The Emergency Planning & Community Right-To-Know Act (EPCRA); 42 U.S.C. 11011 et seq. (1986).
- The Endangered Species Act (ESA); 7 U.S.C. 136; 16 U.S.C. 460 et seq. (1973).
- Federal Insecticide, Fungicide and Rodenticide Act (FIFRA); 7 U.S.C. s/s 135 et seq. (1972).
- Federal Food, Drug, and Cosmetic Act (FFDCA); 21 U.S.C. 301 et seq.
- Food Quality Protection Act (FQPA); Public Law 104–170, Aug. 3, 1996.
- The Freedom of Information Act (FOIA); U.S.C. s/s 552, (1966).
- The Occupational Safety and Health Act (OSHA); 29 U.S.C. 651 et seq. (1970).
- The Oil Pollution Act of 1990 (OPA); 33 U.S.C. 2702 to 2761.
- The Pollution Prevention Act (PPA); 42 U.S.C. 13101 and 13102, s/s et seq. (1990).
- The Resource Conservation and Recovery Act (RCRA); 42 U.S.C. s/s 321 et seq. (1976).
- The Safe Drinking Water Act (SDWA); 42 U.S.C. s/s 300f et seq. (1974).
- The Superfund Amendments and Reauthorization Act (SARA); 42 U.S.C.9601 et seq. (1986).
- The Toxic Substances Control Act (TSCA); 15 U.S.C. s/s 2601 et seq. (1976).

Users may also employ the EPA Web site to view current proposed congressional legislation, the U.S. Code (USC), and the Code of Federal Regulations (CFR).

Air Resources

The EPA maintains a variety of information pertaining to air resources that may be accessed through its Web site. Major headings for searches of this information are found in the following sections.

- Air Pollutants: Aerosols, Asbestos, Carbon Monoxide, Chlorofluorocarbons (CFCs), Criteria Air Pollutants, Ground Level Ozone, Hazardous Air Pollutants (HAPs), Hydrochloroflurocarbons (HCFCs), Nitrogen Oxides (NOx), Particulate Matter, Propellants, Radon, Refrigerants, Substitutes, Sulfur Oxides (SOx), Volatile Organic Compounds (VOCs).
- Air Pollution: Certification Programs, Community Involvement, Industrial Air Pollution, Research, State Implementation Plans, Stationary Sources, Testing, Transboundary Pollution, Urban Air Pollution.
- Air Pollution Control: Abatement, Remediation, Treatment.
- Air Pollution Effects: Acid Rain, Climate Change, Economic Effects, Environmental Effects, Global Warming, Health Effects, Risk Assessment.
- Air Pollution Legal Aspects: Compliance, Enforcement, Guidance, Legislation, Permits, Regulations, Reporting, Standards.
- Air Pollution Monitoring: Emission Factor, Emission Inventory, Emissions, Measurement, Models, Monitoring, World Trade Center Monitoring.
- Air Quality: Air Quality Criteria, Air Quality Models, Attainment, Emission Factor, Emission Inventory, Emissions, Emissions Measurement, Emissions Trading, Measurements, Models, Monitoring, Nonattainment.
- Atmosphere: Climate Change, Global Warming, Ground Level Ozone, Ozone Depletion, Ozone Layer, Ozone Monitoring, Ozone Transport, Smog, Ultra Violet Radiation (UV).
- Indoor Air Pollution: Carbon Monoxide, Environmental Tobacco Smoke, Fireplaces, Radon, Sick Building Syndrome, World Trade Center Dust Cleanup.

- Mobile Sources: Airplanes, Automobiles, Diesels and Locomotives, Engines, Fuels, Inspection and Maintenance, Lawn and Garden Equipment, Marine Engines, Trucks and Buses, Used Oil Recycling, Vehicle Emissions.

Information Systems by Media of Exposure

EPA records are organized along several lines. One method organizes data by the media or route of exposure. Four different exposure media are covered: (1) Air; (2) Prevention, Pesticides, and Toxic Substances; (3) Solid Waste and Emergency Response; and (4) Water. Land exposures are divided among categories 2 and 3. For information on chemicals that may be emitted across multiple media of exposure, see the Envirofacts Master Chemical Integrator (EMCI).

Air

- Acid Rain Emission Tracking System (ETS). A database of SO_2, NOx, and CO_2 emissions from electric utilities, provided on an hourly, quarterly, or annual basis.
- Aerometric Information Retrieval System (AIRS). Computer-based information about airborne pollution in the U.S. and various World Health Organization (WHO) member countries.
- Air Quality Subsystem (AQS). Ambient concentrations of air pollutants and meteorological data from the EPA, state, and local air-monitoring stations.
- AIRS Facility Subsystem (AFS). Emissions and compliance data on air pollution point sources regulated by the EPA, and state and local air regulatory agencies.
- AIRS Graphics (AGWeb). Mapping and charting routine that integrates data from AIRS subsystems.
- AIRS Executive Software. Subset of data extracted from the AIRS database.
- AIRSData. Summaries of six years of air monitoring data, most recent estimates of air pollutant emissions from major point sources, and overall regulatory compliance status for criteria pollutants (carbon monoxide, nitrogen dioxide, sulfur dioxide, ozone, particulate matter, lead).
- Applicability Determination Index. EPA memoranda on compliance issues associated with the New Source Performance Standards (NSPS), National Emission Standards for Hazardous Air Pollutants (with categories for both

NESHAP, Part 61, and MACT, Part 63), and chlorofluorocarbons (CFCs).

- Region 5 (IL, IN, MI, MN, OH, WI) State Implementation Plans of the Clean Air Act. Contains SIP documents and State Clean Air Act cleanup plans.
- Smart Travel Resource Center Database. Transportation and air quality public education information campaigns and programs around the U.S.
- Vehicle and Engine Emission Modeling Software. Modeling software for testing vehicles and non-road engines for emissions.

Prevention, Pesticides and Toxic Substances

- 8(e) TRIAGE. Searchable database of health studies related to Section 8(e) of TSC.
- Chemicals on Reporting Rules (CORR). dBASE (.DBF) files containing information from the Federal Register concerning TSCA regulated chemicals.
- Enviroene Solvent Substitution Data Systems. Accesses a variety of databases containing environmental and safety information on hazardous solvents and their alternatives.
- Enviroene VendInfo. National list of 400 pollution prevention equipment, products, and services.
- FIFRA Section 18 Database. Contains information about current and recent actions under Section 18 of the Federal Insecticide, Fungicide, and Rodenticide Act.
- Pesticide Data Submitters List. Names and addresses of registrants who wish to be notified and offered compensation for use of their data.
- Pesticide Product Information System (PPIS). Information for all U.S. registered pesticide products.
- Pesticide Restricted Use Products (RUP) Report. List of active and canceled pesticide products classified as "Restricted Use."
- TSCATS Standard Reports. Toxic Substances Control Act Test Submissions contains unpublished, nonconfidential studies submitted by U.S. industries to the EPA under the Toxic Substances Control Act (TSCA).
- OPPT Databases and Software. Software from the EPA's Office of Pollution Prevention and Toxics.
- Title III List of Lists: Consolidated List of Chemicals Subject to the Emergency Planning and Community Right-to-Know

Act (EPCRA) and Section 112(r) of the Clean Air Act. List of chemicals subject to emergency planning requirement under the Emergency Planning and Community Right-to-Know Act (EPCRA).

- Toxic Release Inventory. Facility information and chemical reports on air emissions, surface water discharges, releases to land, underground injections, and transfers to off-site locations.

Solid Waste and Emergency Response

- Comprehensive Environmental Response, Compensation, and Liability Information System (CERCLIS) information on hazardous waste sites, site inspections, preliminary assessments, and remediation of hazardous waste sites.
- ECOTOX Threshold Software. Software for calculating ET Thresholds (ETs) for selected chemicals.
- Hazardous Waste Data. Resource Conservation and Recovery Information System (RCRIS) and Biennial Reporting System (BRS) information.
- Municipal ·Solid Waste Factbook. Reference manual on household waste management practices.
- National Response Center. Contact for reporting and gathering information on oil, chemical, radiological, biological, and etiologic discharges into the environment anywhere in the United States and its territories. Reporting information is available online to the public under the Freedom of Information Act (FOIA).
- RCRA Online. Contains over 2900 RCRA letters, memoranda, and Q&As.
- REACH IT. Accesses information on over 500 remediation/site characterization technologies and over 900 technology applications in the Superfund and other Federal programs.
- Reporting on Municipal Solid Waste: A Local Issue. Background information to assist print and broadcast media in understanding municipal solid waste (MSW) issues.

Water

- Better Assessment Science Integrating Point and Nonpoint Sources (BASINS). Environmental modeling, GIS, and national watershed data.
- Center for Subsurface Modeling Support. Publicly available ground-water zone modeling software and services.
- Enhanced Stream Water Quality Model, Windows (QUAL2E). Program for simulating the major reactions of nutrient cycles, algal production, benthic and carbonaceous demand, atmospheric reaeration, and their effects on the dissolved oxygen balance.
- National Contaminant Occurrence Database (NCOD). Database for tracking contaminants in drinking water.
- Safe Drinking Water Information System (SDWIS/FED). The EPA's National regulatory database for the drinking water program.
- STOrage and RETrieval System for Water and Biological Monitoring Data (STORET). Water quality and biological monitoring data.
- Surf Your Watershed. Public access service to help locate, use, and share environmental information on watersheds or communities.
- Water Radioactivity Software. Programs for making technically difficult calculations with a user interface to simplify technical details and offer protection against mathematical errors.

Geographic Information System (GIS) Software and Data
The Geographic Information System (GIS) Software and Data provides four primary GIS-based data and analysis tools.

- American Indian Lands Environmental Support Project (AILESP). GIS data on releases, recent compliance and enforcement histories, and related environmental data for facilities located on or near Indian lands.
- Better Assessment Science Integrating Point and Nonpoint Sources (BASINS). National watershed, environmental assessment, and modeling tool.
- Geospatial Data Clearinghouse. Geospatial GIS data.

- Maps on Demand (MOD). Internet mapping application displays environmental information for the entire United States.

Technical Tools

EPA technical tools provide support for the use of data accessible through information systems by media. These tools are organized along the same lines as media data.

Air

- AIRS Executive Software. Sample of AIRS database.
- Factor Information Retrieval (FIRE) Data System—The Factor Information Retrieval (FIRE). EPA Database management system of recommended emission estimation factors for criteria and hazardous air pollutants. FIRE includes information about industries, emitting processes, emitted chemicals, and emission factors. Allows access to criteria and hazardous air pollutant emission factors obtained from the Compilation of Air Pollutant Emission Factors (AP-42), Locating and Estimating (L&E) series documents, and the retired AFSEF and XATEF documents.
- TANKS. A Windows-based computer software program for estimating volatile organic compound (VOC) and hazardous air pollutant (HAP) emissions from fixed- and floating-roof storage tanks.
- Vehicle and Engine Emission Modeling Software. Modeling software for use in testing vehicles and non-road engines for emissions.

Prevention, Pesticides, and Toxic Substances

- 8(e) TRIAGE. Database of health studies related to Section 8(e) of TSCA.
- Chemicals on Reporting Rules (CORR). Contains two dBASE (.DBF) files related to Federal Register information on chemicals regulated under the Toxic Substances Control Act (TSCA).
- Integrated Risk Information System (IRIS). Database describing human health effects that may result from exposure to substances found in the environment.

- Pesticide Data Submitters List. Names and addresses of registrants who wish to be notified and offered compensation for use of their data.
- Pesticide Product Information System (PPIS). Information on all U.S. registered pesticide products, including registrant name and address, chemical ingredients, toxicity category, product names, distributor brand names, site/pest uses, pesticidal type, formulation code, and registration status.
- Pesticide Restricted Use Products (RUP) Report. List of active and canceled pesticide products classified as "Restricted Use."
- TSCATS Standard Reports. TSCATS (Toxic Substances Control Act Test Submissions) is an index to unpublished, nonconfidential studies submitted by U.S. industries to the EPA under the Toxic Substances Control Act (TSCA).

Solid Waste And Emergency Response

- ECOTOX Threshold Software. Software used to calculate and print tables and sources of Ecotox Thresholds (ETs) for selected chemicals.
- Hazardous Waste Data. Information from the Resource Conservation and Recovery Information System (RCRIS) and the Biennial Reporting System (BRS).
- REACH IT. A database containing information on over 500 remediation or site characterization technologies and over 900 technology applications in the Superfund and other federal programs.
- Reporting on Municipal Solid Waste: A Local Issue. Background information to assist print and broadcast media in understanding municipal solid waste (MSW) issues, including information sources, major laws affecting MSW management, MSW management state-by-state, and compounds and metals for groundwater detection monitoring.

Water

- Center for Subsurface Modeling Support. Source for publicly available ground-water and vadosezone modeling software and services.
- Enhanced Stream Water Quality Model, Windows (QUAL2E). A program used to simulate the major reactions of nutrient cycles, algal production, benthic and carbonaceous

demand, atmospheric reaeration, and their effects on the dissolved oxygen balance.

- National Listing of Fish Consumption Advisories. List of fish consumption advisories for the continental United States, four U.S. Territories, and 12 Canadian provinces and territories.
- STOrage and RETrieval System for Water and Biological Monitoring Data (STORET). Provides data on water quality and biological monitoring.
- Water Radioactivity Software. Programs designed to assist in making technically difficult calculations with a user interface to simplify technical details and offer protection against mathematical errors.

Test Methods and Guidelines

- EPA Test Method Index. EPA test methods.
- Sources of EPA Test Methods. Lists sources cited in the EPA Test Method Index.

EPA Models

These links provide access to various models used by the EPA to calculate exposure levels, risk assessments, chemical concentrations and movement, and fines, among other topics.

- Atmospheric Sciences Modeling Division. Atmospheric models from NOAA's Air Resources Laboratory.
- Center for Exposure Assessment Modeling (CEAM). Predictive exposure assessment models for aquatic, terrestrial, and multimedia pathways for organic chemicals and metals. It includes Littoral Ecosystem Risk Assessment Model for Prediction of Risk of Chemical Stressors Entering the Aquatic Environment Metal Speciation Equilibrium Model for Surface and Ground Water; Numerical Codes for Delineating Wellhead Protection Areas in Agricultural Regions Based on the Assimilative Capacity Criterion.
- Center for Subsurface Modeling Support (CSMoS). Publicly available ground-water and vadose zone modeling software and services, including: Modeling Capture Zones of Ground-Water Well Using Analytic Elements; Parameter Estimation System for Aquifer Restoration Models; Modular Semi-Analytical Model for the Delineation of Wellhead Protection Areas; Soil Venting Model.

- Council on Regulatory Environmental Modeling (CREM). EPA model guidance, development, and application, designed to enhance both internal and external communications on modeling activities.
- Support Center for Regulatory Air Models (SCRAM). Atmospheric air quality dispersion models associated with the Clean Air Act, including Kinetics Model and Ozone Isopleth Plotting Package.
- Vehicle & Engine Emission Modeling Software. Vehicle and engine emission software including MOBILE5, MOBILE6, PART5, Nonroad, and fuel models.
- ABEL Model. Evaluates a corporation's claim that it cannot afford compliance costs, cleanup costs or civil penalties.
- ADL Migration Exposure Model. Estimates the migration of chemicals from polymeric materials as sources of indoor air and water contamination in home environments.
- AQUATOX: A Simulation Model for Aquatic Ecosystems. A freshwater ecosystem simulation model that predicts an effect of various pollutants, such as nutrients and organic toxicants, on the ecosystem, including fish, invertebrates, and aquatic plants.
- Assessment Tools for the Evaluation of Risk (ASTER). Developed to assist regulators in performing ecological risk assessments by providing high-quality data for discrete chemicals.
- BEN Model. Calculates a violator's economic savings from delaying and/or avoiding pollution control expenditures.
- Better Assessment Science Integrating Point and Nonpoint Sources (BASINS). Environmental analysis system for use by state, regional, and local agencies in performing watershed- and water-quality based studies.
- CASHOUT Model. Calculates the present value of cleanup costs for a given Superfund site.
- CHEMFLO-One-Dimensional Water and Chemical Movement in Unsaturated Soils. Screening level model for simulating water and chemical movement in unsaturated soils.
- Chesapeake Bay Community Watershed Model. Watershed model for Chesapeake Bay.
- CORMIX for Mixing Zones. A mixing zone model that can be used to assess water quality impacts from point source discharges at surface or sub-surface levels.

- Enhanced Stream Water Quality Model (QUAL2E). Water quality planning tool for calculating total maximum daily loads (TMDL). Can be used in conjunction with field sampling for identifying the magnitude and quality characteristics of nonpoint sources.
- Hydrologic Evaluation of Landfill Performance Model. Model for evaluating the effectiveness of landfill.
- INDIPAY Model. Evaluates an individual taxpayer's claim that he or she cannot afford compliance costs, cleanup costs, or civil penalties.
- Landfill Air Emissions Estimation Model. Estimates emissions of methane, carbon dioxide, nonmethane organic compounds, and hazardous air pollutants from municipal solid waste landfills.
- MODFLOW and MODFLOW Manual. Twenty problem sets that illustrate MODFLOW modeling principles, input/output specifics, available options, rules of thumb, and common modeling mistakes.
- Multi-Chamber Concentration and Exposure Model. Estimates average and peak indoor air concentrations of chemicals released from products or materials in houses, apartments, townhouses, or other residences.
- Pesticide Analytical Model. Vadose zone modeling of the transport of organic (pesticide) contaminants.
- Prediction of Radiological Effects Resulting from Shallow Trench Operation, Consisting of PRESTO-EPA-CPG Model and PRESTO-EPA-POP Models. Computer model evaluating radiation exposure from contaminated soil layers, including waste disposal, soil cleanup, agricultural land application, and land reclamation.
- PRESTO-EPA-POP: An Operation System for Predicting the Population Health Effects from the Disposal of Radioactive Waste by Shallow Trenches. Model for evaluating radiation exposure from contaminated soil layers, including waste disposal, soil cleanup, agricultural land application, and land reclamation.
- Probabilistic Dilution Model (PDM). Estimates how often a given concentration of concern may be exceeded in receiving streams and was integrated into the ReachScan program.
- Project Model. Calculates the real cost to a defendant of a proposed supplemental environmental project.

- ReachScan with Probabilistic Dilution Model and Endangered Species Database Link. Integrates ReachScan, Probabilistic Dilution Model (PDM), and the Endangered Species Database (ESDB). ReachScan is an integrated surface water modeling and database system designed to estimate surface water concentrations, and determine the presence of endangered species or critical habitats in the county of a releasing facility.
- Regulatory and Investigative Treatment Zone Model (RITZ). Vadose zone modeling of the transport of contaminants associated with oily wastes.
- Retention Curve Computer Code (RETC). Theoretical methods predicting the soil water retention curve and the hydraulic conductivity curve from measured soil water retention data.
- Soil Transport and Fate Database. Information concerning the behavior of organic and some inorganic chemicals in the soil environment.
- Two-Dimensional Finite Element Program for Multiphase Flow and Multicomponent Transport. Two-dimensional flow and transport of three fluid phases: water, nonaqueous phase liquid, and gas.
- Vadoze Zone Leaching Model. Simulation of 1-D water and chemical movement in vadose zone.

Superfund Information Systems (SIS)

Superfund Information Systems provides information from several EPA systems, including the CERCLIS, archived databases, and RODS (Record of Decision System) Online. Data and reports may be viewed, downloaded, and/or ordered. The information systems included are as follows.

- Comprehensive Environmental Response, Compensation, and Liability Information System (CERCLIS). Database of information on Superfund sites. Generates a customized report by site.
- Archived Sites. Sites proposed for listing in the National Priority List, but later removed, may be found using this data.
- Record of Decision System (RODS). Provides detailed information on hazardous waste sites being cleaned up under the Superfund Program. Information includes the chosen remedies for site remediation, detailed site descriptions,

history, contaminants, remedy/remediation action, and action departures.

- Site Information Products. Superfund data (e.g., on CD-ROM) and reports that may be ordered from the EPA using online forms.

Health Risk Assessments

The EPA maintains information on chemical-based health risks from data contained in the Integrated Risk Information System (IRIS). Extensive scientific, exposure, and distribution information is available for the following chemicals: (1) dioxin; (2) drinking water and disinfection by-products; (3) lead; (4) mercury; (5) ozone; (6) particle matter (PM); (7) PCBs; (8) perchlorate; and (9) environmental tobacco smoke.

Reporting Hotlines

When investigating environmental crimes, researchers sometimes encounter events that may need to be reported to the proper authority. In addition, EPA hotlines also provide answers to commonly asked questions. For these reasons, a select list of EPA agency hotlines by topic, and, where appropriate, a brief description, follows.

- Acid Rain Hotline. 202-564-9620 (phone), 202-564-9620 (fax). Forwards technical or policy questions to experienced EPA Acid Rain Division personnel.
- Aerometric Information Retrieval System (AIRS)—Airs Quality Subsystem (AQS)—Hotline. 800-334-2405 (phone). AIRS, the national repository for data on airborne pollution in the United States, is comprised of three major subsystems: Air Quality Subsystem (AQS), Geo-Common Subsystem (GCS) and AIRS Facility System (AFS; separate hotline number, 800-367-1044). AQS contains ambient concentrations of air pollutants and associated meteorological and monitoring site data. GCS includes AIRS reference information; AFS includes emissions, regulatory, and point source permit tracking data.
- Air Risk Information Center Hotline (Air RISC). 919-541-0888 (phone), 919-541-1818 (fax). Technical assistance and information in areas of health, risk, and exposure assessment for toxic and criteria air pollutants.
- Antimicrobial Information Hotline. 703-308-0127 (phone), 703-308-6467 (fax). E-mail: Info_Antimicrobial@epa.gov. Addresses questions concerning current antimicrobial

pesticide issues (health and safety issues, registration and re-registration issues, pesticide laws, rules, and regulations relating to antimicrobials).

- Asbestos Abatement/Management Ombudsman. 800-368-5888, 202-566-2822 (phone).
- Center for Exposure Assessment Modeling (CEAM) Help Desk. 706-355-8400 (phone). E-mail: ceam@epa.gov.
- Clean Air Technology Center (CATC) Infoline (formerly Control Technology Center). 919-541-0800 (phone in English), 919-541-1800 (phone in Spanish), 919-541-0242 (fax). E-mail: catcmail@epa.gov. Technical support and assistance for evaluating air pollution problems and pollution prevention and control technology applications at stationary air pollution sources. It includes the RACT/BACT/LAER Clearinghouse (RBLC), Federal Small Business Assistance Program (SBAP), and International Technical Information Center for Global Greenhouse Gases.
- Clearinghouse for Inventories and Emission Factors (CHIEF). 919-541-5285 (phone), E-mail: info.chief@epa.gov. Information exchange focusing on air emissions from stationary and area sources.
- Emergency Planning and Community Right-To-Know Act (EPCRA) hotline. 800-424-9346 (phone). Information on regulations and programs implemented under: Resource Conservation and Recovery Act (RCRA); Comprehensive Environmental Response Compensation and Liability Act (CERCLA, or Superfund); Emergency Planning and Community Right-to-Know Act (EPCRA); Superfund Amendments Reauthorization Act (SARA) Title III.
- Endangered Species Protection Program (Pesticides) Information Line. 800-447-3813 (phone), E-mail: opp-Web-comments@epa.gov.
- Environmental Financing Information Network (EFIN). 202-564-4994 (phone), E-mail: efin@epa.gov.
- Environmental Justice Hotline. 800-962-6215 (phone), E-mail: environmental-justice-epa@epa.gov.
- EPA Enforcement Economic Models Helpline. 888-ECONSPT (phone), E-mail: benabel@indecon.com. Information and assistance for calculating an individual's, municipality's, or corporation's financial ability to pay environmental penalties. This service is primarily targeted at local, state, and federal agency employees.

- EPA Grants and Fellowships Hotline (NCER Hotline). 800-490-9194 (phone).
- Federal Facilities Docket Hotline. 800-548-1016 (phone).
- Inspector General Hotline. 888-546-8740, 202-566-2476 (phone). Receives complaints alleging fraud, waste, abuse, or mismanagement within the EPA.
- Integrated Risk Information System (IRIS) Hotline. 301-345-2870 (phone), E-mail: Hotline.IRIS@epa.gov. Information on using data included in IRIS regarding human health effects that may result from exposure to various substances found in the environment.
- Methods Information Communication Exchange Service (MICE). 703-676-4690 (phone), 703-318-4682 (fax), E-mail: mice@cpmx.saic.com. Provides information on technical issues regarding the EPA Office of Solid Waste's methods manual (SW-846; *"Test Methods for Evaluating Solid Waste: Physical/Chemical Methods"*).
- National Service Center for Environmental Publications (NSCEP, formerly NCEPI). 800-490-9198 (phone), E-mail: ncepimal@one.net. Distributes over 7,000 EPA publications in various formats.
- National Lead Information Center Hotline. 800-424-LEAD, 800-424-5323 (phone), E-mail: nlic@optimuscorp.com. Provides basic information about lead exposure and poisoning, as well as information for contacting related local and state agencies.
- National Pesticide Information Center. 800-858-7378 (phone), 541-737-0761 (fax), E-mail: npic@ace.orst.edu. Science-based information concerning a wide variety of pesticide-related subjects related to more than 600 active pesticide ingredients found in over 50,000 different products registered for use in the United States since 1947.
- National Poison Control Hotline. 800-222-1222 (phone, emergency only), 202-362-3867 (phone, for administrative and materials requests). Handles emergency calls from concerned citizens about poison prevention.
- National Radon Hotline. 800-SOS-RADON (phone), E-mail: airqual@nsc.org.
- National Response Center Hotline. 800-424-8802 (phone), E-mail: lst-nrcinfo@comdt.uscg.mil. Staffed by the U.S. Coast Guard, NRC receives all reports of releases involving

hazardous substances and oil that trigger the federal notification requirements under several laws.

- Ozone Protection Hotline. 800-296-1996 (phone), E-mail: hotline@tidalwave.net. Offers consultation on ozone protection regulations and requirements under Title VI of the Clean Air Act Amendments (CAAA) of 1990.
- Pollution Prevention Information Clearinghouse (PPIC). 202-566-0799 (phone), 202-566-0794 (fax), E-mail: ppic@epa.gov. PPIC seeks to reduce and eliminate industrial pollutants through technology transfer, education, and public awareness.
- RCRA, Superfund, and EPCRA Hotline. 800-424-9346 (phone). Dedicated to providing information and fielding requests to the appropriate office.
- Safe Drinking Water Hotline. 800-426-4791 (phone), 703-412-3333 (fax), E-mail: hotline-sdwa@epa.gov. Provides information about the EPA's drinking water regulations and other related drinking water and ground water topics.
- Small Business Ombudsman Hotline. 800-368-5888 (phone), E-mail: tessier.larry@epa.gov. Provides information to private citizens, small communities, small business enterprises, and trade associations representing the small business sector regarding regulatory activities.
- STORET Water Quality System Hotline. 800-424-9067 (phone), E-mail: STORET@epa.gov. Information on water quality from the Legacy Data Center (LDC) and STORET for all 50 states and U.S. territories and jurisdictions.
- Tools for Schools (IAQ) Technical Assistance Hotline. 866-837-3721 (phone), e-mail: tfs_help@epa.gov. Technical assistance information hotline for users of the IAQ Tools for Schools Kit.
- Toxic Release Inventory—User Support Service. 202-566-0250 (phone), E-mail: tri.us@epa.gov. TRI-US offers specialized assistance to individuals seeking Toxic Release Inventory (TRI) data collected by the EPA under Section 313 of EPCRA (Emergency Planning and Community Right-To-Know Act).
- Toxic Release Inventory—Community Right To Know (EPCRA) Hotline. 800-424-9346 (phone), E-mail: tri.us@epa.gov.
- Toxic Substances Control Act (TSCA) Hotline. 202-554-1404 (phone), E-mail: tsca-hotline@epa.gov. Technical assistance

and information about programs implemented under the TSCA, the Asbestos School Hazard Abatement Act (ASHAA), the Asbestos Hazard Emergency Response Act (AHERA), the Asbestos School Hazard Abatement Reauthorization Act (ASHARA), the Residential Lead-Based Paint Hazard Reduction Act (Title X of TSCA), and the EPA's 33/50 program.

- WasteWise Helpline. 800-EPA-WISE (phone), E-mail: ww@rcais.net. EPA program through which organizations eliminate costly municipal solid waste, benefiting their bottom line and the environment. WasteWise provides free technical assistance to help develop, implement, and measure waste reduction activities, and offers publicity to successful organizations.
- Wetlands Information Hotline. 800-832-7828 (phone), E-mail: wetlands.helpline@epa.gov. Answers requests for information about wetlands regulation, legislation, and policy pursuant to Section 404 of the Clean Water Act, wetlands values and functions, and wetlands agricultural issues.

EPA Libraries

Headquarters Libraries

- Washington, DC. Headquarters Library; INFOTERRA; Legislative Reference Library; Office of General Counsel Law Library; Office of Prevention, Pesticides and Toxic Substances Library; Office of Water Resource Center
- Libraries in Research Triangle Park, North Carolina
- NERL—Atmospheric Sciences Modeling Division Library; RTP Library Services

Regional Libraries

- Region 1 Library, Boston; Region 1 RCRA Research Library, Boston
- Region 2 Library, New York City
- Region 3 Regional Center for Environmental Information, Philadelphia
- Region 4 Regional Technical Information Center, Atlanta
- Region 5 Library, Chicago
- Region 6 Library, Dallas

- Region 7 Information Resource Center, Kansas City
- Region 8 Environmental Information Service Center, and Technical Library, Denver
- Region 9 Library, San Francisco
- Region 10 Library, Seattle

Laboratory Libraries

- Andrew W. Breidenbach Environmental Research Center Library, Cincinnati
- Environmental Science Center Library, Fort Meade, MD
- NERL—Characterization Research Division Technical Research Center, Las Vegas
- NERL—Ecosystem Research Division Library, Athens, GA
- NHEERL—Atlantic Ecology Division Library, Narragansett, RI
- NHEERL—Gulf Ecology Division Library, Gulf Breeze, FL
- NHEERL—Mid-Continent Ecology Division Library, Duluth, MN
- NHEERL—Western Ecology Division Library, Corvallis, OR
- National Vehicle & Fuel Emissions Laboratory Library, Ann Arbor, MI
- NRMRL—Subsurface Protection and Remediation Division Library, Ada, OK
- Environmental Financing Information Network; National Enforcement Investigations Center Environmental Forensics Library; EPA On-Line Library, www.epa.gov/natlibra/ols.htm.

CHAPTER 9

Sector Facility Indexing Project (SFIP) Data, 2000: SFIP Data Summary for the U.S., Aggregated and by Industry Sub-Sector

The EPA Sector Facility Indexing Project (SFIP) examines the environmental record of a *sample* of businesses in five industries (petroleum refining, iron and steel production, primary nonferrous metals smelting and refining, pulp manufacturing, and automobile assembly) along with a sample of major federal facilities. Taken together, environmental records for 890 facilities are presented in the SFIP. Subdivisions within the industry groupings allow data to be examined with respect to ten industry subgroups or sectors as follows:

Sector	Sector Abbreviation	Number of Facilities
Automobile	Automobile	54
Federal	Federal	273
Integrated iron and steel mills	IISM	20
Aluminum smelters & refineries	Aluminum	23
Copper smelters and refineries	Copper	20
Iron and steel mini-mills	ISMM	96
Lead smelters and refineries	Lead	3
Zinc smelters and refineries	Zinc	3
Petroleum refineries	Petroleum	163
Pulp mills	Pulp	235

Below we discuss the data relative to these ten industry subgroups and the overall SFIP summary.

PURPOSE AND GOALS OF SFIP

According to the EPA, the SFIP was designed to provide the public with enhanced access to environmental records maintained by the agency. It accomplishes this task by centralizing data from several different EPA data sources. The EPA employs the Integrated Data for Enforcement Analysis (IDEA) system to generate SFIP data, and to integrate data on inspection, compliance, and enforcement across facilities regulated under the Clean Air Act (CAA), the Clean Water Act (CWA), the National Pollutant Discharge Elimination System (NPDES), and the Resource Conservation and Recovery Act (RCRA).

It should be noted that SFIP does not contain data for all facilities regulated under the acts listed above as it represents only a sample of facilities. As a result, one of the more appropriate uses of the SFIP is educational. Because SFIP data are easy to manipulate and contain a smaller sample of data than found in other EPA resources, this is a good mechanism for becoming familiar with EPA data before moving on to examinations of larger, more inclusive EPA data sets.

According to the EPA, the primary goals of the SFIP are to:

- enhance public access to facility-level compliance data;
- allow industry and federal facilities to help design self-policing and compliance assistance programs;
- aid government in developing tools to determine compliance patterns and help in the allocation of restricted enforcement resources; and
- improve centralized access to a variety of EPA data.

Because one of the goals of SFIP is to enhance public access to EPA data, the EPA also tracks SFIP data use through a Web log to determine the extent of public interest in accessing EPA data.

The following data and descriptions represent data from the EPA SFIP Web site on October 1, 2002. These data were updated in July 2002, and represent a sample of 890 facilities. Our presentation follows the general EPA data pattern. In addition, we provide the data in summary form with added commentary. We do not, however, provide all available data. Our goal is to showcase examples of the kinds of information that can be extracted from the SFIP. Examples of SFIP data are provided in the final three sections of the chapter.

DEFINITIONS

The following definitions are provided to facilitate understanding SFIP data.

Inspections refers to the average number of federal and state inspections per facility over the past two years that occurred under the Clean Water Act (CWA), the Clean Air Act (CAA), and the Resource Conservation and Recovery Act (RCRA). Inspections are listed separately by act. The total average number of inspections can be created by adding CWA, CAA, and RCRA inspections within any subdivision.

Historical Noncompliance includes the number of quarters in which the average facility was in violation or noncompliance under CAA, CWA, or RCRA over the past two years. The validity of these data are affected by three factors: (1) failure to include state/local data in the EPA's IDEA database; (2) failure of the EPA, and/or state/local regulatory agencies to make site visits to determine compliance status; and (3) facilities tend to be reported as compliant when compliance data is unknown.

Permit Exceedances are derived from self-reported water quality monitoring data required under the CWA. Permit exceedances refers to the number of self-reported water monitoring studies that exceed limits permitted under CWA. These figures represent averages for facilities within each sector.

Current Significant Noncompliance involves measures of Significant Noncompliance (SNC) for the CWA and RCRA, and High Priority Violations (HPV) for the CAA. Both HPV and SNC indicate violations or noncompliance events at facilities that pose a severe level of environmental threat. Ten events can cause a regulated facility to be listed in the CAA and HPV data:

1. Failure to obtain a PSD permit
2. Violation of an Air Toxics requirement
3. Violations by a minor related entity that affects the source's (parent company's) regulatory status
4. Violation of an administrative or judicial order
5. Substantial violations of Title V
6. Failure to submit a Title V application within 60 days of the deadline
7. Testing, monitoring, record keeping, or reporting violations that substantially interfere with enforcement or determination of a facility's compliance requirements

8. Violation of an allowable emission limit detected during a source test
9. Chronic or recalcitrant violations
10. Substantial violations of CAA Section 112 (r) requirements

A facility is removed from HPV when it has demonstrated implementation of a remedy to events that caused the facility to be listed in the HPV data.

Under CWA regulations, four conditions cause a facility to be listed in significant noncompliance (SNC) data: (1) submitting a major report 30 days past its due date; (2) failure to meet a major schedule by 90 days; (3) a major exceedance of selected affluent limits; or (4) failure to comply with the requirements of an enforcement action. A facility is removed from CWA SNC status when the condition that resulted in listing is ameliorated or a formal enforcement action has been taken.

For RCRA, a facility is classified as SNC if it: (1) caused actual exposure or substantial likelihood of exposure to hazardous waste; (2) is a chronic or recalcitrant violator; or (3) deviates substantially from the terms of a permit, order, agreement, or RCRA statutory or regulatory requirement. A facility is removed from RCRA SNC status when the facility is returned to full physical compliance for all violations, and/or the facility remains in compliance with a compliance schedule issued for outstanding violations.

TRI Releases refers to self-reported pounds of one of more than 600 TRI listed chemicals released to air or water directly, land-filled, or injected underground. The accuracy of these data is limited by estimation techniques sometimes employed by individual facilities in their reports. In some cases, we transformed these data into tons (2000 lbs = 1 ton).

Total Waste Generated includes self-reported pounds of TRI listed chemicals contained in production-related waste prior to recycling, treatment, energy recovery, or disposal.

Pollution Spills refers to on-site chemical spills over the past two years obtained from the Emergency Response Notification System (ERNS).

Estimated Surrounding Population includes the estimated population living within three miles of a facility as extracted from Census data. Note that the "surrounding area" data may be set to include populations within one, three, or five miles of the facility. To this data we added the indicator, "potential population mass exposed to hazardous releases." This indicator was calculated by multiplying the average population around a SFIP facility in each classification category (estimated surrounding population) by the number of facilities in each SFIP industrial classification (e.g., all, federal, etc.) to generate an estimate of the number of American citizens potentially exposed to pollutants produced at facilities in each classification.

In the following section, we examine the SFIP data in greater detail. We display these data in a format that follows along with the definitions of the data provided above. All data in the following sections are drawn from the standard SFIP data file.

INSPECTIONS

Table 9.1: SFIP Sector Inspections*			
	CAA	CWA	RCRA
ALL	**1.5**	**2.0**	**1.7**
Automobile	**1.2**	**0.4**	**0.9**
Federal	**1.1**	**1.6**	**2.3**
IISM	**8.4**	**4.2**	**4.6**
Aluminum	**1.9**	**2.0**	**5.1**
Copper	**1.3**	**1.2**	**1.1**
ISMM	**1.2**	**2.2**	**1.6**
Lead	**1.3**	**1.7**	**15.3**
Zinc	**0.7**	**1.5**	**1.7**
Petroleum	**1.6**	**2.4**	**2.3**
Pulp	**1.5**	**2.1**	**0.4**

*Average Annual Number of Inspections per Facility by SFIP Sector and Regulation, 1998-2000.

Overall, there is little variation in the average number of inspections per SFIP facility across the environmental regulation being enforced (i.e., CAA, CWA, RCRA). There is, however, some variation in inspection frequency within each regulation by SFIP sector. For instance, the average number of CAA inspections per facility is 1.5. All facilities fall within +/– 0.4 inspections of this average with the exception of integrated iron and steel mills (IISM), which average 8.4 per facility, and zinc refineries, which average 0.7 CAA inspections per facility. A similar pattern is noticeable for CWA inspections where integrated iron and steel mills (IISM) again have the highest average number of inspections per facility. Automobile facilities have the fewest CWA inspections at 0.4 per facility. Broader variation in inspections can be seen with respect to RCRA where lead smelters, aluminum smelters, and integrated iron and steel mills had a well above average number of inspections per facility, and automobile facilities and pulp mills had a significantly fewer number of RCRA inspections compared to other SFIP facilities.

These data on inspections provide some initial clues concerning the distribution of pollution we can expect to find in the remainder of the SFIP data examined below. The elevated rate of inspections at IISM facilities across all types of regulations indicates that these facilities may be involved in the production of large amounts of toxins, relatively dangerous pollutants, and frequent violations of environmental regulations.

HISTORICAL NONCOMPLIANCE

Table 9.2: Historical Noncompliance*	CAA	CWA	RCRA
ALL	1.6	2.4	2.0
Automobile	0.8	2.8	3.0
Federal	0.8	2.5	2.0
IISM	5.7	5.8	5.8
Aluminum	1.5	1.7	1.0
Copper	0.9	2.2	0.6
ISMM	1.7	2.7	2.1
Lead	0.0	3.7	3.3
Zinc	2.3	2.0	5.3
Petroleum	2.8	2.4	3.4
Pulp	1.6	2.1	0.3

*Average Number of Quarters in Noncompliance Per Facility by SFIP Sector and Regulation, Previous 2 Years (8 Quarters), 1998–2000

Like inspections, there is little variation in historical noncompliance across type of regulation for SFIP facilities in the aggregate. There is much greater variation in noncompliance within a regulation category across sectors. For example, integrated iron and steel mills are well in excess of the average number of quarters in noncompliance across all regulations. Automobile facilities, well below the average for noncompliance under CAA regulations, are well above average for noncompliance under RCRA regulations. Lead smelters, which are reported as being in compliance over the two-year period under CAA, exceed the average for both CWA and RCRA regulations. With the exception of a consistent pattern of historical noncompliance across environmental regulations by integrated iron and steel mills, and the slightly higher than average number of quarters in noncompliance at petroleum facilities, no other violation patterns are easily apparent.

CURRENT SIGNIFICANT NONCOMPLIANCE

Table 9.3: Current Significant Noncompliance*	CAA	CWA	RCRA
ALL	20.0	6.7	5.0
Automobile	6.1	0.0	14.8
Federal	9.4	6.8	2.3
IISM	60.0	45.0	15.0
Aluminum	26.1	4.3	0.0
Copper	6.7	7.7	0.0
ISMM	23.7	6.4	7.4
Lead	0.0	0.0	0.0
Zinc	0.0	0.0	0.0
Petroleum	43.9	6.4	11.2
Pulp	18.2	5.3	0.5

*Average Percent of Facilities in Current Significant Noncompliance by Industry Sector and Regulation, 2000

Current significant noncompliance varies widely across type of regulation. These variations help pinpoint where violations of environmental regulations are most likely. On average, facilities are more likely to be in violation of CAA than CWA (3 times lower) or RCRA (4 times lower). Here, again, integrated iron and steel mills (IISM) have a much higher than average rate of current significant noncompliance across all regulation types: 3 times higher than average for both CAA and RCRA, and nearly 7 times higher than average for CWA. IISM is the only sector far in excess of the CWA average for current significant noncompliance. The automobile, IISM, and petroleum sectors have the highest rates of current significant noncompliance under RCRA. Excluding iron- and steel-related manufacturing, the other metal manufacturing areas have very low rates of current significant noncompliance under both RCRA and CWA.

PERMIT EXCEEDANCES

Table 9.4: Permit Exceedances: Clean Water Act, 1998–2000				
	Pollutants Exceeding Statutory Limits	Regulated Pollutants Released	Release Reports Submitted to EPA	Release Reports Over Statutory Limits
ALL	1.7	14.5	4.6	578
Auto	0.2	2.8	1.0	180
Federal	1.6	13.3	1.0	593
IISM	5.0	30.6	16.6	2380
Aluminum	2.6	20.0	5.5	1123
Copper	0.9	12.7	2.1	796
ISMM	1.7	9.6	4.2	389
Lead	2.7	19.7	6.0	889
Zinc	3.5	16.0	12.5	889
Petroleum	2.7	22.3	6.5	721
Pulp	1.0	12.8	2.2	368

Consistent with the data pattern seen in previous tables, the data on permit exceedances indicate that the integrated iron and steel mill sector is the most likely sector to exceed CWA limits across all four of the measured dimensions.

TRI RELEASES

The TRI covers releases and transfers of specifically identified toxic chemicals. To be sure, general pollution, which includes smog and particle matter, can lead to serious human and environmental health consequences, and are related to outcomes, such as global warming. Exposure to toxic pollutants, which also tend to have long-term environmental persistence (they biodegrade very slowly, and may have half-lives that last for decades), have an added degree of seriousness. Table 9.5, which details the distribution of toxic chemical releases across SFIP sectors, contains several interesting findings.

The automobile sector reports significantly lower than average TRI releases (3 times less than average) and total wastes (6 times less than average), while also reporting that a significantly higher (nearly 3 times) percentage of its TRI releases contain carcinogens. Thus, while automobile facilities are, on average, "cleaner" than other SFIP sectors with respect to toxic chemical releases and transfers, they pose hidden dangers connected to the higher than average level of released carcinogens.

Table 9.5: Toxic Release Inventory and Total Waste Generated*					
	Release	Transfer	Carcin-ogen	Metals	Total Waste
ALL	1,963,467	984,945	2.6	2,116,961	7,371,286
Auto	675,386	663,344	7.4	33,969	1,669,105
Federal	793,413	158,596	2.9	236,762	2,399,948
IISM	1,773,138	2,285,703	1.6	3,514,550	11,024,314
Aluminum	625,687	224,315	1.6	147,114	8,924,931
Copper	52,790,220	343,043	1.1	53,062,237	56,107,799
ISMM	529,166	4,517,116	1.3	4,610,982	5,406,005
Lead	21,556,871	1,791,092	0.6	22,490,100	76,613,477
Zinc	5,859,029	9,986,988	1.1	15,589,442	21,640,219
Petroleum	479,402	134,462	6.1	31,517	6,779,221
Pulp	1,132,759	268,001	6.9	140,736	7,254,252

*Releases, Transfers, Carcinogenic Chemicals, Regulated Metals (total releases and transfers), and Total Waste Product in pounds, 2000. (Carcinogens relate to releases, shown as percentage of releases)

Integrated iron and steel mills report TRI releases near average for SFIP facilities, but report TRI transfers that are more than twice as high as average. They also report 57 percent more total waste than the average SFIP facility. Similarly, iron and steel mini-mills report well above average levels of TRI transfers, and significantly lower than average levels of TRI releases. Consistent with these observations, all facilities involved in the production of metals have higher than average levels of TRI toxic chemical pollution transfers.

With reference to TRI data, copper smelters and refineries stand out for the amount of toxic and total waste produced. Copper facilities report producing 26 times more TRI toxic releases than the average SFIP facility, and 8 times the total waste. Lead smelters and refineries also produce significantly higher than average levels of TRI toxins. Lead facility releases are more than 10 times higher than TRI releases at the average SFIP facility. Lead facilities also report the greatest volume of total waste at 76.6 million pounds—or nearly 11 times higher than the average SFIP facility.

While petroleum facilities report significantly less TRI pollution than other SFIP sectors (because petroleum waste is more likely to be regulated under CAA and CWA) it reports a much higher than average ratio of released carcinogens. Pulp mills also stand out for the high ratio of carcinogens they release.

POLLUTION SPILLS AND POPULATION EXPOSURE

Table 9.6: Pollution Spills: Toxic Waste Accidents and Local Population Exposure Potential

	Facilities with Spills (*N* (%))	Pounds Spilled	Three-Mile Radius	Population Mass
ALL	11.1 (48.2)	40,751	37,467	33,346,530
Auto	1.6 (29.6)	1,339	59,288	3,201,552
Federal	8.4 (53.0)	14,740	42,619	11,634,987
IISM	7.7 (90.0)	4,502	55,360	1,107,200
Aluminum	3.7 (30.4)	27,048	13,915	320,045
Copper	4.1 (35.0)	31,544	12,271	245,420
ISMM	3.0 (25.0)	9,033	39,218	3,764,928
Lead	11.0 (66.7)	17,593	7,922	23,766
Zinc	(MISSING)		29,513	88,538
Petroleum	22.8 (80.4)	87,513	42,686	6,957,818
Pulp	3.1 (34.9)	28,131	23,957	5,629,895

The data presented in Table 9.6 completes the discussion of pollution/toxic chemical releases, transfers, and enforcement by adding information on chemical accidents and the potential population exposed to these accidents. To review, the population exposure potential measures the average number of people residing within three miles of an average SFIP facility within each sector. A three-mile radius was chosen to reflect the population likely to be exposed to both chemical accidents and the highest concentrations of long-term chemical exposure associated with air, water, ground, and toxic waste pollution. It should be made clear that this radius does not include all people who are potentially exposed to the harmful effects pollutants emitted from any specific facility. Indeed, toxic pollutant migration may span great distances (e.g., evidence on dispersion of dioxin generated in Michigan being found in Florida).

The population living within a three-mile radius of a facility provides one measure of harm. A second measure is the mass exposure measure. We created the mass exposure measure to estimate the total number of people across the nation who live within three miles of facilities within each sector. For example, if 7,922 people live within three miles of the average lead smelting and refining facility, and there are three such facilities in the nation, then the mass of people potentially impacted by pollutants from these facilities is 23,766 (7,922 x 3). Following this procedure, we estimate that more than 33 million people live within three miles of all 890 SFIP facilities in the sample. It should be noted that our measure of population exposed may overestimate the number of people exposed to toxins because people in a highly populated area may be counted multiple times if they are exposed to pollution emissions from multiple facilities.

Petroleum sector facilities stand out as the only sector in which facilities have a higher than average number spills per facility. In fact, the average number of spills at petroleum facilities is twice the average. This may reflect the fact that petroleum products are liquid, which would increase the likelihood of chemical spills. However, while metals are not liquids in their final form, they all must pass through a liquid phase. The same is true for many paper pulp products. In contrast, the high number of accidents at petroleum refineries may reflect the level of precautions to prevent spills taken within the petroleum industry.

The petroleum and integrated iron and steel mill (IISM) sectors have the highest percent of facilities experiencing spills. For the IISM sector, 90 percent of facilities experienced chemical spills. For the petroleum sector, the percent of facilities experiencing spills exceeded 80 percent. As a comparison, in the average SFIP sector, 48 percent of facilities experienced chemical spills. Petroleum facilities also have the highest average number of pounds spilled in a chemical accident at more than 87,000 pounds per incident, or more than twice the average SFIP chemical accident. Once again, the petroleum sector is the only sector to exceed the average for this category.

SFIP DATA, AUTOMOBILE ASSEMBLY PLANTS

In this section, we specifically examine SFIP data relative to the automobile assembly sector. For purposes of this example, we focus specific attention on Toxic Release Inventory data for automobile assembly plants for Calendar Year 1998. Given the parameters employed for our search (TRI by facility by chemical released reported) our sample of SFIP automobile facilities is 40 of the original universe of 54. Fourteen facilities were omitted because they did not reach predefined SFIP criteria (i.e., a facility is excluded when it reports TRI emissions of a chemical that less than 14% of facilities in the related subgroup report emitting).

Geographically, the majority of facilities included in the sample were in EPA Region 5 (55%), followed by Region 4 (17.5%), Region 7 (12.5%), Regions 3 and 6 (5% each), and Regions 9 and 2 (2.5% each).

Twenty-five different chemicals were reported as being released by more than 21 percent of automobile assembly facilities in the subsample. These chemicals, and the percent of facilities reporting release of each chemical is as follows: toluene (96%), xylene and isomers (96%), methanol (95%), specified glycol ethers (93%), ethylbenzene (93%), ethylene glycol (93%), 1,2,4-Trimethylbenzene (89%), N-Butyl alcohol (84%), zinc compounds (82%), methyl-isobutyl-ketone (79%), phosphoric acid (79%), sodium nitrate (72%), manganese compounds (70%), benzene (56%), methyl-ethyl-ketone (56%), methyl-tert-butyl ether (53%), nickel compounds (53%), nitrate compounds (49%), lead compounds (37%), N-methyl-2-pyrrolidone (33%), copper (28%), cyclohexane (28%), N-hexane (28%), nitric acid (23%), and diisocyanates (21%).

These 40 facilities reported emitting approximately 60 million pounds of the pollutants listed above. Nearly 40 percent of listed TRI emissions for automobile assembly plants involved xylene. Glycol-ethers and methyl-isobutyl-ketone comprise an additional 26 percent of emissions. Taken together, these three chemicals comprise about 66 percent of reported TRI emissions. Toluene, methanol, ethlybenzene, 1,2,4-trimethlybenzene, and N-butyl alcohol make up 25 percent of reported emissions. Of the 25 listed chemicals, eight chemicals account for more than 90 percent of reported emissions. The 17 remaining chemicals make up less than 10 percent of total reported emissions.

These data are useful in two ways. First, assuming these data are representative of TRI emissions at automobile assembly plants, we could suggest emission reduction policies that are designed to eliminate, minimize, or reduce total TRI emissions in this sector by targeting chemical wastes that constitute the bulk of emissions. From the discussion above, we might focus our efforts on xylene, glycol-ethers, and methyl-isobutyl-ketone. Second, we might employ these data to target the TRI pollutants most harmful to human health emitted by automobile assembly facilities. Here, we might choose to focus attention on benzene and benzene compounds, or lead, even though benzene chemicals make up only 10 percent of emissions, and lead only 1/10 of one percent of total automobile assembly TRI emissions.

Subgroup facility data also lists TRI emissions by facility, and identifies the name and location of each facility. In the automobile assembly subgroup overview data for TRI releases, each facility's SFIP number, name, city, state, TRI number, and EPA region is listed. Using individual facility data, we can determine that three facilities produce more TRI waste, on average, than other facilities. These three facilities are Toyota Motor Manufacturing, Georgetown, Kentucky (EPA Region 4), Ford Motor Company, Claycomo, Missouri (EPA Region 7), and General Motors, Doraville, Georgia (EPA Region 4). Each of these facilities produced more than twice the average number of pounds of TRI pollutants (the average for all included automobile assembly facilities was 1,504,950). The average for the three largest producers was 3,593,702 pounds. In contrast, the three facilities reporting the lowest level of TRI emissions were: Chrysler, Sterling Heights, Michigan (EPA Region 5), Ford, Lorain, Ohio (EPA Region 5), and Chrysler, Belvidere, Illinois (EPA Region 5), with an average of 328,806 pounds of TRI pollutants—or ten times less than the three largest emitters. These differences may have to do with the type of and level of production activity occurring at each facility. It should be noted, however, that the TRI waste-to-production ratios listed in SFIP (in pounds TRI releases and transfers/metric tons production capacity) indicate that the facilities with low outputs also have low waste/production ratios.

For the facilities in our sample, for example, waste-production ratios range from 15.2 at GM's Doraville facility, 9.2 at Ford's Claycomo facility, and 6.7 at Toyota's Georgetown facility, to 2.0 at Chrysler's Sterling Heights facility, 0.9 at Chrysler's Belvidere facility, and 0.3 at Ford's Lorain facility. The average waste-production ratio for sample facilities was 6.2. The three highest waste-production ratios were GM-Doraville, 15.2, GM-Fort Wayne, 13.4, and GM-Pontiac, 13.3. Of major manufacturers, Honda had the lowest waste-production ratio (2.3, N = 2), followed by Chrysler (4.0, N = 8), Ford (6.8, N = 11), and GM (7.6, N = 14).

Individual SFIP reports are also available for each facility. We selected the Chrysler-Newark facility for the purposes of our example. Data for this facility indicate it is linked to the Chrysler-Delaware facility for reporting purposes.

Available information for this facility includes: facility permits and identifiers (e.g., environmental Act, permit ID, name of Act permitted under, facility name, street address); facility characteristics (facility status under each environmental Act, longitude and latitude of permitted facility, SIC codes); inspection and enforcement data, last two years (by Act, inspection dates, penalties, formal enforcement actions over past two years); inspection history (by Act, inspection type, lead agency, date of inspection); compliance summary (by Act, number of quarters in noncompliance); two-year compliance status history (by Act and quarter); formal enforcement actions (by Act, action, agency, date, penalty); EPA formal enforcement cases (by law and section, case number, case type, case name, issue/filing date, settlement date, penalty, Supplemental Environmental Projects [SEP] costs); history of reported chemical releases in pounds per year (since 1992, total air, surface water, underground, land, total on-site releases, total off-site transfers, total releases and transfers); and demographic profile of surrounding three mile area (this may be changed to either one- or five-mile radius; center of latitude and longitude; total persons, land area, water area, population density, housing units, households on public assistance, persons below poverty, percent minority, racial breakdowns, age breakdowns, educational level of residents, income of residents, household incomes). Unfortunately, much of the demographic data for facilities is incomplete, limiting the usefulness of these data for environmental justice analysis. Demographic data may be obtained, however, from the U.S. Census Bureau.

The preceding discussion of SFIP highlights the availability of fruitful data that can be used to examine environmental crime. Researchers are encouraged to experiment with SFIP, and all databases discussed in this work, prior to seeking particular information. A learning curve is involved in accessing most databases, although online help is typically available. Our discussion of SFIP demonstrates how researchers can examine enforcement and compliance actions, as well as harms to the environment. Researchers are encouraged to analyze the data found in SFIP, and perhaps incorporate data from other sources in attempts to design more elaborate research projects. Researchers are also encouraged to use data provided by the Right-to-Know Network, the topic of Chapter 10.

CHAPTER 10

Using the Right-to-Know Network to Access Data

This chapter examines the Right-To-Know Network (RTK; www.rtk.net), and the publicly available environmental data found there. RTK presents EPA data in easily accessible formats.

The purpose of RTK NET is to fulfill the legal requirement of the public use and access language specified in the Emergency Planning and Community Right-To-Know Act or EPCRA. EPCRA was enacted by Congress in 1986 under Title III of the Superfund Amendments and Reauthorization Act. It was designed to enhance public access to information on hazardous chemical waste production and disposal, and to aid states in developing hazardous waste emergency response systems by establishing baselines for routine environmental releases of hazardous chemicals. Ralph Nader's US Public Interest Research Group played a vital role in the implementation of EPCRA.

EPCRA (Sec. 304) requires facilities to report "extremely hazardous substances" in excess of "threshold planning quantity" (40 CFR Part 355, Appendix A and B) to state and local emergency-response planning committees. All information submitted under EPCRA requirements is part of the public record *unless* that information is protected by trade secret (or, in some instances, under laws that may supercede EPCRA, e.g., national security) claims. While it might seem difficult to imagine that a toxic waste would be a trade secret, it would not be hard to imagine, for instance, corporations in the weapons defense industry claiming that their toxic waste is a trade secret.

The EPA employs the data submitted under the requirements of EPCRA to construct the Toxic Release Inventory (TRI). TRI data are one source for the information found on RTK. Several other EPA databases are also employed to construct RTK NET data. These will be examined further in the following sections.

Although RTK data are drawn directly from EPA files, RTK's operators decide how these data are presented, and whether all or only a portion of the available data are presented. In some instances, the EPA limits the data that may be posted on RTK. In most cases, however, RTK NET endeavors to present as much data as possible, and is assisted in this effort by the EPA.

To our knowledge, RTK data is accurate and representative of EPA data. For example, we examined TRI data obtained from both the EPA and RTK and found the data to be an exact match.

ACCESSING AND USING RTK NET

RTK NET can be accessed online at www.rtknet.org. To access RTK NET data, select the DATABASE link from the RTK directory found on the left side of the RTK home page. RTK NET refers to its database page as the "Master Search" page. From this page, users may access 11 different RTK compilations of EPA data. These data sets include:

- Toxic Release Inventory (TRI);
- Biennial Reporting System (BRS);
- Comprehensive Environmental Response, Compensation and Liability Information System (CERCLIS);
- Civil Court Docket (DOCKET);
- Emergency Response Notification System (ERNS);
- Resource Conservation and Recovery Act Information System (RCRIS);
- Toxic Substances Control Act Test Submissions (TSCATS);
- Accidental Release Information Program (ARIP);
- Facility Index System (FACILITY);
- Permit Compliance System (PCS); and
- Risk Management Plan (RMP) Search.

Directions for using, and descriptions of data found in each of these systems are found below. First, a few words of caution about using RTK NET, and some general RTK NET format issues are offered.

PRODUCING RTK NET REPORTS

When generating any report using RTK NET, users have the option of having the output sent to an E-mail address, or viewing the data directly on their monitor. Data may be copied from E-mail or the video screen into other programs.

When examining RTK NET data output, *always* proceed to the end of the data file first and check for the line *END OF REPORT* to ensure that the entire set of requested data has been produced before using the information. If this line does not appear, reenter your request. We have used this data extensively, and rarely encountered this error.

Output Types: Low and High Detail Output Options

For most RTK reports, the user must select whether the information is presented in "low" or "high" detail. For some data sets, the user has the option of selecting a "medium" detail option. In the discussion that follows, we refer only to "high" and "low" detail options. The "medium detail" option, in our opinion, has no specific use, and users should explore the data using the "low detail" option, and request "high detail" searches when they find data of interest.

The "low" detail option provides the basic data an average user would be interested in obtaining in many cases. A selection of "high" detail will, in some cases, produce a disaggregated list of some of the data. For example, a user may be interested in the use of fines to address violations of a specific environmental regulation in the RCRIS database. By employing a "low detail" search for a specific location, a user may find the number of reporting facilities, and the number that have been penalized. They would probably discover that only a handful of facilities in that area received a fine.

Assuming the user would like to learn more about these fines, they should then request a "high detail" search. They could produce the "high detail" search for the entire geographic area, or, if the number of cases in which a penalty has been levied is small, enter each facility's name in the facility search to produce one record for each penalized facility. In this case, the "high detail" data provides information on each fine incident by facility, and, in some databases, disaggregated by type of violation. In some databases, the "high detail" search option will also produce "free field" data that may include qualitative commentary on the facility or case (see for example, CERCLIS, RCRIS, and RMP data). Specific examples of the kind of high detail data available in each data set, and the difference between the "low" and "high" detail data option are discussed for each data set, where applicable.

Output Formats: Text, Comma and Tab Delimited Options

Printout formats may vary across RTK databases. In general, however, three print formats are available for both on-screen and E-mail requests: ASCII (American Standard Code for Information Interchange) text; comma delimited ASCII (Dbase readable); and tab delimited ASCII (Microsoft Excel readable). Unless users plan to employ RTK NET data for analysis, the best option, and the most readable in many cases, is ASCII text.

RTK NET DATABASE DESCRIPTIONS AND EXAMPLES

Researchers will find a great deal of information in the RTK NET database and are encouraged to experiment with the resource to facilitate familiarity.

Toxic Release Inventory (TRI) on RTK NET

The TRI contains data covering the release and transfer of toxic chemicals from manufacturing facilities. A facility is required to report a toxic release of chemicals to air, land, water, or underground to the EPA when the following conditions exist:

- the facility has an Industrial Classification Code (SIC) number 20–39;
- the facility employs 10 or more workers;
- the facility manufacturers or processes more than 25,000 pounds of one of 350 chemicals listed in TRI regulations, or uses more than 10,000 pounds of the 350 listed chemicals in the manufacturing process in one year.

RTK's TRI data may be retrieved using either facility or geographic region (zip code, county, or state). Reports within a region are organized by facility. All RTK NET TRI data are reported by facility, regardless of how the search is produced. The area search allows users to identify all facilities in an area that report under TRI without having to know the names of these facilities. Facility searches are useful when the user knows the name of the facility they want to investigate, or to collect high detail data following a "low detail" search.

RTK NET's TRI database contains the following basic information for each reporting facility. The data produced using a "low detail" search option is limited to the information in this list. The additional information generated using a "high detail" search is described below.

RTK TRI Basic (low detail) information:
- Facility name, mailing name, and address (presented in several distinct data fields);
- EPA region;
- Latitude/longitude;

- Parent company;
- Public contact (name and phone number);
- Technical contact (name and phone number);
- D&B number (Dun & Bradstreet Number);
- Report year;
- TRI ID;
- Primary SIC number;
- Number of submissions;
- Amount of releases and transfer by type of release/transfer (these data are presented in several distinct data fields):
    - total
    - fugitive air
    - stack air
    - water
    - underground
    - land
    - transfer to publicly owned treatment work (POTW)
    - off site transfers
    - total production related waste
    - nonproduction related waste (accidental or remedial)

RTK NET's TRI Web page also provides a link to a Web site operated by the Environmental Defense Fund so that further information on each facility, and information related to health effects of various toxins, may be obtained using another Web-based data tool, *Scorecard*.

As an example of the kind of information obtainable from RTK's TRI database, we provide a brief overview of data we accessed for Hillsborough County, Florida, for the year 2000. The output contained records for 60 facilities required to report under TRI. The report is seven pages long, and contains a facility-based report of released and transferred chemicals, a report of dioxin and dioxin-like emissions (in grams per facility by form of release) for facilities with this specific kind of release, and the name of the dioxin chemicals released at each facility (if applicable).

The facility report lists total emissions at each individual facility by emission type (total, surface water, underground injection, land release, total on-site releases, total off-site releases, and total on and off site releases) and by chemical. For example, the TRI report we produced indicated that 12,379,396 pounds of TRI listed chemicals were released in Hillsborough County in 2000 by the 60 reporting facilities. The majority of these releases were air releases (11,987,696 pounds or 96.8%). The largest contributor to TRI pollution emissions in

Hillsborough County in 2000 was Tampa Electric Company (TECO). TECO operates three facilities in Hillsborough County: Gannon Station, Big Bend Station, and Hooker Point Station. Total TRI pollution emissions for these stations were 8,509,888 pounds, 1,426,699 pounds, and 100,000 pounds, respectively. Together, these three facilities emitted 10,036,587 pounds, or 81% of all TRI emissions in Hillsborough County. These three facilities were also responsible for the majority (90.5%) of dioxin emissions in Tampa for reporting facilities.

RTK TRI (high detail) information:
The "high detail" search option returns additional specific information on the types and amounts of chemicals found at a site, and disposal methods. High detail reports range from a few pages to several dozen pages for facilities/sites that produce, release, and transfer numerous TRI regulated chemicals. As an example, we review the "high detail" TRI for American Laquer & Solvents Co. (ALS).

The high detail report for ALS is five pages in length, compared to its ¾-page low detail TRI. The report indicates that ALS filed four submissions to the EPA in 1987, and that it was no longer doing business by the year 2000. Total chemical releases and transfers at ALS were 73,269 pounds of four chemicals: methyl-ethyl-ketone (12,938 lbs); methyl-isobutyl-ketone (3,950 lbs); toluene (49,935 lbs); and xylene mixed isomers (6,446 lbs). The number of pounds released in fugitive air and stack air emissions is listed for each chemical.

The high detail report contains a series of 14 indicators describing the "activities and uses of toxic chemical at the facility." These 14 indicators are recorded as "Yes/No" data fields. These indicators are as follows:

- Produce (manufacture) the chemical;
- Import (manufacture) the chemical;
- Manufacture the chemical for on-site use/processing;
- Manufacture the chemical for sale/distribution;
- Manufacture the chemical as a by-product;
- Manufacture the chemical as an impurity;
- Process the chemical as a reactant;
- Process the chemical as a formulation component;
- Process the chemical as an article component;
- Process the chemical for repackaging;
- Process the chemical as an impurity;
- Otherwise use the chemical as a chemical processing aid;

- Otherwise use the chemical as a manufacturing aid; or
- Otherwise use the chemical for ancillary or other purposes.

Because ALS's TRI emissions are air-based, the company is not required to complete other data sections indicating the amounts and methods of disposal of its TRI emissions. Companies that produce TRI solid waste chemicals, however, would file such information, and their high detail TRI report would contain information on the amounts and disposal methods for these solid wastes, and would be longer.

Biennial Reporting System (BRS)

The BRS is a waste tracking system designed to record the amount of waste produced, shipped, and received by waste manufacturers and handlers. The BRS is linked to the RCRA (Resource Conservation and Recovery Act), which stipulates the rules and regulations for the treatment, storage, and disposal (TSD) of chemicals identified as toxins under this Act. In effect, BRS data result from implementing the legal requirements for the treatment, disposal, and storage of toxins under the RCRA.

RTK provides five search formats for BRS data: (1) geographic area, (2) facility, (3) industry, (4) generated waste, and (5) received waste. Each format provides similar data aggregated according to the different search criteria the user selects. All data, however, are displayed as facility-specific data. Thus, regardless of the kind of search requested, each output is similar to the extent that each is organized around the reports supplied by each facility (in a region, an industry, or by waste received or waste generated). Thus, whether a user generates data for *Company A* using a geographic area, facility, industry, generated waste, or received waste search, the contents of these data reports will often overlap. In some cases (e.g., waste generated, waste received) the data for a facility will be limited to the search parameter.

To illustrate the "low detail" data format for RTK BRS data, we requested a "geographic area" report for the city of Tampa for the most recent year of data available (1999). The report totaled 18 pages. For the geographic area report, BRS information was provided by facility. The information included:

- Facility identifiers (facility name, street address, county, mailing address; recorded in several distinct data fields);
- EPA ID number;

- Waste generated, managed, shipped by waste type (total and federally regulated; presented in several distinct data fields);
- SIC code(s) (often missing in these data);
- Name and phone number of facility contact;
- Generator status (large or small quantity generator); and
- RCRA storage status, TDR (Treatment, Disposal, and Recycling) status, and TDR exemptions.

As an example of the information extracted from a "low detail" facility record using a geographic area search, we summarize the data listed for the first facility on the Tampa BRS report. This data is reproduced in a format similar to how it would appear on a user's computer monitor.

Facility Name: Amerada Hess Corporation, Tampa Terminal
Location: 504 N. 19th Street
City: Tampa   County: Hillsborough County
State: Florida   Zip Code: 33102
EPA ID: FLD088776588
Mailing Address: 1 Hess Plaza, Environmental Affairs Office
                 Woodbridge, NJ
Data Year: 1999
Total Waste:
      Generated (3.5 tons)
      Shipped (3.5 tons)
Federal Waste:
      Generated (3.5 tons)
      Shipped (3.5 tons)
Contact: Richard L. Siller, 732-750-7748
Generator Status: Large Quantity Generator
Storage Status: No RCRA-permitted or interim storage status
RCRA-TDR Status:
Exempt TDR Status: No on site TDR; no plans to develop on-site storage/treatment

Once these data are extracted by facility, they may be entered into spreadsheets, or other data analysis and management tools, for aggregation into larger geographic units (e.g., zip codes). Complementary data from the U.S. Census can then be incorporated into the data set to facilitate analysis of the relationship between social and economic factors and the location of hazardous waste generation, treatment, storage, and disposal processes.

The "low detail" BRS facility report fills about one-third of a page. In contrast, a high detail BRS can be a dozen pages in length. Selecting the "high detail" search option adds the following information:

List of wastes generated by this facility:
- Waste description
- EPA Waste Codes
- Tons generated
- Tons generated and managed on-site
- This waste was sent off site to:
- System type
- Tons sent
- EPA ID

Upon selecting the "high detail" search option, a list containing the above subfields is generated for each distinct regulated chemical or chemical batch sent to a distinct waste handler.

As an example, we reviewed the "high detail" report for the Bausch and Lomb Pharmaceuticals facility in Tampa for the most recent reporting year available on RTK (1999). Bausch and Lomb listed 16 waste chemical shipments for 1999. Each shipment was sent to the same waste handler, Onyx Environmental Services. The kind of waste, EPA waste code, waste amount, and other information are listed for each individual shipment made by this facility to Onyx Environmental Services.

CERCLIS—Comprehensive Environmental Response Compensation and Liability Information System

CERCLIS contains data produced by enforcing CERCLA, or the Superfund Amendment and Reauthorization Act of 1986. CERCLIS contains data on hazardous waste sites identified as Superfund sites, or inspected for potential inclusion in the Superfund list. It should be noted that RTK NET CERCLIS data do not contain all EPA CERCLIS data, but only the portion of data provided by the EPA to RTK for public inspection.

Data produced using a CERCLIS search can be quite lengthy. For instance, we requested a "low detail" search using RTK's CERCLIS for the city of Tampa which produced a document 126 pages in length. To provide an example of the data contained in "low detail" CERCLIS, we selected one case from the list, Weekly Lumber. Data available included:

- Facility identifiers (site name, street address; this data appears in several independent data fields);
- EPA ID;
- Metropolitan Statistical Area Census Code;
- Congressional district (often missing from the data);
- United States Geological Survey Hyrdo-Unit Number;
- National Priority List (NPL) status;
- Date of discovery (first action);
- Owner; and
- Facility type (federal/not federal).

Using the "high detail" search option, users may generate additional site information. "High detail" CERCLIS data for the Weekly Lumber facility contained specific free-field details, related details, and a history of site actions as follows:

Site notes: "This site is an abandoned lumber treatment facility which operated under two separate owners from 1963 to 1989. Copper, Chromium, Arsenic in soil, surface water and ground water (DLR 7-19-94)."

List of alias names for site: Pitch Pine Lumber
List of "operable units" and actions as follows:
Unit: Sitewide

Action 1:	Discovery
End Date:	07/19/1994
Action Lead:	State, Fund Assisted
Action 2:	Integrated Assessment
Start Date:	03/06/1995
End Date:	03/06/1995
Action Qualifier:	High
Action Lead:	EPA Fund Financed
Plan Status:	Primary
Action 3:	Administrative records
Start Date:	02/02/1996
End Date:	02/02/1996
Action Qualifier:	Admin. Record Compiled for a Removal Event
Action Lead:	EPA Fund Financed

Action 4:	HRS Package
Planned Start Date:	03/15/1995
Planned End Date:	08/16/1995
Start Date:	03/20/1995 (Actual)
End Date:	12/18/1995 (Actual)
Planned Start	2Q 1995
Planned End	4Q 1995
Action Qualifier:	NFRAP (No further remedial action planned)
Action Lead:	EPA Fund Financed

Action 5:	Site Inspection
State Date:	08/02/1994
End Date:	04/12/1995
Action Qualifier:	High
Action Lead:	EPA Fund Financed

Action 6:	Preliminary Assessment
Start Date:	07/19/1994
End Date:	10/06/1994
Action Qualifier:	High
Action Lead:	EPA Fund Financed

Action 7:	Removal
Planned Start Date:	05/03/1995
Planned End Date:	08/03/1995
Start Date:	05/18/1995 (Actual)
End Date:	12/14/1995 (Actual)
Planned Start	3Q 1995
Planned End	4Q 1995
Action Qualifier:	Cleanup
Plan Status:	Primary
Action Urgency:	Non-time critical

As can be seen from this record, a number of different types of EPA inspections, assessment, and actions (seven in total) occurred at this site, culminating in a site cleanup. The cleanup prevented the site from being listed on the National Priorities List (NPL).

DOCKET

DOCKET allows users to access information about cases filed against facilities by the EPA. Three types of DOCKET searches are available through RTK: (1) facility/area; (2) defendant; and (3) case. The "Facility search" allows users to search for cases against individual facilities, or in predefined geographic regions (zip code, city, or state). The "Defendant search" allows users to search for cases by a defendant's name. The "Case search" allows users to search for cases that violate a particular law, involve a specific violation or pollutant type, or by case number.

Of particular interest in DOCKET search records are the data items identified in the output as "result." In this data field, the user finds the final result or conclusion of a specific case. These results include: (1) consent instrument with penalty; (2) consent instrument without penalty; (3) consent instrument with specified cost recovery; (4) dismissed by tribunal; and (5) specified cost recovery. These data are useful for examining case outcomes, and when linked with other data sets, such as Census data, can be used to conduct environmental justice research; or when linked with corporate financial records, can be used to analyze the relationship between corporate assets and case outcomes.

DOCKET also lists the penalty amount and Superfund cost awarded, if any. Additional information in "low detail" DOCKET data include:

- Administrative action number;
- Case name;
- File date;
- Conclusion date;
- Name of first defendant (use "high detail" search option to list all defendants);
- The law(s) under which violators were charged;
- Name of first facility in action (use "high detail" search option to list all facilities charged within an action); and
- Facility address and identifiers (presented across several data fields)

The "high detail" search option in DOCKET produces limited additional information pertaining to facility aliases and the complete list of defendants and facilities named in a specific action.

The Emergency Response Notification System (ERNS)

ERNS data is a record of reported emergencies resulting from the unplanned release of toxic pollutants into the environment. ERNS records may be searched by: (1) area; (2) discharger; or (3) material discharged. A "low detail" ERNS search returns basic information about the spill, including:

- Date;
- Time;
- Street address;
- City, state, zip code;
- Substance spilled;
- CHRIS code;
- Amount spilled; and
- ERNS report ID number

Accidental chemical spills are sometimes reported by multiple parties (e.g., the facility; state or local authorities; members of the public) meaning a specific chemical release/spill may appear in the ERNS database more than once. Thus, it is important to cross-reference case information to remove multiple reports of the same incident from the data before analysis. Multiple reports, however, may be useful to researchers interested in identifying the characteristics of releases/spills reported by multiple parties.

A "high detail" ERNS report returns "further information" describing the situation, environmental media involved, and cause of the accident. As an example, we reproduce a "high detail" data description from a spill reported at Cargill's Bartow, Florida facility, October 10, 1997, as this data would appear on a user's computer monitor:

Environmental Media Involved (T/F or True/False) –
Air: T Land: F Water: F Groundwater: F Facility: F
   Other: F
Waterways/other:
Transportation Mode: Fixed Facility
Causes of incident (T/F or True/False):
Trans. Accident: F Equipment Failure: F Dumping: F
   Unknown: F
Operator error: F Natural Phenomenon: F Other: F
Event Description: Valve on granulator/valve not closed by
   worker
Miscellaneous: Area within plant evacuated
Action taken: Secured valve

As can be seen from these data, there is some inaccuracy in the reporting of events in ERNS. For example, in the release/spill described above, it is clearly noted that the event occurred because a "valve [was] not closed by worker." Yet, in the "cause of incident section," the person reporting the event recorded that there was no operator error involved (Operator Error: "F"). Our brief examination of a sample of cases from the Tampa ERNS (25, nonrandom) where the event description implied "operator error" failed to yield a single case where the report also listed operator error as the cause of the event. It is, however, unclear whether this kind of error occurs because of reporting practices by responding facilities or agencies, or recording errors and practices of EPA staff. It is possible, for instance, that the default response for "cause of accident" questions is false, and must be changed to "True (T)" by EPA staff, and that this detail is overlooked in recording the data. In any event, one of the drawbacks of ERNS data is that there are no reliability checks of the data once the data have been recorded.

RCRIS—Resource Conservation and Recovery Information

RCRIS data compiles information that generators, transporters, treaters, storers, and disposers of hazardous waste must report under the Resource Conservation and Recovery Act (RCRA). It should be noted that RCRIS data are restricted to land-based disposal of hazardous waste. RCRIS is used by the EPA: (1) to track handler permits and compliance with Federal and State regulations, (2) to track required cleanup actions, (3) for program management and assessment purposes, (4) as a hazardous waste land-disposal inventory, (5) for assessing and implementing facility management and planning guidelines and plans, (6) for environmental program assessment, and (7) to support implementation of the RCRA.

RTK NET RCRIS searches may be performed in one of three ways: (1) geographic area, (2) facility, or (3) industry. In RCRIS data, facilities are referred to as "handlers." All data, regardless of how it is requested, is reported by facility within each search option.

It is important to note that RCRIS data are not differentiated by year; that is, data are not recorded with respect to time as a unit of measurement. The unit of analysis is the handler, and all data relevant to a specific handler are returned when requesting a RCRIS search. This restricts the use of this data set for certain types of analyses, and individuals who are interested in time-dependent relations are directed to use BRS data. In effect, RCRIS data provide a cumulative record for handlers of hazardous waste, and may have some use for studies of the long-term behavior (e.g., recidivism and compliance) of handlers, but cannot be used to assess certain time-dependent hypotheses.

Basic or "low detail" RTK RCRIS data contain the usual facility information (location, address, owner, handler ID, facility contact, SIC code, generator status, TSD status) along with longitude and latitude indicators. In addition, RCRIS "low detail" data indicate the:

- Number of hazardous waste disposal permits held by a facility;
- Number of recorded violations;
- Number of penalties assessed against the facility/handler;
- Total dollar amount of penalties;
- Number of enforcement actions to date; and
- Date information first recorded for handler.

Our request for a "low detail" RCRIS report for the city of Tampa resulted in a 48-page report. As an example of the "low detail" RCRIS data, we review the RCRIS data for Ashland Chemical Incorporated of Tampa. Located at 5125 West Hanna Avenue (latitude, 2800060; longitude, 08231080), Ashland's SIC code, 5172, indicates its primary operation (refer to Census Bureau data for definitions of SIC codes). Ashland is a small-quantity generator (SQG), with treatment/storage status (TSD status). It uses private land disposal methods, and holds three hazardous waste permits. It began providing information under the RCRA in 1986. Since that time, it has four recorded violations, been penalized six times, faced six enforcement actions and one corrective action, and received penalties in the amount of $16,524.

The "high detail" search returns additional information on each violation and penalty, permit conditions, and additional information on EPA and State inspections. The high detail report for Ashland Chemical Incorporated contained five pages of additional information on this handler. As an example of the kind of information that may be retrieved, part of Ashland's violation record reads as follows:

> Violation Date: 01/16/92   Citation
> Violation Area: Generator—All Requirements
> Relative Priority of Violation (9 = highest) = 9
> Date document of compliance was/is to be submitted:
>   04/15/1992
> Date on which compliance verified: 06/11/92
> Violation Class: 1

        Enforcement Actions for this violation:
            State enforcement actions issued on 03/22/1990
            Type of action: written informal administrative action
            Penalty: $824 Type: final monetary penalty
            Penalty: $824 Type: proposed monetary penalty

Users should produce a "low detail" search, and employ that data to identify sites that require the user to gather further information through the "high detail" search option since the majority of facilities will not have a violation record. As noted in our example, a "high detail" RCRIS search for an individual facility can be several pages in length. For the city of Tampa, for example, the "high detail" RCRIS search report nears 200 pages in length—or four times the length of the "low detail" search.

TSCATS—Toxic Substances Control Act Test Submissions
TSCATS allows users to search EPA data using chemical names and regional delimiters to search for hazardous waste emissions that qualify as toxic substances under the Toxic Substances Control Act. The TSCATS chemical search allows users to vary a number of different parameters to construct customized searches. These parameters include:

- Submitter name;
- Contractor name;
- Submission type (e.g., report, test results);
- Document number (if known, or select "all");
- Microfiche number (if known, or select "all");
- Category name (specific chemical category);
- Chemical name (specific chemical);
- CAS number (if known, or select "all");
- Study type;
- Organism (organism effected, or select "all");
- Route (effect pathway, or select "all");
- Level of detail (high or low); and
- Output type (text, comma delimited, tab delimited).

As an example, we requested a TSCATS report for the category name "lead" with no geographic parameter restrictions (e.g., we set all other parameters to "all"). This should produce data on all reports made to TSCATS for the chemical category "lead" for the entire U.S. A 58-page report followed listing various reports on lead and lead compounds.

The information produced by TSCATS allows users to identify reports that have been produced on specific chemicals so that they may refer to, or request these reports to aid their research efforts. TSCATS does not provide the reports. Given current Web-based technology and the Web's role in providing information access, future improvements to TSCATS should include an online library where these reports may be directly accessed.

ARIP—Accidental Release Information Program

ARIP data describe chemical accidents that have been both reported to and confirmed by the EPA. RTK NET's ARIP does not contain all reports made to the EPA under the Accidental Chemical Release (ACR) program maintained through the Emergency Response Notification System (ERNS), which may limit its usefulness for some types of research (see for example, Lynch, Stretesky, and Hammond's 2000 study which employs ERNS data on accidental chemical releases).

RTK NET's ARIP may be searched by geographic area, facility, or chemical. Search options include low and high detail reports. The low detail reports yield the following basic information about accidental chemical releases:

- Reporting year;
- Facility name, location, and other identifying information (e.g., Dun & Bradstreet number; this information appears in several different data fields);
- SIC code;
- Owner;
- Number of employees;
- Primary product;
- Release start date;
- Release end date;
- Chemical name;
- CAS number (for released chemical; this information may be used in a TSCATS search to identify additional sources of information about chemicals);
- Concentration (of released chemical);
- Physical state (of released chemical);
- Amount released by release type (air, surface water, land, treatment facility, total; this information appears in several distinct data fields);

- Number injured, hospitalized, dead, evacuated, and placed in shelters by type of victim (responders, employees, contractors, public, total; this information appears in several distinct data fields); and
- Cost of reported property damage and/or loss.

A high detail report returns the following additional information:

- List of names, dates, and times for authorities notified of the release (this information is presented in several distinct data fields);
- Applicable ERNS, NRC, or ARIP number;
- Latitude and longitude of release;
- Cause of release (listed either as equipment failure or operator error);
- Location of loss of containment (e.g., equipment involved);
- EPA region;
- ERNS reporting date and time (if applicable);
- When release occurred (description of events leading to release);
- Status of process line (effect of release on facility operations);
- How release discovered;
- Immediate response to release;
- End effects of release;
- Method of communication with public;
- Training, procedures, and management used before this release;
- New training, procedures, and management used after this release;
- Engineering systems or controls used before this release; and
- New engineering systems or controls used after this release.

Some of the data in the high detail report may be in free field format.

There were nine ARIP incidents reported between 1989 and 1995 for the city of Tampa. Four incidents were reported as involving victims or costs. We aggregated these reports to illustrate the total number of victims and costs for Tampa:

- Number injured, 3;
- Number hospitalized, 2;
- Number of deaths, 0;
- Number evacuated, 100 (all in one incident);

- Number placed in shelters, 0;
- Costs to facilities, $13,095;
- Costs to public, $0.

Considering these data, facilities in Tampa appear not to experience an unusual number of accidental chemical releases (for conflicting evidence produced using ERNS, see Lynch, Stretesky, and Hammond, 2000). These data, however, raise some serious question about the calculation of costs involved in ARIP reported incidents.

First, each ACR incident involves some cost, if only because a facility loses chemicals with value into the environment (not to mention the loss of productivity that accompanies responding to an ACR). Second, all costs listed by reporting facilities include only the facility's costs; none report public costs. Clearly, each incident has some public costs. For example, each incident involved the time of governmental personnel who record this information. Some incidents require a response and physical presence of public employees who respond to ACRs. As a result, the validity of ARIP cost data should be questioned, and users are cautioned against using this information as a true indication of the costs of ACR incidents.

FINDS

The FINDS database is an easy-to-use facility locator, and includes three search options: (1) geographic area; (2) facility; and (3) industry. The "low detail" FINDS search option returns a list of the names, addresses, and ID numbers for all facilities regulated by the EPA for the requested search. The "high detail" FINDS search option returns all the information contained in the "low detail" search option, plus a list of aliases for each facility, each facility's SIC code, and a list of regulations that each facility must meet.

For research purposes, the FINDS system is useful for generating a list of facilities in an area that can then be matched against other EPA databases to determine facility reporting patterns, and to ensure that a complete data set has been extracted for an area or industry.

PCS—Water Permit Compliance System

The EPA's Permit Compliance System (PCS) data is designed to track surface water permits issued under the National Pollutant Discharge Elimination System (NPDES) as governed by the Clean Water Act (CWA). PCS data are entered directly into the system by individual states or EPA regions. As a result, the PCS suffers from some data quality/reliability issues. For example, it is known that PCS data are inconsistent across states because each state or EPA region may have to meet different reporting requirements concerning the data that must be entered into PCS. Data may also be subject to variations in regional enforcement programs.

PCS data are aggregated by states from Discharge Monitoring Reports (DMR) completed by individual facilities. Individual facilities report their effluent discharges on the DMR to EPA regional offices or state regulators. The EPA aggregates these reports into Quarterly Noncompliance Reports (QNCR). For the purposes of the PCS, the EPA classifies water emitters as "major," "minor," and "no rating points."

PCS searches may be performed by "geographic area," "facility," or record of "noncompliance." To illustrate the type of data obtained, we performed a PCS geographic area search for the city of Tampa. PCS data for Tampa indicated the existence of 159 facilities with NPDES water discharge permits. The facilities include, but are not limited to, fertilizer producers and farm suppliers; power plants; gas stations, automobile repair shops, truck stops, and quick-lube/oil change facilities; car washes; U.S. military bases; flooring companies; grocery stores; quick-marts; seafood markets; automobile rentals; food and beverage processing, canning, and bottling; golf courses; transportation industries (e.g., railroad); private and public water processors (e.g., sewage discharge systems); coal mining; metal processors; ship yards; mobile home operators; and any other facility that discharges water-based waste.

The "low detail" PCS reports contain the following information fields:

- Facility name;
- Location (city, state, county, in distinct data fields);
- NPDES ID;
- Permit type;
- Date on which facility became inactive (if applicable);
- Indication of facility status ("major," "minor," "no rating points");
- Facility type (industrial, municipal, other);
- Owner type (private, public);
- Application type (Standard or Short, and Type A, B, or C);
- SIC code;
- EPA region;
- Mailing address;
- River basin area;

- Receiving waters;
- Longitude and latitude (if available);
- Average design flow (if available; measured in millions of gallons per day);
- Date first permit issued;
- Facility contact (name and phone number);
- Number of times permit reissued (if applicable; if not 0 or missing);
- Industrial category (2-digit SIC code);
- United State Geological Survey Hydrologic Basin code;
- Number of outfalls for permit (number of effluent emission points);
- Number of parameter limits specified on permit;
- Number of enforcement actions against permit (if not 0);
- Number of inspections of permit (if not 0);
- Number of quarters in noncompliance (last 13 quarters for minor facilities; last 21 quarters for major facilities);
- Compliance schedule violations (if not 0);
- Number of DMR effluent or non-receipt violations (if not 0).

It should be noted that all fields listed above followed by the phase "if not 0" indicate that this data will be absent from any facility report if no such action has occurred at that facility. Additional notes in the "low detail" PCS indicate:

- Whether the facility discharges to a major estuary or estuary drainage area;
- If the permit was issued directly by the EPA;
- If the facility was provided with federal monies for construction;
- Whether the facility is on final effluent limits;
- Whether a municipal compliance plan schedule was to take effect, or if the plan was delayed, and date of actual implementation;
- Whether an evidentiary hearing is required or anticipated concerning a permit;
- Outcomes of evidentiary hearings; and
- Pretreatment program status, and other miscellaneous notes.

Some of these additional data fields are in free field format.

The "low detail" PCS report for the city of Tampa's 159 existing and closed facilities was 63 pages in length. The report quality for each facility varied dramatically in terms of completeness, and also appeared to vary by facility type. Generally, public facility reports contained the greatest number of completed data fields. The lack of consistency in these reports provides some indication of data reliability and validity issues in PCS data.

Another indicator of validity problems are the data entered under the field "Number of DMR effluent or non-receipt reports." It is unclear whether these represent DMR effluent reports, or the failure to file a required DMR effluent report (or both). For example, several facilities in Tampa have DMR effluent or non-receipt reports larger than 50. Since some of the permits involved were issued as early as 1973, it is impossible to tell whether these involve non-reports (since there are 85 reporting quarters during this time period), or actual reports of DMR effluent emissions. It should be noted as well that despite a significant number of facilities with large numbers of DMR effluent or non-reports, the number of inspections and violations appears quite low. Consider the data in Table 10-1, which was constructed from the PCS report for Tampa.

The number of facilities with DMR effluent/nonreporting violations is 28 (17.6% of all permitted facilities in Tampa). The average PCS facility with DMR effluent violations/nonreports had 3.2 outfalls, 20 parameter limits, 9 inspections, 2.8 enforcement actions, was in noncompliance over 7 of the last 13 quarters, and had 41.36 DMR effluent/nonreport violations. In comparison, the 131 facilities without DMR effluent/nonreporting violations averaged 1.07 inspections (more than eight times lower; it should be noted that 45% of inspections for facilities without DMR violations occurred at only two facilities, while an additional 25% of inspections occurred at four other facilities, and the remaining 125 facilities faced only 42 inspections), 0.21 enforcement actions (ten times lower), and 0 quarters in noncompliance. Clearly, facilities that report DMR violations (either due to nonreporting or exceeding effluent limits) are more likely to be inspected, and when inspected, to be penalized with an enforcement action.

The data in Table 10-1 also highlight two issues about facilities with DMR violations: (1) facilities that report fewer DMR effluents or have fewer nonreports are more likely to be in quarterly compliance than facilities with a higher number of DMR effluent or nonreports; and (2) there is little to no relationship between DMR/nonreports and inspection and violation frequency.

To provide an example of the information contained in the PCS facility report, we review information reported for the Citgo Petroleum facility, at Tampa Terminal in Sparkman's Channel (physical location, longitude +2749000, latitude –0822400; 801 McCloskey Blvd., Tampa, FL, 33605). The permit for this facility was first issued in October 1974, and was reissued one time. The facility is located in EPA Region 4, U.S. Geological Survey Basin Code, 03100206. The facility's NPDES permit number is FL000531. The permit for this facility was issued directly by the U.S. EPA. The facility is classified as a minor facility.

FL000531 empties effluents into Sparkman Channel, which is part of the Southeast Tampa Bay water basin. The permit under which the facility operates has 15 effluent restrictions. Over the past 13 quarters, this facility has been in noncompliance eight times. Given the number of restrictions and the high probability of noncompliance at this facility, and the large number of DMR effluent/nonreport violations (262), a large number of inspections and violations would be expected. During the life of the permit, however, only four inspections were made, and two enforcement actions taken. Clearly, this facility is a persistent violator of its NPDES permit, though it faces few penalties.

The "high detail" report for the city of Tampa is nearly 1000 pages in length. "High" and "low" detail reports contain the same basic data fields. The difference between the two types of reports is the additional information presented for each facility related to inspections, enforcement actions, non-compliance events, DMR reports and measures, monitoring events and reports, and outfalls (discharge pipes) found in the "high detail" report. Each is reported by date, with information concerning the outcome, reason for an event, chemical measures, and so on.

Earlier, we noted that the DMR measures in the "low detail" report were difficult to interpret because it was unclear whether a facility had filed a DMR report noting effluent outputs, or because it had failed to file the required DMR report. The "high detail" PCS reports can be used to clarify which of these conditions holds. In the "high detail" report, each DMR is listed, and indicates whether effluents were reported, or whether the facility failed to file a DMR. While this determination can be made, the task may be time consuming. Consider, for example, facility FL00531 listed in Table 10-1. This facility had 262 DMR effluent nonreports that would have to be sorted to determine whether it was in noncompliance for failure to report a DMR or for DMR effluent outputs.

Table 10-1: Facilities with DMR Effluent and Nonreport Violations under the Permit Compliance System, City of Tampa Florida, by Facility NPDES ID, 1974-2000.										
Facility NPDES	O	PL	I	EA	QN	DR	CS	PF	PR	YI	YC
FL00531	3	15	4	2	8	262	1	Y	1	1974	—
FL01627	4	36	7	4	10	106	0	N	0	1974	—
FL36820	2	24	22	7	7*	81	0	N	0	1984	—
FL00469	2	20	9	1	8	75	0	N	1	1974	—
FL33073	1	10	5	0	13	72	0	N	0	1977	1983
FL41220	1	22	6	5	13	67	2	N	0	M	1995
FL00591	3	12	6	2	8	66	0	Y	1	1974	—
FL32425	5	50	5	3	8	60	0	N	0	1975	—
FL39896	1	20	12	13	8	59	0	N	0	M	—
FL34746	4	40	5	6	8	53	0	N	0	1978	—
FL38652	1	3	10	4	8	40	0	N	0	1984	—
FL40614	2	25	16	2	8	37	0	N	0	M	—
FL43931	4	9	0	0	6	31	0	N	0	M	—
FL39110	3	10	5	4	8	21	0	N	0	1984	1995
FL39918	1	7	7	2	8	21	0	N	0	M	1995
FL35149	3	4	1	0	4	16	0	Y	0	1977	—
FL00825	6	3	17	0	3*	15	0	N	M	1976	—
FL61191	7	7	1	3	7	15	0	Y	0	M	—
FL20940	4	55	53	2	6*	13	0	N	0	1974	—
FL30023	1	10	8	2	13	9	0	N	0	1975	1988
FL37702	3	12	3	2	2	7	0	Y	0	1985	—
FL00710	1	4	6	2	8	6	0	N	1	1973	1994
FL34622	18	45	7	2	2	6	0	Y	2	1978	—
FL42927	1	8	2	1	6	5	0	N	0	M	1994
FL01392	2	22	5	1	2	5	0	N	0	1974	1997
FL00647	1	9	17	4	2	5	0	N	1	1974	—
FL01384	3	59	8	2	2	3	0	N	2	1974	—
FL29319	M	M	11	3	12	2	0	N	0	1975	1992
Mean	3	20	9	3	7	41	17	—	—	1977	

*Ranked by number of NPDES violations/nonreports. (N=28). (See note at end of Table for descriptions of data contained in each column).

Key: **O**–*Outfalls*. The number of points at which a facility releases effluents; **PL** – *Parameter limits*. The limits placed on a permit; **I**–*Inspections*. The number of times a facility has been inspected under a given permit; **EA**–*Enforcement actions*. The number of enforcement actions against a facility under a given permit; **QN**–*Quarters in noncompliance*. For minor facilities, the number of quarters is limited to 13. For major facilities, the maximum number of quarterly reports presented is 21. The latter facilities are designated with a "*"; **DR**–*DMR effluent violations, or DMR nonreporting violations*. The number of times a facility either reports effluent limits above permit parameter limits, and/or the number of times a facility failed to file a DMR report; **CS**– *Compliance schedule violations*. The number of times a facility failed to comply with imposed pollution limit schedules; **PF**–*EPA Permitted Facility*. Is the permit under which this facility operates issued directly by the U.S. EPA? (yes, no); **PR**–*Permit reissues*. Number of times the permit for this facility was reissued; **YI**–*Year of Issue*. Year in which the permit for this facility was first issued; **YC**–*Year Closed*. Year in which this facility ceased operation (if applicable). **M**–*Missing Information*.

Risk Management Plan (RMP) Search

A RMP search allows users to locate risk management plans for facilities using one of three types of searches: (1) geographic area; (2) facility; or (3) full text. Risk management plans describe a facility's interpretation of the potential hazards at a facility, the potential risk to the community, and the plan of action the facility employs to prevent and respond to potential environmental hazardous releases. The quality of these plans varies from one facility to the next. RMPs also vary in length.

Risk management plans are required under 40 CFR Part 68.155, and under the Process Safety Management regulations maintained by the Occupational Safety and Health Administration (OSHA; regulation 1910.119) where applicable. Facilities employing or storing hazardous chemicals that have the potential to damage the surrounding physical, human, or animal environment are required to maintain a RMP.

A RMP search returns information to the user by E-mail. All reports are facility specific, regardless of how the information is generated (all search options ultimately require the user to access an RMP by facility. The user has the option of how to obtain the facility RMP by performing one of the three types of searches noted above).

A RMP describes: (1) general plant equipment; (2) plan goals; (3) on-site regulated substances (names of chemicals and amounts); (4) worst case scenario results summary; (5) alternative release scenarios; and (6) accidental release prevention programs and chemical-specific prevention plans.

Typically, RMPs are quite general and do not completely describe the potential impact of a chemical accident. For example, Americold Logistic's (plant number 80527), which uses liquid ammonia to refrigerate food products, reports the following in its RMP:

> Worst case scenario: "Release of the maximum quantity of ammonia that can be stored in a vessel (accounting for administrative controls) – 6627 pounds in 10 minutes. No passive migration measures were used. The most pessimistic meteorological conditions were used: 1.5 meters/second wind speed, and F stability. Reference Table 15 from EPA RMP Off-Site Consequences Analysis Guidance Document. See Appendix A. The toxic endpoint was determined using the EPA's "RMP-Comp" computer program downloaded from their Web site. Distance to toxic endpoint: the one hour, time average concentration of 200 ppm (0.14 mg/L) reached 1.4 miles."

Users will notice that no mention is made of the potential human harm that may occur in the surrounding environment (possible injuries or deaths), the need to have a plan for community evacuation in the event of a worst case scenario, the potential impact on the surrounding environment, the need for emergency equipment, or the financial costs that might be associated with a worst case scenario. These kinds of descriptions are possible given that the average prevailing wind speed and directions for geographic locations in the U.S. may be easily obtained. This data can then be used to plot a dispersion plume. Census data can then be used to estimate the number of inhabitants in the area affected by the plume. In effect, these plans leave much to be desired, especially for residents who live near facilities where the release of hazardous chemicals remains possible.

It is a good idea for community members to be familiar with the RMPs in their areas, and to examine them when selecting potential home sites. Community members can use this information to their own personal advantage, and also pressure local governments and facilities to establish more appropriate emergency response plans.

ADDITIONAL RESOURCES AT RTK NET

RTK NET also offers users access to several additional resources and databases. On the menu bar on the left side of the "Master Search" page, users will see a link labeled "Resources." Accessing this link takes the user to the resources page. Each link provided on the resource page takes the user to other Web sites that contain information useful for understanding, using, and interpreting data on RTK NET. A brief description of the links found on the RTK NET resource page follows.

- *CERLIS/Superfund.* A direct link the EPA's Superfund data.
- *DOCKET.* A direct link to the EPA's DOCKET data.
- *Census Bureau's Landview.* A direct link to information about the Census Bureau's Landview Geographic Information System (GIS) software and data. This system is useful for any environmental hazard research. Using Landview, users can plot environmental hazard data against Census Bureau data (once the data in the two systems have been integrated). Landview software may also be downloaded from the Census Bureau.
- *Landview Tutorial and Technical Documents.* Further information on the use of the Census Bureau's Landview software and data.
- *RCRA.* A direct link to the EPA's RCRA data.
- *TRI.* A direct link the EPA's TRI data.
- *The Right Stuff.* A RTK NET document that describes various ways in which RTK NET data have been employed by users to address environmental health issues.
- *New Jersey Health Information Fact Sheet.* Chemical-related health information describing plans and policies that can employed to help reduce and respond to environmental chemical exposure health risks.
- *EPA's IRIS System.* IRIS (Integrated Risk Information System) provides information on the known health risks associated with specific chemicals.
- *United Auto Workers (UAW) Health and Safety Chemical Information Page.* Maintained by the United Auto Workers Union, this page contains information and links to information on hazardous chemicals commonly found in the production of automobiles and automobile parts. This information is also applicable to other industries.
- *EPA Sector Facility Indexing Project.* See Chapter 9.
- *FedStats.* Provides access to numerous online sources of federal information useful for studying environmental hazards, including the Centers for Disease Control and Prevention (CDCP), the Occupational Safety and Health Administration (OSHA), the Department of Housing and Urban Development

(HUD), which contains information on public housing facilities, and the Department of Justice, which oversees criminal cases against environmental offenders.

- *U.S. Census Bureau FactFinder.* FactFinder is a Web-based means of accessing commonly used online Census Bureau data. Some links will take users to Census Bureau pages that can be used to purchase data sets on CD-ROM.

Census Bureau data have numerous uses when combined with environmental hazard data available through RTK NET. Census Bureau data can be used to add variables to environmental hazard data that describe the area in which hazards are and are not located. For example, if we wanted to determine the characteristics of zip codes within an area containing environmental hazards, and to determine if zip codes with certain characteristics were more likely to have environmental hazards than zip codes without those characteristics, we would need a Census Bureau file with the suspected characteristics for all zip codes in the geographic area. We would then merge this data with environmental hazard location data. This analysis could be performed for one specific kind of hazard, or for several different hazards either individually or in an aggregated form. This is the kind of analysis researchers perform when they examine the issue of environmental justice.

These data could also be used to examine other kinds of environmental justice issues, such as the potential link between the distribution of hazardous waste sites (treated separately as hazardous waste production, treatment, storage and disposal facilities, or in aggregate form) and the probability of certain kinds of diseases. Criminologists have also recently employed these kinds of data to examine the spatial association between lead (Pb)—a chemical known to cause aggressive behavior in humans, and to be related to numerous conditions associated with learning disorders—and the distribution of violent crime rates (see Stretesky and Lynch, 2001).

RTK NET IN GENERAL

RTK NET provides easy access to a number of different EPA databases. This chapter reviewed these databases and their uses. To demonstrate the extent of available data, consider that we downloaded approximately 1,500 pages of data in preparing this chapter with a focus on Hillsborough County and the City of Tampa. There is a great deal of research that can be performed using RTK NET data; enough it would appear, to keep any army of researchers busy for decades. The format of RTK NET may be more valuable to researchers than to members of the general public.

Another important Web-based resource is *Scorecard*. While *Scorecard* contains many of the same data sets as RTK NET, it has the advantage of using a higher level of Web-based technology making it a more appropriate starting point for members of the public or those beginning their venture into the study of environmental hazards. For this reason, we discuss the *Scorecard* Web site in the following chapter. To be sure, however, RTK NET remains an invaluable source of information for researchers because it is formatted to allow data to be extracted in ways that are compatible with many statistical analysis packages.

CHAPTER 11

The Scorecard Network

This chapter provides a guide to the *Scorecard* Web site, the most easily navigated major environmental Web site that can be used to access environmental hazard, pollution, and health data. The site's design is appealing and well laid out, and contains numerous links to a variety of agencies that collect and publish environmental and health data, and to data specially prepared for presentation on *Scorecard*. And, while the presentation of data and facts on *Scorecard* is not oriented toward researchers (e.g., data are often not in a downloadable format), the site usually contains a link to the original data if it is Web accessible. *Scorecard* is not only well-designed and accessible, it's also a great place to begin researching a problem, and a versatile and useful research tool even for advanced researchers.

Scorecard is maintained by Environmental Defense, a nonprofit organization with over 300,000 members nationwide. The following facts about Environmental Defense were taken from the organization's Web site. Founded in 1967, Environmental Defense unites perspectives on science, law, and economics to create innovative, equitable, and cost-effective solutions to society's most urgent environmental problems. It helped launch the environmental movement by winning a ban on the pesticide DDT. Currently, Environmental Defense has more PhD scientists and economists on staff than any related organization. Environmental Defense supports sustainable development, social justice, and the environmental rights of the poor and people of color.

SCORECARD HOME PAGE

Scorecard can be accessed via the Internet at www.scorecard.org. The home page is simple to understand and contains: a description of a leading environmental issue and/or a summary of some recent research; a moving list of ten communities most affected by a designated toxic health threat (the featured threat topic is rotational); a main navigation menu (bottom center of home page); and a direct-link search that allows users to retrieve information on toxic health threats by communities.

The home page is designed around the main navigation menu, which provides nine links to major sources of information maintained on *Scorecard*:

1. Criteria Air Pollutants
2. Hazardous Air Pollutants
3. Lead Hazards
4. Land Contamination (Superfund)
5. Animal Waste from Factory Farms
6. Toxic Releases from Industrial Facilities (TRI)
7. Clean Water Act Status
8. Watershed Indicators
9. Setting Environmental Priorities

By selecting links 1 through 6, the user is taken to a search page for the specific hazard (link 7 reviews water quality issues using a design similar to the descriptions that follow). Each of these search pages is designed using the same format. Thus, once you master the use of any the first six user areas, the remaining areas operate in a similar manner. As a result, and consistent with the purpose of this chapter and in an effort to avoid redundancy, we restrict our in-depth review of *Scorecard* procedures and information to section 1 above, "Criteria Air Pollutants."

Before beginning our review, we direct those seeking additional information on using *Scorecard* to the "Scorecard Guide" which may be accessed through the "FAQs" link on any subpage. This guide may be used online, or downloaded for review at a later date.

CRITERIA AIR POLLUTANTS

Select the "Criteria Air Pollutants" link from the main menu on the *Scorecard* home page to access this section. Criteria air pollutants are defined as the six most common air pollutants in the United States responsible for smog, soot, poor air quality, and aggravated health conditions (e.g., difficulty breathing, heart and lung disease, and premature mortality). The introduction to this section notes that while air quality has improved in the United States throughout the 1990s, 100 million Americans continue to be exposed to environments with unhealthy air quality.

The six criteria air pollutants are: carbon monoxide, lead, nitrogen oxide, ozone, particle matter (PM), and sulfur dioxide. As discussed earlier, the maximum allowable limits for these six criteria air pollutants are defined by the National Ambient Air Quality Standards (NAAQS). Locations unable to meet the standards designated in NAAQS are classified as non-attainment areas.

Facts About Criteria Air Pollutants

Below, we present some basic facts about the six criteria air pollutants obtained by selecting the link "About the Chemicals" from the links located on the left-side of the "Criteria Air Pollutants" page. Further information on each of these chemicals is available in *Scorecard's* "Chemical Profile" database (discussed below).

Carbon Monoxide (*CO*): Poisonous gas produced by the incomplete combustion of carbons contained in fuels. CO's adverse impact on humans occurs by reducing the delivery of oxygen to organs and tissues. Seventy-seven percent of CO emissions are from transportation sources, followed by incinerators, wood-burning stoves, and industrial sources. Persistent exposure to elevated levels of carbon monoxide may cause cardiovascular disease, and impairment of visual perception, manual dexterity, and learning and performance of complex tasks. NAAQS standard for CO is 9 ppm (8 hour average) and 35 ppm (1 hour average).

Lead (*Pb*): Lead is a widely used soft metal and a persistent environmental toxin. Environmental lead levels have decreased dramatically over the past decade. Despite this decrease, lead pollution remains a serious environmental health threat because of its persistence in the environment, and the low level exposure required to produce negative health consequences. Non-ferrous smelters, battery plants, and gasoline additives are the major sources of lead pollution in the United States. In localized environments, lead contamination may result from exposure to lead-based paint (primarily in homes built before the 1950s), ceramic, pewter, and leaded-crystal products, among other items found in the home including some hair-coloring agents. Lead has been linked to a number of adverse health effects including learning disabilities, lowered IQ, school failure and dropping out, certain congenital defects, aggressive and violent behavior, disruptive classroom behavior, and criminal and delinquent behavior (see Stretesky and Lynch, 2001). Animal studies have also uncovered evidence of lead's carcinogenic (cancer-causing), teratogenic (birth defect–causing), and mutagenic (genetic mutation–causing) effects.

The NAAQS for lead is 1.5 micrograms/cubic meters of air (quarterly average).

Nitrogen Dioxide (NO_2) and other *Nitrogen Oxides* (NO_x): NO_2 is a product of combustion. Exposure to NO_2 may reduce resistance to respiratory infections and cause bronchitis and pneumonia. The NAAQS for NO_2 is .0053 ppm (annual mean). NO_x compounds have been implicated as a primary source of acid rain (resulting in the deterioration of ecosystems) and ozone production (smog, also defined as a respiratory toxicant), and form during the combustion of fuels at high temperatures. Its major sources are transportation, fossil fuel, electrical utilities, and industrial boilers.

Ozone (O_3): Ozone, a major component of smog, is not a direct environmental pollutant. It forms when various VOCs (see below) and NO_x compounds are exposed to sunlight. Health effects associated with lower level atmospheric concentrations of ozone include damage to lung tissues and reduced lung function.

Volatile Organic Compound (*VOC*): VOCs are implicated in the production of ozone, and may also be related to carcinogenesis. Automobiles, dry cleaning facilities, chemical manufacturing plants, and paint shops are the primary sources of VOCs. NAAQS for ozone is 0.012 ppm (1 hour average) and 0.08 ppm (8 hour average).

Particle Matter (*PM*): PM is designated as PM-10 (matter less than 10 microns) and PM-2.5 (matter less than 2.5 microns). In general, human health risks increase as the size of PM declines. Exposure to PM impairs lung function, aggravates existing cardiovascular and respiratory diseases, reduces the immune system's function, and may cause cancer and premature mortality. NAAQS for PM-10 is 50 micrograms/cubic meter of air (annual mean) and 150 micrograms/cubic meter of air (24 hour average). NAAQS for PM-2.5 is 15 micrograms/cubic meter of air (annual mean) and 65 micrograms/cubic meter of air (24 hour average).

Sulfur Dioxide (SO_2): Sulfur dioxide is released by the burning of coal and diesel fuels that contain sulfur. Major sources of this pollutant include steel mills and refineries, pulp and paper mills, oil- and coal-based power plants, and nonferrous smelters. Health effects include the aggravation of existing respiratory and cardiovascular diseases. Sulfur dioxide also contributes to the production of acid rain. The NAAQS for sulfur dioxide is 0.03 ppm (annual mean), 0.14 ppm (24 hour average), and 0.50 ppm (3 hour average).

CRITERIA AIR POLLUTANTS (CAP) "POLLUTION LOCATOR" HOME PAGE

The home page for any of the main menu pollution items is reached by accessing that pollutant's link on the *Scorecard* home page. Accessing any of these links leads to a page called the "Pollution Locator" home page for the specific environmental pollutant selected.

As noted, we limit our example to the "Criteria Air Pollutants" link. We do so because the consistent design of this Web site is applicable across all listed pollution areas, and to minimize overlap with discussions of specific data sets provided in previous chapters.

To begin, select the "Criteria Air Pollution" link from the *Scorecard* home page. Once you select this link, a page titled "POLLUTION LOCATOR/Criteria Air Pollutants" will appear (if you selected the "Lead Hazards" link, for example, this page would read "POLLUTION LOCATOR/Lead Hazards").

The "criteria air pollution" (or CAP) locator page has a menu on the left-side to allow easy navigation of CAP information. Many of the pages, however, also contain embedded links that are not always directly accessible from this menu. For example, the first line of text on the CAP page contains a link to a brief description of the six air pollutants addressed in CAPS data (see discussion in previous section of this chapter). The CAP Pollution Locator page provides three ways to access CAPs data.

The most obvious navigation choice is the large U.S. map located at the bottom-center of the page. Use this map by selecting a state to access information on that state. Alternatives include selecting the two links embedded in the text on this page. The first embedded text link is labeled "Provide Your Zip Code." This option takes you to CAP information for the zip code you entered. The second embedded link option is labeled "Pollution Locator," which leads to the "Pollution Locator Search Engine." This page may also be accessed by using the navigation bar on the left-side of the CAP Pollution Locator page.

Pollution Locator State Report

The Pollution Locator State Report is reached by accessing the map described in the previous section. For purposes of this example, we selected Florida. The page for each state is laid out in exactly the same manner, and any state the user selects will contain the information reviewed below.

The page for each state is divided into eight sections. The first is entitled "Criteria Air Pollutant Report: [State Name]." This section contains seven links: (1) Map Locating the Pollution Sources; (2) Air Quality Ranking: Health Risks, Exposure and Emissions; (3) Environmental Justice Analysis for [State]; (4) Health Risks; (5) 1999 Emissions Summary of Criteria Air Pollutants; (6) Take Action; and (7) Links. These hotlinks take you down the remainder of the page to the information provided in each section, and the page can be easily navigated without the use of this tool. Below we discuss the information provided in several of these links.

Map Link
Accessing the link "Map Locating the Pollution Sources" leads to a color-coded map for the requested state. Here, a user may get a visual "feel" for the data, and map the location of selected indicators within a specific state.

Air Quality Link
The "Air Quality Link" takes you further down this page to several measures of air quality for the selected state. Basically, the air quality data are presented in a large histogram. The axis of the histogram represents the percentage ranking for the requested state relative to all states for seven different pollution indicators: person days in exceedance of national air quality standard for; (1) ozone; (2) carbon monoxide; (3) nitrogen oxides; (4) PM-2.5; (5) PM-10; (6) sulfur dioxide; and (7) VOC. The range for each division on the pollutant ranking scale is 10 percent (e.g., 0–10%, 10–20%, etc.), with higher percentiles suggesting worse air quality. For example, the data reveals that Florida is between the:

- 40th and 50th percentile of states for ozone emissions;
- 90th and 100th percentile of states for carbon dioxide emissions;
- 90th and 100th percentile of states for nitrogen oxide emissions;
- 90th and 100th percentile of states for PM-2.5 emissions;
- 70th and 80th percentile of states for PM-10 emissions;
- 90th and 100th percentile of states for sulfur dioxide emissions;
- 90th and 100th percentile of states for VOC emissions.

These data clearly indicate that Florida is among the "dirtiest/worst" states (a *Scorecard* pollution classification) with respect to the concentrations of these air pollutants. From these data we can conclude that the leaders of Florida's government could be doing much more to ensure that the state's citizens are protected from exposure to noxious air pollutants. In fact, these data would lead to the conclusion that Florida's political leaders have performed their jobs extremely poorly since it is the duty of public officials to protect the citizens they serve and to place their interests above those of polluting industries, especially those incapable of conforming with legal requirements (for details on corporations meeting legal requirements of environmental laws, see the data for Florida in chapters on SFIP, ECHO, and RTK NET).

The state report section also contains links to some additional pollution indicator information. Those not satisfied with the general state ranking provided above may access one of four additional links found here to obtain further criteria air pollution information. We present these links as they appear in the "Pollution Locator/Criteria Air Pollutants/State Report/Florida" heading. Italicized words indicate hotlinks embedded in the text.

- Rank states by criteria air pollutant *health risk* or *emissions*.
- Rank counties in FLORIDA by criteria air pollutant *health risks*, *exposures*, or *emissions*.
- Rank facilities in FLORIDA by criteria air pollutant *emissions*.
- Rank monitoring stations in FLORIDA by criteria air pollutant *exposures*.

To illustrate the information produced by using these additional links, we selected the "health risks," "exposures," and "emissions" links for counties in Florida. The "emissions" link took us to a page where the top 25 most polluted counties in Florida were listed. This list can be generated for any of the six criteria pollutants. For example, Dade County ranks as the number one county for VOC pollutants with 103,586 tons, followed by Broward County (71,771 tons), and Hillsborough County (61,532 tons).

The "exposures" link provides a ranking of counties in the selected state for one of several different exposure measures (user-selected from a drop-down menu). We selected the standardized PSI (Pollution Standards Index) measure from the drop-down menu. The PSI is a standardized measure of air quality created by the EPA to describe the general health effects associated with specific pollution conditions and levels. When the PSI is high, a health advisory report is issued for an area, and is often broadcast on news and weather reports. PSI standardized scale values range from 0 to 500, and provide an estimate of air quality from the level of five criteria air pollutants (combined PM measures, ozone, nitrogen oxide, sulfur dioxide, and carbon monoxide) recorded in local air samples. PSI health indicator values are as follows: (1) Good, 0–50; (2) Moderate, 51–100; (3) Unhealthy, 101–200; (4) Very Unhealthy, 201–300; and (5) Hazardous, 301+. As an example, the average daily PSI for five Florida Counties (Escambia, Bay, Manatee, Sarasota, and Hamilton) were "Unhealthy" during 2000. No counties in Florida ranked higher than "unhealthy" on the basis of daily averages using the PSI.

Selecting the "health risks" link provides a list of counties where criteria air pollutants exceed NAAQS standards (a more complete discussion of the health risk link is provided below). The list may be created to reflect "all" or any specific criteria air pollutant using a drop-down menu. The "health risk" data are presented in "person days in exceedance of NAAQS." This number (which we call the PDE) is generated by the EPA. The PDE is obtained by multiplying the number of days when the concentration of a criteria air pollutant in a county exceeds NAAQS standards, by the number of people who live in the area. The PDE thus provides an estimate of the number of people living in the selected location who are affected by a hazard, weighted by the size of the population. For example, if an area exceeds NAAQS standards only one day in a year, and 100,000 people live in that area, then the PDE would be 100,000. If the same area had an excessive NAAQS reading for the remaining five criteria pollutants for one day each, the total PDE for the area would be 600,000 (100,000 x 6). Hillsborough County has the highest PDE among counties in Florida, with a PDE of 1,001,555. On an average day, this figure means that nearly 2750 people (1,001,555/365) are exposed to one specific or a combination of the six criteria pollutants in excess of NAAQS standards.

Environmental Justice Link

Within the State Pollution Locator section, users may also select the "Environmental Justice Analysis" link. Environmental Justice Analysis examines the distribution of pollution hazards and risks relative to the distribution of populations. Questions surrounding environmental justice include whether pollution is unevenly distributed, and whether this distribution reflects patterns of discrimination related to race, class, or other indicators of power differentials in society.

A number of different pollution distribution indicators appear when a user selects the environmental justice link. The list of indicators for Florida is reproduced in Table 11-1. This table indicates several findings for Florida in general. Caution should be exercised in interpreting these data since they represent only bivariate relationships.

First, the most persistent overall indicators of exposure to environmental hazards in Florida are poverty and income (poverty and income have the highest, most consistent series of positive values). Second, the largest differences in environmental hazard exposure across Florida involve race/ethnicity differences for the distribution of Superfund sites, and facilities emitting criteria air pollutants (indicated by the large, positive ratios of 3.78 and 2.50, respectively). The race/ethnicity ratio of Superfund site locations is nearly twice as large as the next largest ratio (1.96 for the distribution of Superfund sites by poverty status).

Third, for facilities emitting criteria air pollutants, the race/ethnicity ratio is substantially larger than the ratio for any other pairing for facilities emitting criteria air pollutants. Fourth, the combined measure "children in poverty" addresses an often-overlooked environmental justice issue, one that may have lasting or life-long impacts. Children in poverty ratios indicate that children who live below the poverty level in Florida are more likely to be exposed to high levels of pollutants. Overall, these data indicate that race/ethnicity and class variables possess substantive importance in terms of understanding the distribution of environmental pollution in Florida.

Certain measures used in this table, however, fail to adequately represent the impact of class and race on the distribution of environmental hazards in Florida (i.e., home ownership and job classification). The lack of strong relationships for these variables may be conditioned by race/ethnicity. In other words, if we reexamined this relationship and divided home ownership or job classifications by race/ethnicity (e.g., working-class people of color, white, working-class people, non-working–class people of color, non-working–class white people) a very different picture of the distribution of environmental hazards is likely to emerge.

Finally, it should be noted that the relationships depicted in this table reflect how variables used to produce these data were defined. For example, the cutoff point for low and high-income families is defined as $15,000, with low-income families earning less than $15,000, and high-income families earning more than $15,000. Clearly, this definition has its limits and lumps together a diverse array of family incomes in the high-income category. Families earning $15,000 a year do not have the opportunity to live in the same neighborhoods as families earning $50,000 or more per year, and treating these families as if they were equivalent may hide important income linked relationships. Indeed, it is likely that families earning $15,000 to $20,000 per year are more likely to live in neighborhoods similar to families earning $10,000 to $14,000 per year than families earning more than $50,000 per year.

It is also likely that proximity to hazardous waste sites and the ratios presented in Table 11-1 would be substantially different if income was defined differently. From previous research we performed using this data for the state of Florida, we would suggest that *Scorecard's* income divisions are likely to attenuate the relationship between income and proximity to hazardous waste sites. These same criticisms apply to several other categories used in *Scorecard's* environmental justice data.

Because the definition of variables and the limitations of those definitions can have a strong impact on the outcomes of an analysis, *Scorecard* provides access to the definitions for the various categories employed in Table 11-1 using hotlinks embedded on this page, as well as a link to a section on the "limits of the data" under the environmental justice link. Using these links, we created a summary of these definitions (see Table 11-2) as presented on *Scorecard*.

Table 11-1: Distribution of Environmental Burdens in Florida		
Distribution of BURDENS By RACE/ETHNICITY		**Ratio**
Releases of Toxic Chemical	(indicator of chemical releases)	−0.52*
People of Color	130000	
Whites	250000	
Cancer Risks from Hazardous Pollution	(added risk per 100,000)	1.47
People of Color	280	
Whites	190	
Superfund Sites	(sites per square mile)	3.78
People of Color	0.14	
Whites	0.04	
Facilities Emitting Criteria Air Pollutants	(facilities per square mile)	2.50
People of Color	1	
Whites	0.4	

Distribution of BURDENS by INCOME		Ratio
Releases of Toxic Chemical	(indicator of chemical releases)	−1.05*
Low Income Families	230000	
High Income Families	220000	
Cancer Risks from Hazardous Pollution	(added risk per 100,000)	1.15
Low Income Families	230	
High Income Families	200	
Superfund Sites	(sites per square mile)	1.78
Low Income Families	0.09	
High Income Families	0.05	
Facilities Emitting Criteria Air Pollutants	(facilities per square mile)	1.62
Low Income Families	0.76	
High Income Families	0.47	

Distribution of BURDENS by POVERTY		Ratio
Releases of Toxic Chemical	(indicator of chemical releases)	1.23
Families Below Poverty	270000	
Families Above Poverty	220000	
Cancer Risks from Hazardous Pollution	(added risk per 100,000)	1.14
Families Below Poverty	240	
Families Above Poverty	210	
Superfund Sites	(sites per square mile)	1.96
Families Below Poverty	0.11	
Families Above Poverty	0.06	
Facilities Emitting Criteria Air Pollutants	(facilities per square mile)	1.85
Families Below Poverty	0.89	
Families Above Poverty	0.48	

Distribution of BURDENS by CHILDHOOD POVERTY		Ratio
Releases of Toxic Chemical	(indicator of chemical releases)	1.08
Kids Below Poverty	280000	
Kids Above Poverty	260000	

Cancer Risks from Hazardous Pollution	(added risk per 100,000)	1.19
Kids Below Poverty	250	
Kids Above Poverty	210	
Superfund Sites	(sites per square mile)	1.83
Kids Below Poverty	0.11	
Kids Above Poverty	0.06	
Facilities Emitting Criteria Air Pollutants	(facilities per square mile)	1.88
Kids Below Poverty	0.94	
Kids Above Poverty	0.50	

Distribution of BURDENS by EDUCATION		**Ratio**
Releases of Toxic Chemical	(indicator of chemical releases)	1.00
Non-High School Graduates	200000	
High School Graduates	200000	
Cancer Risks from Hazardous Pollution	(added risk per 100,000)	1.10
Non-High School Graduates	230	
High School Graduates	210	
Superfund Sites	(sites per square mile)	1.90
Non-High School Graduates	0.10	
High School Graduates	0.05	
Facilities Emitting Criteria Air Pollutants	(facilities per square mile)	1.59
Non-High School Graduates	0.78	
High School Graduates	0.49	

Distribution of BURDENS by JOB CLASSIFICATION		**Ratio**
Releases of Toxic Chemical	(indicator of chemical releases)	1.05
Working Class People	220000	
Non-Working Class People	210000	
Cancer Risks from Hazardous Pollution	(added risk per 100,000)	1.05
Working Class People	220	
Non-Working Class People	210	

Superfund Sites	(sites per square mile)	1.39
Working Class People	0.07	
Non-Working Class People	0.05	
Facilities Emitting Criteria Air Pollutants	(facilities per square mile)	1.26
Working Class People	0.59	
Non-Working Class People	0.47	

Distribution of BURDENS by HOME OWNERSHIP **Ratio**

Releases of Toxic Chemical	(indicator of chemical releases)	1.41
Renters	240000	
Homeowners	170000	
Cancer Risks from Hazardous Pollution	(added risk per 100,000)	−0.88*
Renters	210	
Homeowners	240	
Superfund Sites	(sites per square mile)	−0.63*
Renters	0.05	
Homeowners	0.08	
Facilities Emitting Criteria Air Pollutants	(facilities per square mile)	−0.63*
Renters	0.48	
Homeowners	0.76	

*Negative signs were added to ratios where the group with more resources/power is disadvantaged.

Table 11-2: Summary of Definitions Used in the Environmental Justice Analysis Link*

Race/ethnicity: (people of color; whites). People of color include non-white (African-Americans, Asians, Hispanics/Latinos, Native Americans, and others) racial/ethnic groups.

Income: (low income; high income). Low-income families earned less than $15,000 annually; high-income families earned more than $15,000 annually.

Poverty: (families below poverty; families above poverty). Families are divided into those above and below poverty using the 1990 Census designation of poverty-level family income for a family of four as $12,575/annually.

Childhood Poverty: (children below poverty; children above poverty). The distribution of children below age 18 living above and below the Census definition of poverty.

Education: (non-high school graduates; high school graduates). The percentage of residents over 25 years of age who completed or failed to complete high school.

Job Classification: (working class; non-working class). Percentage of residents who are working class (e.g., clerical, sales, support staff, private household and other services, craft and transportation workers, laborers) and non-working class.

Homeownership: (renter; home owner). Owner-occupied versus renter-occupied housing units.

Cancer Risks from Air Pollutants: (include hazardous air pollutants or HAPs). HAPs are chemicals that cause adverse human health consequences, including, but not limited to birth defects. The EPA has estimated the concentration of nearly 200 HAPs for over 60,000 U.S. Census tracts. *Scorecard*'s cancer risk measure combines these data with data on chemical toxicity to produce a weighted population estimate of the average added lifetime cancer risk in a Census tract attributable to outdoor air pollution hazards.

Releases of Toxic Chemicals: An indicator (not actual releases in pounds) measuring TRI releases of 650 different chemicals reported by manufacturers that includes a boundary of one mile from the border of each Census tract.

Superfund Sites: The number of Superfund sites per square mile.

Facilities Emitting Criteria Air Pollutants: The number of facilities emitting any of the six criteria air pollutants per square mile.

*Data by *Scorecard* (All variables listed below are dichotomous variables)

Scorecards' environmental justice information may also be searched using the "Community Center/Environmental Justice/Locator for Unequal Burdens." This page allows the user to select specific parameters for a data search. Users may select one of the predefined demographic categories (people of color, people below poverty, renters, kids in poverty, working class) for a selected area (entire U.S., by state, or from a list of specific counties), and all or one of the pollution risks (cancer risks from hazardous air pollutants, releases of toxic chemicals [TRI], Superfund sites, facilities emitting criteria air pollutants).

Health Risks Link
The next portion of the state pollution locator section details the "Health Risks" measures. Here, a summary of population health risks measured by "person days in exceedance of NAAQS" regulations are

summarized. For Florida, the data in this section are limited to two indicators, lead and ozone, because these are the two criteria air pollutant indicators for which Florida counties exceed NAAQS limits. For example, this information indicates that the quarterly average for air lead was in excess of NAAQS standards for 1,011,555 person days. Above, we encountered this figure when reviewing the PDE data, which indicated that Hillsborough County had a PDE of 1,011,555. Taken together, these two figures reveal that Hillsborough County's PDE was also a measure of lead exposure in that county, that Hillsborough County must only be out of compliance for air lead, and that Hillsborough County is the only county in Florida out of compliance for NAAQS lead emission standards.

Summary of Criteria Air Pollutants Link
Following the "Health Risk" section, users will find a section entitled "Summary of Criteria Air Pollutants" for the selected state. This table displays tons of pollutants per year for four pollution categories: mobile, area, point, and all. Mobile sources include automobiles and trucks. Area pollutants are stationary air pollution emitters. Point source pollutants are water pollutants with an identifiable, direct facility source. The "all" category is a sum of these three pollution sources. In this table, criteria air pollutants are displayed by their source or origin (e.g., mobile, etc.). As an example, the data for Florida are as follows (last reporting year, 1999; see Table 11-3):

Table 11-3: Summary of Criteria Air Pollutants By Source/Origin—Florida

	Mobile	Area	Point	All
Carbon Monoxide	4,808,725	979,936	74,422	5,863,083
Nitrogen Oxides	678,983	61,110	373,354	1,113,447
PM-2.5	95,425	116,443	15,151	227,019
PM-10	341,205	204,469	23,225	568,899
Sulfur Dioxide	65,103	38,115	802,475	905,693
VOC	543,028	376,162	27,154	946,344

Added together, these data indicate that 9,624,485 tons of criteria air pollutants were emitted into Florida's ambient air in 1999. By any standard, this is a great deal of pollution, and the negative health consequences of this level of pollution on Floridians are significant. Indeed, this figure helps us to understand the data in the "Air Quality

Rankings" section, which indicated that Florida is among the "dirtiest/worse" states in the nation in terms of air pollution.

Taking Action

The pollution locator section closes with two sections that allow users to "Take Action." In these sections, the user may elect to "E-mail the EPA," "E-mail the Governor of [the selected State]," "Join an online discussion about [the selected State]," "E-mail a Scorecard Community Report to a Friend," "Network with Environmental Groups," "Contribute to Environmental Defense," "Volunteer with Environmental Groups in Your Area," and "Learn How to Use Scorecard to Find out about Toxins in Your Community." Taking action is an important aspect of environmental research, and this Web site, unlike those discussed earlier, helps promote the active participation of researchers and members of the general public in environmental action.

ADDITIONAL SCORECARD INFORMATION

Aside from the information found on the "Pollution Locator State Reports" link, other information is included on the "CAP Pollution Locator Homepage." The following addresses the links of interest to those researching environmental crime.

Regulatory Controls

The "Regulatory Controls" link takes users to the following: (1) a list of federal regulatory programs; (2) California's regulatory programs; (3) a list of environmental hazards; (4) a target list of chemicals that should be reduced or eliminated according to national or international organizations (see following discussion for details on these links).

Pollution Locator Search Engine

In place of the above links, a user may select to search for pollution information using the "Pollution Locator Search Engine." This search engine allows users to define the parameters of a search, and returns much more specific information than the general links described above.

Using the pollution locator search engine, users may search for pollution-related information and data using one of three alternatives: (1) zip code search; (2) geographic area search; or (3) company search. The zip code search is the most straightforward of the three. Here, a user simply enters the zip code for the area in which they are interested in generating information, and accesses the "Go" button. Under the "geographic area search," users have five search options: (1) a general state search; (2) a county search within a state; (3) a watershed search; (4) a watershed search within a state; and (5) a watershed search within a county. Finally, users may search for pollution hazards by company, by entering either the company field name, or limiting the search for a company's pollution record to a specific state.

Setting Priorities

The "setting priorities" menu option takes the user to a series of data that can be employed to determine the priority of public health risks associated with environmental pollution and hazards. After selecting this link from the menu on the Pollution Locator page, a page with a regionalized U.S. map appears. Users may click on any region within the United States to access priority setting data. We selected the southeast region of the U.S. to illustrate the nature of these data. Several pages of links and data were displayed on the screen after selecting this link.

The first series of links direct users to comparative rankings of current environmental problems in the selected region for three issues: (1) human health; (2) ecology; and (3) welfare. Within each of these areas, health risks are divided by "seriousness." For example, human health risks are divided into: (1) higher risk; (2) medium-higher risk; (3) medium risk; (4) medium-lower risk; and (5) lower risk. Specific conditions are listed under each of these risk types. Users may select "general" or "area specific" link options that relate to each risk. For instance, the first "higher risk" human health issue is "indoor air pollution." Users may review "general" information about indoor air pollution, or "area specific" information. Table 11-5 summarizes the risk factors listed for each of the three main priorities. While the risk factors are repeated in each of the three areas, this listing can be used to select issues that have the highest average rank across the three areas. For example, if we assigned values to each risk category (higher risk = 1, medium-higher risk = 2, medium risk = 3, medium-lower risk = 4, and lower risk = 5), we could determine the overall priority of a specific issue. As an example, let us select a few risk exposure issues: radon, pesticides, airborne lead, global warming, and Superfund sites. The rankings for each issue by area are displayed in Table 11-4. Following the weighting procedure described above, and the average issue weight shown in Table 11-4, we would treat pesticides and global warming as the highest priority issues across these three areas, followed by radon, Superfund sites, and airborne lead.

Additional links in this section describe the project's purpose, the ranking process, participants in the ranking process, and EPA contact information for the selected region.

Table 11-4: Example of the Use of Setting Priorities Data found on *Scorecard*

	Human Health	Ecology	Welfare	Average
Pesticides	2	2	3	2.33
Radon	1	5	3	3.00
Airborne Lead	3	4	5	4.00
Superfund Sites	3	3	5	3.67
Global Warming	5	1	1	2.33

(See Table 11-5 for a complete list of priorities by type and issue.)

Table 11-5: Risk Priorities as Defined in *Scorecard* Used for Setting Priorities on Human Health, Ecology and Welfare

<u>High Risk</u>

Human Health: Indoor Air Pollution; Radon

Ecology :   Degradation of terrestrial habitat and wetlands; global warming; stratospheric ozone depletion

Welfare: Acid deposition; drinking water; global warming; nonpoint source pollution; ozone/ carbon monoxide; particle matter; stratospheric ozone depletion

<u>Medium-High Risk</u>

Human Health: Acid deposition; drinking water; ozone/ carbon monoxide; pesticides; stratospheric ozone depletion; toxic air pollution

Ecology: Acid deposition; industrial wastewater; nonpoint source pollution; ozone/carbon monoxide; pesticides

Welfare: None

Medium Risk

Human Health: Airborne lead; groundwater; hazardous waste; industrial solid waste sites; industrial wastewater; municipal solid waste sites; nonpoint source pollution; municipal waste water; particle matter; Superfund sites

Ecology: Accidental chemical releases; groundwater; hazardous waste; industrial solid waste sites; storage tanks; Superfund sites; toxic air pollutants

Welfare: Accidental chemical releases; degradation of terrestrial habitat and wetlands; indoor air pollution; industrial solid waste sites; industrial wastewater; municipal solid waste sites; municipal wastewater; odor/noise pollution; pesticides; radon

Medium-Low Risk

Human Health: Accidental chemical releases; odor/noise pollution; radiation; storage tanks

Ecology: Airborne lead; particle matter; radiation

Welfare: None

Low Risk

Human Health: Degradation of terrestrial habitat and wetlands; global warming

Ecology: Drinking water; indoor air pollution; odor/noise pollution; radon

Welfare: Airborne lead; degradation of wetlands; hazardous waste; radiation; storage tanks; Superfund sites; toxic air pollutants

Pollution Rankings Link
Scorecard also allows users to directly access its "pollution rankings" database. The pollution ranking database is easy to use, and consists of a series of four drop-down menus. The purpose of this device is to rank geographic areas in terms of one of four types of pollutants: (1) hazardous air pollutants; (2) criteria air pollutants; (3) emissions of toxic chemicals, and (4) animal wastes. In recent years, animal wastes have become an increasing health concern, especially in rural areas, and *Scorecard's* inclusion of data pertaining to this issue is relevant to these recent environmental justice concerns. The drop-down menus in this section allow the user to create a geographic rank for the above hazards for either: (1) states, (2) counties, (3) zip codes, or (4) facilities.

About the Chemicals
Scorecard's databases contain information on more than 7100 chemicals (for a list of these chemicals, follow the link on the "About the Chemicals" main Web page). This list includes all chemicals regulated under major environmental laws, and large-use quantity chemicals. The "About the Chemicals" link leads to two search engines. The first allows users to search for information about a chemical by name or the chemical's standard identification number (Chemical Abstracts Service, or CAS registry number). The second allows users to generate a ranked list for chemical releases by type of release and area ("Rank Chemicals by Reported Environmental Release in the United States").

Health Effects Link
Information on various health effects associated with chemicals and pollutants can be obtained by accessing the "Health Effects" link on the left-side menu of the Criteria Air Pollutants home page. The Health Effects main page contains twelve health link effects. These links are organized by type of effect: (1) cancer; (2) cardiovascular or blood toxicity; (3) developmental toxicity; (4) endocrine toxicity; (5) gastrointestinal or liver toxicity; (6) immunotoxicity; (7) kidney toxicity; (8) musculoskeletal toxicity; (9) neurotoxicity; (10) reproductive toxicity; (11) respiratory toxicity; and (12) skin or sense organ toxicity.
    The health effects information maintained on this Web site is vast, and represents an up-to-date and comprehensive examination of health issues. Numerous links are embedded in the pages that follow selection of each health link.

Regulatory Controls Link

Users should select this link to learn more about the regulatory controls that apply to toxic and hazardous pollutants. Links to (1) federal agencies; (2) California state agencies; (3) a list of environmental hazards, and (4) a target list of hazardous chemicals identified by national and international organizations are provided.

The "Federal Agencies" link connects users to twelve agencies and/or regulations: (1) Occupational and Safety Health Act; (2) Clean Air Act—Regulated Toxic, Explosive or Flammable Substances; (3) Clean Air Act—Criteria Air Pollutants; (4) Superfund Act—Extremely Hazardous Substances; (5) Clean Air Act—Hazardous Air Pollutants; (6) Resource Conservation and Recovery Act—Hazardous Constituents; (7) Superfund Act—Hazardous Substances; (8) Department of Transportation—Inhalation Hazards; (9) Safe Drinking Water Act—Maximum Contamination Levels; (10) Federal Insecticide, Fungicide and Rodenticide Act—Registered Pesticides; (11) Clean Water Act—Priority Pollutants; and (12) Toxic Release Inventory—Regulated Chemicals. These links allows users to access regulatory rules without having to hunt through government agency Web sites.

Scorecard provides one of the most comprehensive and navigable Web sites related to environmental hazards and pollution. It should be evident from the length of this chapter, which focused on the material in one of the seven most relevant databases maintained by *Scorecard*, that the amount of online data available through this Web site is immense. It would be difficult for any one individual to master or analyze all of the available data. This chapter provides further evidence to our claim that there is an extraordinary amount of environmental crime, pollution, health and justice data that criminologists have failed to draw upon in their discussions and analyses of these issues.

CHAPTER 12

Corporate Average Fuel Economy Standards: Protecting the Environment by Regulating Engine Efficiency Through Mile Per Gallon Requirements

The majority of chapters in this book have examined laws, regulations, and data that fall under the direct purview of the Environmental Protection Agency. The EPA, however, is not the only agency charged with enforcing laws and regulations that impact the environment. Every state, for example, has its own independent agency that enforces environmental laws and regulations. The connection between these state agencies and the enforcement of environmental regulations is fairly apparent. In other cases, however, it is not immediately clear how an agency acts to protect the environment. For instance, it is probably clear how policies concerning the disposal of nuclear waste, enforced by the Nuclear Regulatory Commission (NRC), contributes to environmental protection and elevated levels of human safety. Once we know that the Department of the Interior (DOI) is responsible for protecting public lands, endangered species, national parks, and energy resources, we can easily comprehend the important role this agency plays in protecting the environment. It may be less clear, however, how an agency such as the National Highway Traffic Safety Administration (NHTSA), a branch of the U.S. Department of Transportation (DOT), plays a role in environmental protection.

In order to clarify and explore this role, this chapter examines the NHTSA's responsibilities in rule-making and enforcement efforts stemming from the Corporate Average Fuel Economy (CAFE) standards. This chapter differs from the preceding five chapters in that we go beyond identifying environmental crime data. In particular, we use CAFE data to demonstrate how researchers can employ environmental crime data, and subsequently offer policy recommendations for greater environmental protection.

CAFE LEGAL BACKGROUND

In 1975, the U.S. Congress passed the Energy Policy and Conservation Act (EPCA; Public Law 94-163; 42 USC 116). As part of its directive, the EPCA mandated that passenger cars and light trucks (which included pickup trucks and sport-utility vehicles [SUVs] weighing less than 8,500 pounds) meet fuel efficiency requirements. The EPA was initially charged with helping establish this program. The fuel efficiency program became the responsibility of the Secretary of Transportation, the chief executive officer of the Department of Transportation, under the Motor Vehicle Information and Cost Savings Act (49 USC Subtitle VI , Part C, Chapter 329, "Automobile Fuel Economy").

The impetus behind CAFE or fuel economy standards lay in two related issues: the OPEC oil embargo of the mid-1970s, and elevated levels of air pollution found in U.S. cities during the same period. The idea was quite simple. Increased vehicle fuel efficiency would decrease U.S. reliance on foreign sources of oil, which would also decrease the impacts of an oil embargo on the U.S. economy. At the same time, an increase in vehicle fuel efficiency would decrease gas consumption, leading to lower levels of automobile pollution. The burning of fossil fuels in combustion engines produces several noxious by-products linked to the production of smog, human diseases (including elevated levels of cancer), and environmental degradation that can damage items from consumer goods and buildings, to forests and wildlife. Thus, forcing vehicle manufacturers to meet fuel efficiency standards would have two beneficial outcomes for the American public: one economic, the other health-related. In effect, CAFE is not only an economic policy, it is, simultaneously, a public health, environmental, and energy policy.

We should make it clear that CAFE is not typically discussed as an environmental policy. For example, when members of the general public are exposed to information about CAFE it usually comes from conservative groups and automakers who argue that CAFE should be repealed because it stifles Americans' freedom of choice, or is bad for American automobile manufacturers. These groups miss the point that consumer freedoms are part of a delicate balance of choices, and that it is perfectly reasonable and, indeed, expected that choices that endanger the freedom of a majority of the population should be limited. In this case, driving gas-guzzling vehicles that emit high levels of noxious pollutants endanger the freedom of Americans who don't drive gas-guzzlers to have access to clean air and more healthy living environments. More relevant to this book is the fact that most academics and legal experts who examine environmental policies do not examine CAFE standards and enforcement (as an example of this omission, see Findlay & Farber, 2000; Ferrey, 1997). They also miss the point that CAFE can have beneficial consequences not only for American businesses, but also for the majority of Americans through decreased rates of disease. We added a discussion of CAFE to this book in an effort to broaden research into this and similarly neglected aspects of environmental regulations, law, and crime.

HISTORICAL BACKGROUND

The events leading up to the creation of CAFE standards are rather complex and enmeshed with a series of events and EPA deadlines for implementing air pollution standards. The story begins with preparations for the 1972 Presidential campaign. The Democrats selected Senator Edwin Muskie to run against the incumbent, Richard Nixon. At that time, air pollution had become an issue of increasing public and scientific concern. The effects of air pollution were plainly visible to the general public. Backed by popular support and scientific studies, Muskie had become an active leader in the effort to create national air pollution regulations. In contrast, the first few years of the Nixon administration saw few serious actions on the environmental front. As a result, there was growing support for Muskie's presidential bid. This scenario changed dramatically mid-way through 1970 when Nixon signed a Presidential order creating the EPA *after* Congress had failed to implement the required legislation. With this triumph in hand, Nixon recovered on environmental issues enough to win re-election. His action also set into motion a series of pollution regulations.

The order Nixon signed required the newly created EPA to establish air pollution standards within 180 days. This was accomplished through the National Ambient Air Quality Standards (NAAQS), which were incorporated into the Clean Air Act (CAA). As part of this Act, EPA executives were charged with reducing automobile emissions to improve air quality. The EPA proposed automobile air emission standards to which American automakers objected, claiming that they could not successfully be met. Outspoken critics, such as Lee Iacocca, then President of Ford Motor Company, argued that complying with the proposed standards could force the

American automobile industry to shut down. Especially contentious were proposed standards concerning lead emissions found in automobile exhaust. Meeting the proposed standard would require the cooperation of the oil industry, which would be forced to reformulate the contents of gasoline to meet new legal requirements.

As part of its efforts to reduce air pollution, the EPA also proposed vehicle fuel efficiency standards, which would be based on vehicle miles per gallon (mpg) estimates, as part of the CAA. The Big Three automakers—GM, Ford, and Chrysler—argued that they could not manufacture automobiles that met the proposed mpg standards. In her book, *When Smoke Ran Like Water*, Devra Davis (2002, p. 116), a former National Academy of Sciences Scholar, recounts the story. She notes that after complaining that they would be unable to meet the proposed EPA mpg standard because it was technically impossible, someone at the meeting pointed out that Japanese automakers had met the proposed standard two years earlier.

> In response...one Senate witness from GM reportedly said 'Oh sure, they can do that with their little bitty Japanese cars, but not with a real big American Car. The slap did not sit well with Soichiro Honda [Owner of Honda Motors]. He bought a Chevrolet Impala, shipped it...to Japan, and had...engineers replace the existing cylinder head to prove that their [Honda's] system could handle bigger, heavier cars.

The experiment worked. Faced with the fact that Japanese technology could work in American vehicles, U.S. automakers shifted their attack to the new unleaded gasoline regulations (Davis, 2002, pp. 117–120). Despite assurances from Ford's President, Lee Iacocca, that automakers could not make a vehicle that could meet both the mpg and lead emissions requirements, both Honda and Mazda had already accomplished the task. While U.S. automakers fought these regulatory efforts, and Lee Iacocca made his stance very clear, it wasn't long before engineers at GM solved both problems using the catalytic converter. The converter not only lowered automobile emissions, but it also increased fuel efficiency. For the moment, the disagreement over automobile emission standards and vehicle fuel efficiency ended, and the EPA had won an important battle. This battle, however, continually resurfaces, highlighted by the claim that any increase in CAFE would prove disastrous to the American automobile industry.

WHAT EXACTLY IS CAFE?

CAFE is a means of quantifying a manufacturer's passenger car and light truck fleet fuel efficiency. In effect, CAFE measures the average mpg achieved by all vehicles a manufacturer sells during a calendar year. CAFE calculations are quite complex, and the exact formulas employed to make these calculations do not need to be reviewed here. Basically, what CAFE measures is a fleet's (that is, the passenger cars and light trucks sold by a manufacturer) average mpg weighted by sales for each vehicle in the fleet. The NHTSA receives the data needed to make these calculations from the EPA. In turn, the EPA gets its data directly from manufacturers who are required by law to report the results of laboratory tests on vehicle fuel efficiency (mpg achieved in controlled laboratory experiments) to the EPA. The EPA then adjusts the data from the laboratory tests to estimate the mpg expected during real world driving conditions (these adjustments correct for drag, road conditions, and other real world factors that detract from laboratory mpg tests). The NHTSA uses these data to determine which automakers will be fined for failing to comply with the requirements of CAFE regulations. We discuss these fines later in this chapter.

In determining the final CAFE "score" for a manufacturer, the NHTSA applies several different adjustments. For example, a CAFE fuel efficiency rating for a manufacturer is adjusted to reflect a credit allowance for manufacturers that produce alternative fuel vehicles. A CAFE score is also adjusted to reflect credits a manufacturer may have earned during the previous three years. A manufacturer can earn CAFE credits by producing a fleet of vehicles that exceed CAFE limits in a given year. These credits can then be applied against years in which the manufacturer fails to meet CAFE requirements (with a three-year limit).

When CAFE standards were first implemented in 1978 under Title V of the Motor Vehicle Information and Cost Savings Act, the fleet fuel efficiency standard was set at 18.0 mpg (see Table 12-1 for CAFE standards by year for both passenger cars and light trucks). The NHTSA, however, was granted authority to alter CAFE standards. By 1990, NHTSA had raised the standard to 27.5 mpg for passenger cars, and 20.0 mpg for light trucks. Congress effectively froze the NHTSA's ability to alter CAFE standards from 1996 through 2001 by failing to appropriate funds for this purpose. Currently, the CAFE standard for passenger cars has not changed since 1990.

Later in this chapter, we discuss the relationship between CAFE standards and annual average fleet mpg. At this point, it bears mention that automakers seem to increase fleet mpg only in response to CAFE requirements, and not because doing so has sweeping economic implications or health consequences for the American public.

Table 12-1: CAFE Fuel Efficiency Standards for Passenger Cars and Light Trucks, 1978–2003, in MPG Fleet Average		
Model Year	**Passenger Cars**	**Light Trucks**
1978	18.0	—
1979	19.0	16.8*
1980	20.0	15.5*
1981	22.0	16.2*
1982	24.0	17.5
1983	26.0	19.0
1984	27.0	20.0
1985	27.5	19.5
1986	26.0	20.0
1987	26.0	20.5
1988	26.0	20.5
1989	26.5	20.5
1990	27.5	20.0
1991	27.5	20.2
1992	27.5	20.2
1993	27.5	20.4
1994	27.5	20.5
1995	27.5	20.6
1996-2003	27.5	20.7

* Our estimate of a combined CAFE standard for 1979–1981. For these years, CAFE standards were set independently for 2-wheel and 4-wheel drive light trucks. For purposes of this Table, we combined these distinct CAFE averages for these years.

THE TALE OF TWO CAFES

We examine two distinct periods in the history of CAFE regulations, 1978–1988 and 1989–2001, to demonstrate how automakers responded to changing CAFE standards. As noted in Table 12-1, during the first period, CAFE requirements were raised on a regular basis. Increasing these requirements had important effects on average fleet fuel efficiency. During the second period of stagnant CAFE standards, average fleet mpg has remained relatively constant. At the same time, engine horsepower increased, and manufacturers pushed light-truck and SUV sales which neutralized the effects of CAFE.

CAFE, 1978–1988

CAFE standards increased substantially from 18 mpg to 26 mpg (or by approximately 44%) from 1978–1988. During this period, average total fleet fuel economy (that is, the mpg average for all vehicles sold in a year) for all (domestic and foreign) passenger cars and trucks increased from 19.9 to 28.8 mpg. Over this period, the average curb weight for vehicles in the United States declined from 3349 pounds to 2831 pounds (or by approximately 15.5%). This decrease in weight helped conserve fuel and increase fleet mpg averages. In addition, average engine sizes also declined from 260 cubic inches to 161 cubic inches (or by approximately 38%). Despite the dramatic decrease in engine size, the ratio of horsepower to weight rose (from 3.68 in 1978 to 4.11 in 1988), indicating that new engine technology produced more horsepower from smaller engines while providing greater combustion efficiency.

Overall, engines got smaller, cars got more powerful relative to their weight, and mpg averages improved, while cars got slightly smaller (there was a 4.4% reduction in interior vehicle space from 1978–1988). In sum, it appears that CAFE had dramatic effects on improving vehicle fuel efficiency while improving horsepower/weight ratios and having negligible impacts on interior vehicle space.

CAFE, 1989–2001

From 1989 through 2001, CAFE standards changed only slightly, moving from 26.5 mpg to 27.5 mpg. During this period, average total fleet fuel economy (that is, the mpg average for all vehicles sold in a year) for all (domestic and foreign) passenger cars and trucks remained relatively constant, fluctuating between 27.9 and 28.8 mpg. Over this period, the average curb weight for vehicles in the United States increased from 2878 pounds to 3148 pounds (or by approximately 9.4%). This increase in weight, which reflected a growing light truck/SUV sales market segment, was one cause of stagnation in overall sales weighted fuel efficiency. In addition, average engine size also increased slightly from 163 cubic inches to 165 cubic inches (or by approximately 1%). At the same time, the ratio of horsepower to weight rose significantly from 4.24 hp/100 pounds to 5.16 hp/100 pounds, or by 22 percent. New engine technologies produced much more horsepower from engines that remained relatively constant in size. This shift indicated that automakers were more interested in using engine technology to increase horsepower rather than fuel efficiency. While average vehicle weight increased, average vehicle interior space remained constant. Overall, engines got more powerful relative to their weight, vehicles weighed more, engine size and vehicle interior space remained constant, while fuel efficiency stagnated.

From 1978 through 1988, CAFE regulations had a significant impact on average fuel economy increases for vehicles sold in the U.S. Fleet fuel economy increased by 44 percent over this time. Likewise, the CAFE standard for this period rose 44 percent. In contrast, the CAFE standard for the period covering 1989 through 2001 increased less than 3 percent. During this period, average fleet fuel economy increased by less than 1/10th of one percent.

As an example of this problem, consider the issue of voluntary increases in fuel efficiency promoted by automakers. In 2000, Ford Motor Company pledged to boost the fuel economy of its SUVs 25 percent by 2005. By April 2003, and in the midst of a sales decline, Ford backed off its original pledge, and instead offered the promise of a 20 to 30 percent fuel efficiency improvement across its entire vehicle line by 2010 ("Ford's Vow Ignores...," 2003). Clearly, the effectiveness of CAFE has been eroded in recent years, which has contributed to the need for other mechanisms to lower air pollution concentrations. Automakers have not voluntarily improved vehicle fuel efficiency absent of government regulation. Efforts to increase CAFE standards could also force automobile manufacturers to pay greater attention to the association between vehicle fuel efficiency, air pollution, and public health.

THE LIGHT TRUCK-SUV EFFECT

Over the past two decades the increase in sales of light trucks, which includes SUVs, has presented a threat to the environment, and to American reliance on foreign oil. In 1979, light trucks constituted only 9.8 percent of the automobile industry's new car sales. The market share for light trucks doubled a mere three years later in 1982. Since the late 1970s vehicle sales have continually shifted toward light trucks. During the late 1970s, this shift was marked by people looking for inexpensive, fuel efficient vehicles, and a number of small trucks were introduced to fulfill this market niche. Lower fuel prices, however, stimulated interest in Jeep-like SUVs, and the boom was on. The SUV became the "cool," less efficient, alternative to the family station wagon. At the same time, the plain, small, fuel-efficient truck gave way to the brooding, fender flaring, macho pickup, and moved sales from the country-side to urban and suburban neighborhoods. Taken together, these trends made the light truck into an urban/suburban vehicle, which recently captured a 50 percent share of new car sales, to the detriment of clean air efforts. This shift in sales has had a dramatic impact on the intentions of CAFE standards.

At the time CAFE was conceived, light trucks made up a small percentage of the automobile market. Providing an exception for light trucks, which were required to meet lowered CAFE standards, seemed reasonable. This was especially true given that light trucks were used in rural areas, or places with lower levels of noxious air pollution, and were typically owned by people who needed work vehicles or inexpensive forms of transportation. Today, the situation has changed dramatically. SUVs, which are classified as light trucks, are now seen as family vehicles, and many are offered at the upper end of the market as luxury vehicles. Thus, it makes less sense to view light trucks, and in particular SUVs, as requiring exemption from more stringent CAFE standards.

Lower CAFE averages for light truck fleets follow the general pattern discussed above in the section "A Tale of Two CAFEs." From 1979 through 1988, light truck average fuel economy rose to over 28 mpg, or by approximately 30 percent. From 1989 through 2001, however, average fuel economy for light trucks fell 7 percent. Because of the less rigorous light truck CAFE requirements, light truck manufacturers have not been required to produce engines that are as efficient as those found in passenger cars. In effect, CAFE "loopholes" have allowed automakers to build vehicles that are not in keeping within the spirit of CAFE regulations. They have also allowed manufacturers to shift the production of more inefficient vehicles to the light truck category. SUVs, for example, are often built on truck frames so that they can be classified as light trucks and, as a result, meet lesser CAFE requirements for fuel efficiency.

One of the most glaring instances of this practice is DaimlerChrysler's PT Cruiser, a vehicle, which for all practical purposes appears to be a passenger vehicle (station wagon), but is classified as a light truck. Though it looks like a classic station wagon, the Cruiser is classified as a truck because it is built on a truck frame. As a result, the Cruiser is only required to meet CAFE standards for light trucks rather than passenger cars, even though its 4 cylinder, 2.4 liter engine with 21 city and 29 highway mpg is a model of efficiency for the light truck class (which features numerous vehicles that achieve less than 15 mpg in city or highway driving). Building the Cruiser on a truck frame allows DaimlerChrysler to accumulate additional CAFE credits.

Light trucks and SUVs do not have to be gas guzzlers. According to a 1999 study by Jason Mark, senior transportation analyst for the

Union of Concerned Scientists ("Greener SUVs: A Blueprint for Cleaner, More Efficient Light Trucks"):

> the average truck on the road today emits 47 percent more smog-forming exhaust and 43 percent more global warming pollution than the average car. Combined with the growing sales of SUVs and other light trucks, the environmental gap between trucks and cars has resulted in an additional:
> *1.8 million tons/year of smog-forming pollutants
> *237 million tons/year of global warming gases
> *18.4 billion gallons/year of gasoline use
> (www.ucsusa.org/clean_vehicles/cars_and_suvs/).

Mark argues that fitting SUVs with existing technology that costs less than $1000 would increase the fuel efficiency of SUVs to more than 28 mpg. This increased cost is offset by consumer fuel cost savings estimated to be more than $3000 over the vehicle's lifetime. Furthermore, this technology would also contribute to a 32 percent decline in vehicle emissions related to global warming, and a 76 percent reduction in smog-related emissions.

· As an example of the effect of the growing light truck/SUV market share of automobile sales, consider Table 12-2 that provides a simple illustration of the impact of the growing SUV/light truck market on air pollution. Vehicles produce two types of gases that have negative environmental impacts: those related to smog formation and those related to global warming (GW). Mark (2003, p. 6) notes that on average, light trucks/SUVs produce 1.4 times more smog-related pollutants and 2.4 times more global warming pollutants than the average passenger vehicle. To keep our comparison simple, we assumed that a car produces 1 unit of smog pollution and 2 units of global warming pollution. Following Mark, this means that the average SUV/light truck produces 1.4 smog pollution units and 4.8 global warming units.

As Table 12-2 illustrates, given lower CAFE standards for SUVs/light trucks, a simple shift in the composition of new vehicle sales accounts for a rise in pollution produced by new vehicles of 14.5 percent when comparing 1990 and 2002. This table also illustrates the dangers of not revising SUV/light truck CAFE standards given their increased market share of U.S. vehicle sales.

Table 12-2: Change in Air Pollution (Smog and Global Warming) Due to Shifts in New Vehicle Sales, 1990 and 2002, For Every 100 Vehicles Sold								
	Cars Sold	SUVs Sold	Car Smog	Car GW	SUV Smog	SUV GW	Total Car	Total SUV	Total All
1990	70	30	70	140	42	144	210	186	396
2002	52	48	52	104	67	230	156	297	453
%Dif	−25	60	−26	−26	60	60	−26	60	15

In short, we can learn to modify SUVs to be environmentally friendly while maintaining their basic size, or learn to live without SUVs as currently designed because of their dramatic environmental and human health consequences.

CAFE, FOREIGN AND DOMESTIC PASSENGER CARS AND LIGHT TRUCKS

When CAFE regulations were being proposed, U.S. automakers objected, claiming that the suggested standards could not be met. Once it was established that these standards could be met, and that Japanese automakers had already created vehicles that met the proposed standards, U.S. automakers altered their approach and argued that they would be disadvantaged by the foreign competition offered by Japanese automakers. In the decades that followed, however, U.S. automakers learned to cope with CAFE.

From 1978 through 2001, the mpg fleet average for domestic-produced vehicles increased from 18.7 to 28.8 mpg—a notable 54 percent increase in fuel efficiency. In contrast, the average fleet mpg for foreign vehicles increased from 27.3 to 28.4—or by only 4 percent—over the same time period. More specifically, foreign vehicles demonstrated large increases in fleet mpg between 1978 and 1983. From 1983 to 1988, the average fleet mpg for foreign vehicles declined, leveled off from 1989–1997, and declined again from 1998 through 2001. In contrast, domestic automakers' fleet average has shown a rather consistent increase over the entire period (with a few deviations). In recent years, however, domestic fleet mpg has also leveled off as well. Today, domestic and foreign fleet mpg averages are nearly equivalent.

According to the Union of Concerned Scientists, "While new cars and light trucks emit about 90 percent fewer pollutants than three decades ago, total vehicle miles driven have more than doubled since

1970 and are expected to increase another 25 percent by 2010" (www.ucsusa.org/clean_vehicles/cars_and_suvs/). Furthermore,

> Despite decades of air pollution control efforts, at least 92 million Americans still live in areas with chronic smog problems. The EPA predicts that by the year 2010, even with the benefit of current and anticipated control programs, more than 93 million people will live in areas that violate health standards for ozone (urban smog), and more than 55 million Americans will suffer from unhealthy levels of fine particle pollution. This pollution is especially harmful to children and senior citizens.

These dangers demonstrate the importance of discussing and reconsidering CAFE pollution standards.

COMPLIANCE WITH CAFE

In this section, we examine compliance with CAFE regulations. Manufacturers who fail to sell enough vehicles that meet CAFE standards are liable for a civil penalty. The civil penalty is calculated at a rate of $5.50 per every $1/10^{th}$ of a mpg for each vehicle in noncompliance. For example, if a manufacturer produces and sells 1 million vehicles that did not comply with CAFE, and the violation exceedance is 1 mpg per vehicle, then the manufacture is liable for a civil fine for each 1 mpg for each vehicle. Since there are ten $1/10^{ths}$ in a mile, the fine per vehicle is 10 x $ 5.50, or $55.00. This is not a large sum, and is probably not large enough to deter either manufacturers or consumers from buying a vehicle that falls 1 mpg below CAFE. The total fine to the manufacture, however, is $55 million. This might be considered a substantial sum of money if manufacturers did not simply pass these costs off to consumers by raising the price of vehicles. We must also remember, however, that the manufacture can apply credits toward this amount, so that the fine may be reduced by selling other vehicles that exceed CAFE standards. We will return to a further discussion of costs to consumers later in this chapter.

Table 12-3 displays CAFE fines collected between 1983 and 1999 by manufacturer, and by year in Table 12-4. It should be noted that these are collected fines, not necessarily all levied fines. Some levied fines are offset by the use of CAFE credits. Because of the lag between the time of vehicle sales, the levying of fines, and their collection, CAFE data is never complete for the most recent years, and some outstanding (uncollected) fines may not be displayed in the table that follows (see, Burns and Lynch, 2002).

As Table 12-4 shows, CAFE fines declined in recent years. This decline is due to a shift from passenger car to light truck/SUV sales, which have lower aggregate CAFE requirements, and decreased potential fines.

Vehicle manufacturers paid more than $500 million in CAFE fines from 1983 through 1999. This seems like a large sum with a potential for reducing the number of CAFE violations. As noted earlier, however, CAFE fines are, to be sure, paid indirectly by consumers, meaning that vehicle manufacturers can successfully pass these fines along to car buyers without experiencing any direct financial impacts. This ability minimizes the deterrent effects of CAFE fines.

Table 12-3: CAFE Fines Collected, by Manufacturer, 1983-1999, ordered by Total Fines Paid (rounded to nearest whole dollar)

Manufacturer	Fines Paid	# Fines	Avg. Fine
Mercedes	$199,027,448	16	$12,439,215
BMW	141,267,374	13	10,866,721
Volvo	56,421,280	9	6,269,031
Jaguar	40,069,650	7	5,813,786
Porsche	25,210,877	15	1,680,725
Range Rover	23,092,237	13	1,776,326
Fiat	7,942,890	15	529,526
Sterling	4,309,780	5	861,956
Peugeot	2,854,205	8	356,776
Volkswagen	401,060	3	133,687
PAS Inc.	294,500	1	294,500
Lotus	123,581	3	41,194
Maserati	121,600	2	60,800
Panzo	26,918	5	5,384
Vector	4,350	3	1,450
Autokraft	2,590	1	2,590
Consulier	150	3	50
Sun	45	1	45

*Callaway Cars Inc., received a fine of $20,400 in 1990 that was later rebated, and therefore, is not included in this table.

Table 12-4: CAFE Fines Paid by Year Paid		
Year	# of Manufacturers Fined	$ Fines Paid
1983	1	57,970
1984	1	5,958,020
1985	4	15,564,540
1986	6	29,871,815
1987	8	31,260,530
1988	8	44,519,450
1989	11	47,500,515
1990	9	48,308,615
1991	12	42,241,770
1992	9	38,286,565
1993	10	28,688,380
1994	7	31,498,570
1995	8	40,787,510
1996	6	19,301,930
1997	10	36,211,850
1998	7	21,571,402
1999	5	19,375,021

*Note: The number of fines listed in Tables 12-3 and 12-4 are not equivalent. Fines in Table 12-3 are aggregated by manufacturer and count discrete fine incidents, which included multiple incidents in the same year. Fines in Table 12-4 are aggregated by year, not manufacturer, which eliminates multiple fine counts within any given year.

Vehicle buyers are largely unaware that the price they are paying for their vehicles has been affected by CAFE fines levied against manufactures. Modifications to the CAFE program suggested below would help correct this situation, and might generate greater consumer interest in fuel economy. We argue that making consumers more aware of CAFE and its intentions would create a situation in which manufacturers would be required to pay greater attention to CAFE and vehicle fuel efficiency standards.

To some extent, the "culprits" behind CAFE violations include consumers who purchase vehicles from manufacturers who do not comply with CAFE requirements. Consumers, however, should generally be considered "unwitting" accomplices, since they are typically unaware of the existence of CAFE regulations, or that the fine that these regulations stipulate impacts the prices of the vehicles they purchase.

The purchasers of certain types of CAFE noncompliant vehicles share a common characteristic: they are generally very well-off economically. Consider, for instance, that of the 124 separate fine incidents listed in Table 12-3, over 90 were levied on luxury cars or upper-end automobile manufacturers (Mercedes, BMW, Jaguar, Volvo, Porsche, Range Rover, Sterling, PAS, Lotus, Maserati, Panzo, and Vector). Consumers purchasing vehicles produced by these manufacturers are generally better able to afford higher CAFE fines than, for example, independent farmers, small contractors, and laborers who rely on their vehicles for work.

In the next section, we propose several revisions to existing CAFE regulations that we believe can make CAFE standards more effective in the effort to reduce pollution.

CAFE POLICY RECOMMENDATIONS

Changes in environmental regulation require sound policy initiatives, thorough implementation, and monitoring. Ineffective policies based on public or political pressures often results in setbacks that may cause extensive environmental damage. To date, research has identified a weak relationship between policy goals and policy effectiveness (e.g., Larson, 1980; Pressman & Wildavsky, 1973). Several economists, for example, argue that "regulatory policies do not exhibit their desired and expected outcomes" (Ringquist, 1993, p. 1023).

Throughout this book, we have examined a variety of data sources useful for studying environmental crime. One of the primary purposes of studying environmental crimes is to understand why they happen with the intent to prevent these behaviors in the future. Thus, the end result of studying environmental crimes are policies designed to protect the environment, reduce environmental degradation, and improve environmental health to benefit humans. With that goal in mind, this section examines policy initiatives and alterations that can make CAFE a more effective mechanism for protecting the environment. We offer these recommendations with the goals of maximizing the effectiveness of CAFE standards and demonstrating how policy recommendations can emerge from data analysis.

We are proceeding from the assumption that in order for CAFE to become a more effective means for protecting the environment, it must include mechanisms that change the behavior of both automobile manufacturers and automobile consumers. As illustrated earlier, the history of CAFE regulations are characterized by two distinct periods: an early, effective period characterized by substantial mpg gains and decreased pollution emissions, and a later ineffective period characterized by declining vehicle mpg and increasing rates of pollution emissions. We also identified classification concerns that hamper the effectiveness of CAFE standards. Below, we suggest some policies that are designed to make CAFE more effective by increasing fuel efficiency and lowering vehicle emissions.

In particular, we call for a more logical classification of different types of vehicles, raising the passenger car standards, raising CAFE fines, offering consumer rebates, eliminating trading allowances, and making CAFE more visible. Because we have no technical expertise in automobile technology, we do not tackle the issue of alternatively fueled vehicles in these recommendations. Our suggestions go beyond the recent announcements made by NHTSA concerning new CAFE requirements for light trucks (21.0 mpg in 2005, 21.6 mpg in 2006, and 22.2 mpg in 2007).

Reclassify Vehicles

One of the reasons CAFE has become ineffective in recent years has to do with changing vehicle market structures and the unwillingness of legislators and regulators to respond to those changes by reforming CAFE. Specifically, the popularity of light trucks and SUVs has done much to undermine the goals of CAFE regulations. When CAFE regulations were first proposed, light trucks comprised a small percentage (less than 7%) of vehicle sales in the United States. Further, these vehicles were primarily used in the pursuit of livelihoods, and were owned by farmers, laborers, and small business owners. We must also consider that when used as farm vehicles, light trucks do not contribute to the problem of urban air pollution. For these reasons, it made sense to separate light trucks from passenger cars and to establish different CAFE requirements for these two separate vehicle classes.

Most light trucks are now family vehicles, and no longer primarily serve the independent worker or farmer. SUVs, however, have been able to maintain their status as trucks because of a loophole in the law that is exploited by vehicle manufacturers (they are built on truck frames). Given the role of the SUV in today's society and market place, we suggest that pickup trucks and SUVs be placed into separate categories. We also recommend that CAFE standards for SUVs be raised to 27.5 mpg, which would force manufactures to pay greater attention to fuel economy issues for a significant portion of the new car market.

Recognize a Luxury Category

As noted above, the intent of CAFE exemptions for light trucks was to provide a safeguard against disadvantaging the small business owner, independent laborer, and farmer through excessive CAFE penalties. In today's market, a mechanism for achieving this goal must be created. One way to do this is to divide light trucks into groups that distinguish luxury SUVs and pickups from other SUVs and pickups. Luxury SUVs and pickups can be distinguished, for example, by the standard equipment found in the vehicle, the number of cylinders, or vehicle price. Because these vehicles are generally less efficient than passenger cars, persons purchasing these vehicles should be made to pay a higher CAFE fine for their choice of polluting the environment. Does the local farmer drive his $52,000 Lincoln Blackwood or Cadillac Escalade around the farm? Are you loading up your family into the 7 mpg, $105,000 Hummer convertible this morning to take the kids off to school?

Separate Passenger Cars and Mini-Vans

Consistent with our argument concerning light trucks/SUVs, we suggest separating passenger cars and mini-vans. Because it is not the intention of our reforms to penalize the family, but to improve air quality standards to benefit all families, mini-van CAFE requirements should be set to 24.5. This would also allow the passenger car CAFE requirement to be raised in an effort to reduce pollution.

Raise The Passenger Car Standard

As noted, engine technology has been employed in two ways by automobile manufacturers across two distinct periods in the history of CAFE: to improve gas mileage by making smaller, more efficient engines; and to boost the horsepower produced by smaller engines. The boost in horsepower occurred during a period when CAFE standards were relatively unchanged. During that period, gas mileage also remained relatively unchanged. Automakers also turned their attention to building bigger SUVs and light trucks. This trend seems to imply that without an outside impetus, automakers tend to overlook the social benefits of more efficient engines as a mechanism for reducing air pollution. Generally, automakers must be forced to take socially beneficial actions. The Union of Concerned Scientists, for example, argued that:

> Automakers have a history of not incorporating cost effective technologies that benefit consumer safety and the environment

until they are required to do so. As a result, government has
had to step in to protect consumers by setting safety, fuel
economy and emissions standards. One of the most recent in a
line of examples is the air-bag that is now required in all new
vehicles – automakers resisted this technology even in the face
of clear demonstration of its safety benefits and calls from
consumers   for   safer   vehicles.   (www.ucsusa.org/
clean_vehicles/cars_and_suvs).

A similar conclusion was reached by Burns (1999).

Average new passenger vehicle fuel efficiency peaked in 1988, and
is now less than it was ten years ago (www.ucsusa.org/
clean_vehicles/cars_and_suvs). Automakers would like us to believe
that this trend reflects consumer demand, and in response we were
provided with more SUVs. What most consumers demand, however,
are safe and efficient vehicles. Many SUVs are neither safe nor
efficient.

In its report, *Drilling in Detroit*, the Union of Concerned Scientists
argued:

> Relying on hybrid electric vehicle technologies could bring
> the fleet to at least 55 miles per gallon. Such a fleet would
> more than double current fuel economy levels and could save
> consumers between $3,500 and over $6,500 in fuel costs.
> Hybrid electric vehicle technologies could enable a family car
> to reach nearly 60 mpg, while an SUV could cross the 50 mpg
> mark. A simultaneous move to fuel cell vehicles could lead to
> a tripling of the fuel economy of family cars and could
> significantly   reduce   fuel   costs   for   all   drivers
> (www.ucsusa.org/clean_vehicles/cars_and_suvs/pageID=228).

Given current levels of engine and automobile design technology, and
the probability of being able to improve on that technology, these
scientists recommend raising CAFE to 40 mpg by 2012, and 55 mpg by
2020.

Raising CAFE Fines
Raising   CAFE   standards   alone   is   an   insufficient   response.
Manufacturers are unlikely to comply with these standards unless
financial penalties for noncompliance are also increased. These
penalties can be used to raise the cost of buying noncompliant vehicles
so that consumers will also alter their purchasing behaviors. These fines

can also be put to beneficial uses, such as providing funds needed for other environmental programs.

Consumer Rebates
The current CAFE system provides penalties but not incentives to purchase fuel efficient vehicles. Incentives should be offered to consumers who buy fuel efficient vehicles rated above CAFE standards (i.e., environmentally friendly vehicles) as a reward for helping to protect the environment. This program could be paid for through funds generated by raising CAFE fines.

End The Trading Allowance
Many different environmental programs have attempted to employ trading allowances to accomplish their task. For example, General Motors can apply CAFE credits earned through the sale of Chevrolets to its Cadillac division. Such trading allowances tend to simply shift the burden of purchasing fuel-efficient vehicles from more wealthy consumers (e.g., Cadillac buyers) to less wealthy consumers (e.g., Chevrolet buyers). The ability to trade CAFE credits allows a manufacturer to make one segment of its vehicle market fuel efficient while neglecting the fuel efficiency of its overall product line.

Make CAFE More Visible
One of the primary reasons that CAFE is not an effective policy is because it is a relatively unknown regulation among members of the general public. Most people do not know that vehicles that do not meet fuel efficiency standards are subject to fines. They also don't know that they pay this fine when they purchase a vehicle. This can be easily corrected by requiring vehicles that do not meet CAFE standards, and which therefore are subject to a fine, to clearly state how much extra the manufacturer is charging for this vehicle in order to pay the fine the company estimates it will owe at the end of the year.

We offer these policy recommendations with the intent to further the effectiveness of CAFE standards. The implementation of CAFE was a noble effort on behalf of policy makers, although CAFE standards do not appear to be maximizing their potential effectiveness. We concur with Ringquist's (1993, p. 1025) suggestion that "Implementation is the crucial link between public policies and their associated outcomes," and based on our assessment of CAFE, hope that our policy recommendations receive due consideration.

CAFE IN GENERAL

At current use levels, it is estimated that there are 30 to 50 years of oil reserves remaining below the earth's surface. Regulations designed to preserve this energy are needed to preserve society as it is now constructed. CAFE is one policy designed to help achieve this goal. CAFE, however, is also designed to help reduce levels of noxious air pollutants linked to global warming and several diseases. Thus, CAFE is an environment, energy, and public health policy rolled into one.

CAFE is a misunderstood, underutilized, and often misrepresented regulation. In contrast to auto manufacturers' claims, CAFE saved American consumers $92 billion by reducing gasoline use by 60 billion gallons, while each gallon of saved gas prevented 24 pounds of global warming pollutants from being released (www.ucsusa.org/clean_vehicles/cars_and_suvs). The Union of Concerned Scientists estimated that CAFE requirements also created jobs in the automobile sector. Further, there is no relation between increased fuel economy and decreased fleet safety as automakers predicted. Rather, CAFE legislation caused vehicles to become more efficient, lightweight and safer simultaneously (through enhanced construction technologies). Likewise, CAFE did not, as automakers predicted, cause a decline in vehicle choice. Rather, during CAFE's "lifetime," the number of vehicles offered to consumers expanded.

CAFE has helped achieve important air pollution and environmental objectives. In recent years, however, as CAFE has been undermined, its effects have diminished and even reversed. Given its past success, and future potential, it is time to reinvigorate and strengthen CAFE regulations for the good of the majority of American citizens, and the health and well-being of future generations.

It is also time for those who study violations of law to focus on a broader range of studies that examine the impact and practices of environmental regulators, similar to what is offered above. Such studies, we believe, are becoming increasingly necessary and probable with enhanced Internet access to governmental data. Further, these studies are also needed to support the contentions of environmental and corporate crime researchers.

CHAPTER 13

A Look Toward The Future of Environmental Crime

In discussing strategic issues facing the American Society of Criminology, former-Vice President Todd Clear noted, "Too much of contemporary public policy legislation is based upon mistaken ideas about the causes and prevention of crime, and far too much of the public debate on crime policy rests on fallacious images of criminality and criminal justice" (2001, p. 3). This statement reflects the concern of many criminologists who believe their work is generally ignored by policy-makers. But, if the average criminologist who studies the crimes that concern the public—street crimes—laments the lack of impact their research has on crime policy, the environmental crime researcher stands on the edge of the abyss ready to jump, having had virtually no impact on public policy.

Environmental criminologists face a substantial challenge if they seek to have their work affect public policy. To do so, they have to change perceptions about crime among the general public, the news media, and other criminologists. These are not small tasks. In addition, they must alter funding priorities so that the government directs research monies toward the study of environmental crimes. Additionally, they must alert policy-makers to the undue influence corporations currently have in shaping laws about what will and will not be considered environmental crime.

It seems that environmental crime issues are continually overshadowed by the drama of conventional crime. Highlighted by the media in daily news reports on television and in the printed media, street crimes are also the focus of many television crime shows, from real-life "documentaries" such as *COPS* and other shows featuring high-speed police chases, to the weekly series including *NYPD Blue*, *CSI: Crime Scene Investigation*, and *Law and Order*. Movies such as *Erin Brockovich*, and *A Civil Action*, which focus on environmental crimes, are rare. Rather, crime movies are typically dominated by the unreal action thriller that sensationalizes crimes or the hunt for the criminal (e.g., *2 Fast 2 Furious*, and the *Lethal Weapon* movie series), or features the rarest of criminal events (e.g., *The Italian Job*, *The Silence of the Lambs*, and *Natural Born Killers*). The problem of overcoming the obstacles presented by popular culture's shaping of public opinion about crime should not be minimized.

The effort to change how environmental crime is perceived among policy-makers, the public, and criminologists is one example of a future priority environmental crime researchers must address. In the remainder of this chapter, we examine some future priorities to provide guidance for continuing research efforts on environmental crimes. Included among priority issues in the coming years are the potential move toward community justice, local efforts to address environmental crime, future directions for EPA reform, and consideration of ecological issues within the context of sustainable development. The chapter concludes with a look at new and evolving environmental issues, and our projections for the future of environmental crime.

RESEARCH

David Simon (2000) calls for further research to test the applicability of existing theoretical frameworks to environmental crime. Specifically, he suggests that Mertonian anomie theory (Messner & Rosenfeld, 1994) and differential association are among the approaches that could further our understanding of organizationally situated environmental crime. In particular, Simon (2000, p. 644) notes that "Ecological crime provides something of a laboratory for testing and refining these two theories of organizational behavior."

Rebovich (e.g., 1998, 2002) identified several areas of environmental crime for future research. He suggests, for instance, that researchers examine the components found in the environmental crime reduction equation (i.e., "tighten environmental legislation + tougher enforcement + increase legitimate disposal alternatives = reduced rates of environmental offenses"), to determine where penalty severity reduced the number of environmental offenses. He also believes researchers should examine a number of additional issues: (1) future challenges likely to be faced by environmental law enforcement; (2) international environmental crime and the global enforcement and deterrence efforts taken in response to those acts; (3) the factors impacting the likelihood of successful prosecution of environmental crimes; (4) the procedures government officials use to relegate criminal cases to civil courts; and (5) recidivism rates to measure the effectiveness of various sanctions. Many of the issues Rebovich identified could be examined using the data discussed throughout this book and through efforts to collect other forms of relevant data.

In discussing the future of prosecuting environmental crime Rebovich (2002) argues that future environmental crime research ought to: (1) examine the behavior and characteristics of the environmental criminal in the same way we identify the characteristics of the ordinary criminal offender; (2) identify business types (e.g., size, number of employees, receipts, profits) and orientations (e.g., mining, automobile, etc.), competitive/monopolistic sector (e.g., trade associations, lobbying group), and locations of businesses likely to engage in environmental crime; (3) examine prosecutorial decisions to charge suspects accused of environmental crimes, and the effectiveness of environmental crime prosecutions; (4) examine the penalties assessed for environmental crimes; (5) assess the effect of intermediate environmental sanctions; and (6) examine the effectiveness of preventive actions.

Rebovich (2002) suggests that much will be expected of tomorrow's environmental prosecutor. These expectations will include an enhanced emphasis on law enforcement duties that not only uphold the letter of the law, but which also protect public health. These diverse goals will likely result in the environmental prosecutor feeling pressure to appeal to a variety of groups and interests. As the environmental prosecutor's role evolves, research must be redirected to provide information to address these often-competing goals (Rebovich, 2002). This research can be useful to future environmental prosecutors much like "Past environmental crime studies have afforded some rewarding insights into the metamorphosis of environmental criminality and the strategies developed concerning environmental crime control" (Rebovich, 2002, p. 344). Rebovich (1998, p. 352) also suggests that additional research attention be directed toward the ways in which enforcement efforts might impede the successful apprehension and prosecution of offenders.

Of primary importance is the need for a comprehensive and accurate database on the characteristics of offenders and offenses, and the investigative, prosecutorial, and sentencing efforts focused on environmental crimes across multiple levels of government. Once collected and analyzed, these data could prove invaluable for deterring future violations and facilitate the investigation of environmental crimes. The effort to contribute to this project was one impetus behind this book.

Improvements in the EPA data collection process and databases would also provide an enhanced research arena for environmental crime. To be sure, the EPA has made numerous improvements to its data collection and dissemination practices. Mintz (1995, pp. 119–130), however, provides an insightful account of the limitations of EPA data and offers directions for maximizing the effectiveness of data collection. In discussing the EPA's system of evaluating its accomplishments using simple numerical indicators, Mintz (1995, p. 199) notes:

> EPA officials keep a record of the number of administrative orders, civil referrals, and criminal referrals issued or made by the agency over the course of a fiscal year, as well as the total amounts of administrative and civil penalties it has assessed against environmental violators. These figures, which play a role in EPA's internal allocation of resources, are then made available to the Congress and interested members of the public. This system, which has been widely referred to as "bean counting," has been subject to extensive and sometimes heated criticism, both from within the agency and from outside it.

Mintz notes the unreliability of environmental indicators as a primary measure of the effectiveness of EPA enforcement efforts, adding that "no single enforcement measure can provide a fair and balanced picture of the efficiency and effectiveness of EPA enforcement programs" (p. 124).

In offering suggestions for improvements in environmental data collection and agency self-assessment practices, Mintz notes that the EPA and state environmental regulatory agencies should continue collecting data they already focus on, but also include information on the number of pollution sources subject to regulation, greater information on pollution sources inspected, greater detail regarding rates of compliance and recidivism, and various other environmental enforcement information. Mintz argues that no single indicator offers adequate assessment of EPA actions. Collectively, however, numerous measures provide greater direction for the agency and more information on which evaluations of the agency can be made. Mintz acknowledges that these increases in data collection will require additional resources for the EPA and state agencies. Increased resources for data collection and dissemination, however, are likely not the top priority for any agency constantly facing budget cuts.

Mintz's call for enhanced EPA data collection is supported by Rosenbaum (2003, p. 180), who notes:

The rapidly evolving environmental sciences have had a paradoxical impact on the EPA and its mission. The environmental movement has caused the United States to give a much higher scientific priority to basic and applied environmental research than existed before 1970. These sciences now provide an essential technical base on which competent environmental regulation must be grounded.

At the same time, this rising tide of ecological science can produce new data indicating that prior policy decisions may have been based on inadequate information and must be revised.

Rosenbaum's argument can be expanded to include all environmental regulatory agencies and law enforcement groups. Advanced statistical analyses and greater interest in researching environmental issues dictate that useful data be collected and subsequently made available to researchers to analyze their potential impact on policy practices.

RESEARCH ON COMMUNITY JUSTICE

By incorporating a more comprehensive approach to ecological issues, community justice efforts will benefit from recent grassroots environmental efforts. Bullard and Wright (1993, p. 836) suggest that research endeavors should include the public as an equal partner in attempts to build trust with affected communities. They argue that research examining environmental harms within the context of community justice should be geared toward helping troubled communities. In this case, researchers are acting as agents of change (a position we discuss in our concluding chapter), using their research to alter the course of history. This requires researchers to move beyond the traditional treatment of the affected community as "subjects," and that they view this opportunity as something more than just another publication. Bullard and Wright (1993, p. 836) note that "We need a holistic methodology for documenting, remediating, and preventing environmental health problems," suggesting the following recommendations as an entry point to approaching community justice (p. 837):

- Ensuring public participation in research projects, with a particular emphasis on gathering input from the population under study.

- Encouraging both regional and national congressional discussion of individuals, groups, and communities affected or at-risk of facing environmental harms.
- Developing and maintaining a "Division or 'Bureau of Environmental Statistics'" under the direction of the EPA, with the intent to collect and collate environment and health-related information on at-risk groups.
- Conducting follow-up research evaluations of earlier research regarding at-risk groups and communities, with particular consideration to the inconclusiveness of many government-sponsored studies regarding the dangers associated with physical proximity to hazardous waste.

The EPA has made some progress in this area. For instance, the agency's Office of Research and Development, the "scientific and research arm of the EPA," is designed to identify, understand and solve environmental problems, integrate the work of the office's scientific partners (e.g., academia, other agencies, and nations), and "provide leadership in addressing emerging environmental issues and in advancing the science and technology of risk assessment and risk management" (www.epa.gov/ord/htm/aboutord.htm). Further, the creation of the agency's Office of Environmental Information denotes a promising step toward enhanced data dissemination practices. Despite these efforts, much work remains.

LOCAL EFFORTS

Several researchers identify the need to address environmental issues at the local level, as opposed to the historical practice of relying on federal and state agencies to confront environmental issues. In summing up the future of environmental regulation, Edwards (1998, p. 50) focuses on the importance of recognizing the impact of environmental harms at the local level and the uncertainty of environmental protection:

> The preservation and conservation themes originating with the Progressive Conservation Movement are easily identified in the modern environmental movement. Public support for environmental protection remains stable but has shifted from the national level to the local level. Tired of having their wells poisoned by unregulated and irresponsible chemical handlers, members of local communities have become active in

demanding action from the government. While actions have been taken to implement environmental protection laws and regulations, some are eventually called into question as knowledge about the environment increases.

To some, further environmental laws and regulation must be balanced with enhanced enforcement efforts at the local level. Epstein (1998), for instance, argues that hiring enough state enforcement agents to ensure compliance and protection would require a daunting investment, especially since state resources for environmental protection efforts are (currently and historically) underfunded. He argues that the most logical enforcement strategy is to use mechanisms already in place, state and local law enforcement agencies, adding that state and local police officers may provide the best means for increasing community awareness of environmental violations and for decreasing the number of violations people commit because they think no one is looking. Adding these duties to those of local police makes sense (because police have intimate knowledge of the communities they serve), and would help dissolve the stereotype concerning the difference between the impact and seriousness of environmental and street crime on society.

Hammett and Epstein (1993, p. xi–xii) also offer recommendations to help local authorities enhance their responses to environmental crime. They recommend: (1) local prosecutors, law enforcement officials, and regulators devote further attention and commitment to environmental crime, (2) an overall "Heightened public awareness of environmental crime," and (3) improved information exchange between those charged with addressing environmental crimes. In general, these recommendations highlight the need for information dissemination with regard to environmental crime. Many of these issues could be empirically evaluated through available data.

EPA REFORM

Many authors have offered direction for EPA reform efforts, although as stated throughout this work, the EPA does not operate in a vacuum and is subject to various powerful influences including the public, Congress, the Executive Office of the federal government, and industry. Nevertheless, calls for reform should be duly considered in light of the problems faced by the agency and the need for enhanced regulatory efforts.

In his examination of potential reforms at the EPA, Rosenbaum (2003, pp. 194–196) provides direction for the agency with regard to more efficient and effective environmental regulation. Although he openly admits his suggested areas of EPA reform have been proposed by most major independent commissions that have examined the EPA since 1990 (Rosenbaum, 2003), they nevertheless provide a starting point for reorientation of EPA regulations. Among other things, Rosenbaum calls for an EPA-congressional charter that would clearly define the agency's mission, and provide relief for the EPA from unreasonable regulatory deadlines, administrative rules, and program objectives put forth in congressional environmental legislation. Following Bullard and Wright (1993), Rosenbaum (2003) also calls for the EPA to increase its environmental monitoring, data collection, and data interpretation efforts. Rosenbaum notes that the creation of the Office of Environmental Information signifies a step in this direction, although he calls for additional personnel and funding to support more elaborate federal- and state-level efforts to improve existing data sources and develop new ones. He further argues that the EPA should offer incentives and resources to improve the quality of environmental information collected at the state level.

Rosenbaum (2003, p. 195) further argues that the EPA establish an organizational culture that is "more receptive to alternative, innovative approaches to environmental prosecution" and less dependent on command-and-control regulation. In anticipating how the EPA can prepare for reform efforts, Rosenbaum notes that Congress may be the most influential agency shaping EPA reform, an argument supported by Mintz (1995, p. 127) who states that given the EPA's "...often stormy history of adversarial relationships with Congress, EPA's top leaders would be well advised to cultivate a smooth working partnership with interested lawmakers on Capitol Hill." These calls for enhanced efforts are reflective of calls for improvement within the EPA by numerous researchers. Whether they come to fruition depends on many factors, including the actions of future EPA directors and all others with a role in shaping future EPA efforts.

These are but a few of the many issues facing environmental protection in the future. While the actions taken at the local level offer promise for active involvement among groups historically absent from activism, there remains numerous issues worthy of proactive efforts to prevent future problems, and several promising alternatives/responses.

SUSTAINABLE DEVELOPMENT

Perhaps one of the most promising and pressing issues concerning environmental regulation and protection is sustainable development. In their informative discussion of this issue, Vig and Kraft (2003, p. 391) argue that "The concept of sustainable development has emerged as the most widely recognized framework for addressing environmental concerns throughout the world." Broadly defined by Paehlke (2003, p. 57) as "the capacity to continuously produce the necessities of a quality human existence within the bounds of a natural world of undiminished quality," sustainable development involves long-range planning as opposed to immediate reactions. Paehlke (2003, p. 58) adds that:

> Environmental sustainability encompasses high performance levels within three measurable sets of environmental values: (1) human health (especially as affected by air and water quality and the purity and naturalness of food), (2) ecosystem health (the protection of habitat, wilderness, and biodiversity), and (3) resource sustainability. Resource sustainability, the narrower sense of sustainability, is achieved through the effective management of society's total material and energy requirements.

Vig and Kraft (2003) argue that sustainable development requires, at minimum, coordination among government agencies with the intent to prevent departments from working toward conflicting purposes, and that "sustainable development supercedes environmental policy in the sense that all public policy and private activities ultimately must be concerned with environmental sustainability" (p. 392). They add that sustainable development has many meanings and deserves greater discussion and research than has occurred to this point, and that concrete indicators are required for measuring progress toward sustainability in various areas (Vig & Kraft, 2003). The need for future research in this area dictates a more interdisciplinary approach to ecological issues than we have seen in the past. Such an interdisciplinary approach results in the need for data collection from a variety of fields and resources. This issue is briefly addressed below.

NEW AND EVOLVING ISSUES

A look to the future of environmental issues remains incomplete absent a look at "problems" likely to impact the environment. We use the term "problems" loosely due to the possibility of proactive efforts which could successfully address several of these issues prior to their becoming problematic, or at the very least mitigate their impact. Our account of these issues is taken from the work of Vig and Kraft (2003) who note that various environmental issues remain unresolved despite three decades of progress. They provide a non-exhaustive list of some of the most important problems expected to confront the United States in the future, with a particular emphasis on sustainable development (pp. 393-397):

- **Energy Consumption and Climate Change** (e.g., the impact of fossil fuel burning including its potential impact on global climate change).
- **Biodiversity and Endangered Species** (e.g., climate change and loss of biodiversity are considered the greatest long-term threats to the global environment).
- **Clean Water and Wetlands** (e.g., it remains unclear if overall surface water quality has improved in the U.S. despite three decades of regulation in this area).
- **Hazardous and Nuclear Waste** (e.g., storing, treating, and disposing of hazardous and toxic wastes remains problematic despite increasing efforts by manufacturers to reduce the use of hazardous and toxic materials).
- **Suburban Sprawl and Sustainable Communities** (e.g., community-based initiatives and the relationship between "smart growth" and continued development of the environment).
- **Environmental Justice** (see Chapter 2).
- **International Leadership and Global Security** (e.g., there remains many issues requiring more intensive international cooperation).

Vig and Kraft (2003) argue that the future is not as gloomy as it may seem from these and other impending problems. They note that professionals from several fields (e.g., economists, business leaders, government officials, and environmental professionals) believe "that more efficient and cost-effective methods are necessary in order to address the expanding environmental agenda" (Vig & Kraft, 2003, p. 399). To demonstrate that all is not gloomy, Vig and Kraft (2003, pp. 399-403) identify seven areas in which new policy efforts are receiving significant attention:

- Pollution Prevention
- Risk Assessment and the Precautionary Principle
- Environmental Taxes, Incentives, and Markets
- Devolution to States and Communities
- Collaborative Planning
- Environmental Research and Technology Development
- Sustainability Indicators

Their work on identifying problems and noting proposed and current solutions is commendable. We strongly urge that environmental research, and all research for that matter, continue to not only identify areas of concern but offer sound solutions to address current or potential problems.

OUR LOOK TO THE FUTURE

In light of these (and other) projections and our experience in this area, we offer our look to the future with a particular emphasis on issues pertaining to studies of environmental crime. Our projections, along with others previously mentioned in this work, are non-exhaustive and many have been discussed in previous accounts of projected environmental crime issues. Our offering, where feasible, considers recent developments already impacting studies of environmental crime.

Increased Environmental Crime Research
Empirical research on environmental crime dates back to the mid-1980s and early 1990s, a brief history by any account. In addressing future directions for environmental crime research, Rebovich (1998) adds that basically no empirical studies observed environmental crimes and government responses to these offenses prior to the mid-1980s. Rebovich (1998, p. 351) sums up the situation regarding empirical assessments of environmental crime enforcement efforts in suggesting that:

> Research in this area is in its infancy, and much work remains to be done. Thus far, attention has mainly been focused on characterizing typical offenders, delineating the methods for committing criminal acts, and determining how alleged offenders are handled in the criminal justice system. While this research provides a notable preliminary step, more specific attention is needed.

It is suggested that the increased research focus on environmental crime, including responses to such actions, will likely result in more effective regulation of the environment. It remains important for sound research to be supported by relevant policy approaches. The EPA and others have taken steps toward facilitating such research, particularly through offering grants and providing other avenues of support for empirical evaluations. The growing body of ecological research must be accessible to those in government and the general public to enable proper consideration of future environmental regulatory direction. Similar to current efforts to seek proper remedial efforts for violators of more traditional laws, it is argued that we continue to seek the proper means to ensure that the environment is protected from those who seek to harm it, and we find the most effective means to address those who violate environmental laws.

Based on the increasing body of environmental studies and the awareness of agencies such as the EPA to make data available to the public, it is felt that the growing body of environmental crime research will continue to expand. Supported by increased funding opportunities (e.g., EPA grants) and increased use of data available via the Internet, research in this area is projected to increase in the forthcoming years. The existence and development of academic programs focused on environmental issues, and the increasing frequency with which environmental crime and justice research appears in scholarly journals suggest the area is becoming well-grounded among researchers.

A primary obstacle to increased research in this area is the recent government practice of removing "sensitive" material from public access. In light of recent events such as the September 11, 2001 terrorist attacks and the war with Iraq, and with the corresponding concern for homeland security, public agencies throughout the nation have removed documents from public access. While much information remains freely available, some restrictions are projected to continue in light of our concern for terrorism. While this seems to contradict our suggestion that data are widely available for studying environmental crime, and that research in this area will continue to grow, only certain "sensitive" information has been removed and there remains available to the public a wealth of untapped information that would provide little, if any support to terrorist activities. Researchers should keep in mind the utility of the Freedom of Information Act if they are unable to locate information they need.

Potentially Enhanced Regulatory Efforts

Recent concern for homeland security may result in enhanced regulation of industry. One of the most promising results of recent events is the effort to organize federal law enforcement activities that impact the efficiency and effectiveness of environmental regulations. It is believed that government agents will become more involved in social control efforts, not necessarily out of concern for ecological destruction, but as a security issue. Any intrusion into industry for the purposes of national security could have the secondary effect of exposing harms to the environment, or could possibly deter violators who recognize their vulnerability to exposure given the government's greater involvement in their practices. Not all areas of industry are affected by recent events; however, it is felt that greater formal social control efforts could result in enhanced environmental regulation.

The Continued Influence of Politics

Environmental crime enforcement efforts will likely continue to be influenced by the party affiliation of those controlling the presidency and Congress. Following an established pattern, Republicans will continue to promote less regulation (e.g., the new power plant rules President Bush supported that went into effect in late August, 2003) than Democratic parties, although public opinion has, and will be a wildcard in this trend. Few presidents (or politicians at any level) have been able to ignore public concern for the environment (though some have tried). Should society become increasingly concerned about environmental issues, the party affiliation of the president (or the congressional majority) will have limited impact on environmental regulation. It is unfortunate, but it may take another significant environmental disaster (e.g., the damage caused by the Exxon *Valdez*) before we see any substantial increase in public concern for the environment.

An Increased Focus on Global Environmentalism

The rise of globalism in many fields of study and society in general means that environmental regulation on a global basis will no longer be merely a topic of discussion, but instead a long overdue reality. The need to look beyond national boundaries is becoming popular in many countries, and global environmentalism is perhaps one of the primary areas of concern. Recent protests against the World Trade Organization (e.g., Vogel, 2003), the recent "World Summit on Sustainable Development" (e.g., Taylor, 2002), and the overall move toward global trade and commerce serve as evidence of this argument. Much work remains in this area, as finding common ground among countries regarding any issue can be problematic. In light of the recent decision by President Bush to withdraw the United States from the Kyoto Protocol on climate change (Vig, 2003), the United States, in particular, as a world leader in production and manufactured goods must consider its role in global environmentalism.

Increased Interdisciplinary Study of Environmental Issues

In addition to the need for environmental issues to be addressed in international terms, there is also a need for different fields of study to break down the traditional walls hampering interdisciplinary research and work together in more effective research efforts. For instance, Elkington (1998) argues that environmental sustainability involves three sets of environmental values: resource sustainability, ecosystem health, and human health. Given the varied nature of the fields involved with these values, studying and researching these areas requires input from several perspectives, and is necessary to assess the impact of efforts surrounding sustainable development. One would be hard-pressed to find researchers who maintain expertise in each of these particular areas, thus cooperative research efforts are needed among the humanities and sciences.

Greater Societal Consideration of Sustainable Development

It is anticipated that the concept of sustainable development will grow in popularity and cross-discipline studies will provide insight regarding the effectiveness of this innovative approach. The complex nature of environmental crime dictates the incorporation of knowledge from a variety of disciplines. For instance, criminologists and criminal justice researchers, by nature of their training, are generally unaware of the meaning behind many environmental indicators, while most environmental researchers are unfamiliar with criminal behavior and legal studies. The Delphi Technique is an appropriate research methodology that brings together researchers from relevant fields of study to forecast future trends. It is argued, and hoped, that research of this nature can be conducted to not only forecast accurately, but also to study recent phenomena.

F. Scott Fitzgerald once noted that "Optimism is the content of small men in high places." No doubt our look at the future is, in places, overly optimistic and somewhat simplistic. We leave the hard core forecasting to futurist researchers who give due consideration to all relevant variables, including political, social, and economic factors.

CHAPTER 14

In Conclusion...

This book has guided readers through some of the central concerns, laws, harms, and data on environmental crime. The primary purpose of discussing legal issues was to provide a context for the data we desired to bring to the attention of criminologists and other social scientists. We have also provided numerous examples of the kinds of data, and output researchers can derive from the data we have examined, in the hope of stimulating research into the neglected issue of environmental crime. We introduced, but did not fully discuss issues of harm, which we address more completely below.

As stated earlier, the study of environmental crimes is a relatively recent area of research. The study of environmental law also has a short history, spanning only a quarter of a century. When researchers first became interested in environmental crime, they had to employ their skills and imaginations (and some luck) to discover sources of data that could be used to describe and study these acts. Today, many environmental crime data sets are available to the public through the Internet, creating easier access for researchers and opening this area for new investigations and replications of existing research findings.

Historically, the study of crime has focused almost exclusively on crimes most likely to be committed by the lower classes. Though this criticism was levied thirty years ago, it remains true today. It bears mention that in the late 1930s, Sutherland made a similar claim about corporate crime in general. Over the 75 years that have elapsed since that time, criminologists and sociologists still pay precious little attention to issues of corporate crime, and even less to environmental crime. It is safe to estimate that in any given year, 95 percent of academic research on crime involves ordinary crime or street crime. These are the crimes most likely to involve criminals from relatively powerless social and economic positions. In contrast, environmental crimes, which are typically committed by the most economically and socially powerful, remain neglected academic subjects.

PERCEIVING CRIMINAL VICTIMIZATION

You have every right to feel upset when someone steals or vandalizes your property. Maybe you worked long and hard to be able to afford your vehicle; perhaps the property had some significant value as a memento; or, perhaps you felt something larger. Perhaps you felt that your social rights were violated or that you have been harmed in some way that is not easily described in terms of financial loss. Whatever the reason for your emotional state, you feel a sense of victimization. But, let us take a moment to place the harms that result from these common criminal acts in perspective.

The average financial loss a person incurs from acts of theft or vandalism ranges from a few dollars for larceny thefts, to several thousand dollars for motor vehicle theft (before insurance coverage is included). Besides the financial loss, a stolen car is an inconvenience. Your victimization may leave you feeling unsafe at home for a period of time if you were the victim of a burglary. In response to any of these forms of criminal victimization, you may say "Why me?" Let's put this feeling into context.

Maybe you are unlucky enough to be among the 3 percent of New York City residents who were the victims of larceny-theft; or the 1.5 percent of New Yorkers who had their motor vehicle stolen; or the 1.4 percent who had their dwelling burglarized (note that these are simple percentages that do not take account of multiple victimizations of the same person. Doing so would lower these percentages, but probably not substantially). After all, there are 10 million other people in New York City who could have been the victims of these acts in addition to you. Why you and not someone else? There is a bright side—at least you weren't among the most unlucky crime victims—the 2 percent of New York City residents who were the victims of violent crimes that included murder, rape, assault, and robbery. Or, are you really that lucky after all?

Residents of major U.S. cities are exposed to a broad spectrum of pollution. They breathe polluted air; they may drink polluted water; they may live in housing built on a former landfill or on or near a hazardous waste site, or near an industry that emits toxins. Each time a person who lives in these circumstances takes a breath or a drink, every moment they live on contaminated ground, they are being violently, although silently victimized by pollution. They are victims of toxic or environmental crimes. Many more people share this experience than that of being the victim of common or street crime.

Because environmental crimes don't confront us in the same way as ordinary street crimes like theft, we may be unaware we are being victimized. We may see our victimization, if we perceive being a victim at all, as the result of our own choice (if it was your choice) of living in a large city. Then again, no one asked you if it was acceptable for them to pollute the air you breathe, or the water you drink, or to manufacture products that create toxic by-products near your residence. Like the street criminal who steals your property, the environmental criminal doesn't ask for your permission, at least not directly. S/he may ask your governmental representatives for permission to victimize you by lobbying for reduced air pollution thresholds, or seeking higher limits on pollutions permits they hold. And, when given permission to victimize you, it is not against the law to generate pollution, at least not from a strictly legal standpoint or from the perspective of criminal law. After all, the person/entity in question has a permit! Still, if the laws that are supposed to protect you are lax, does this mean that you are not being victimized? We, as citizens, should expect to be protected from environmental crime and the violence it creates.

ENVIRONMENTAL VIOLENCE

When you are the victim of an environmental crime, you are the victim of violence. Environmental crimes cause you to be exposed to chemicals that harm your body. Exposure to various air, water, and soil pollutants can cause you to suffer from potentially lethal diseases and illnesses. Scientists, for example, have found that death rates increase with the number of days of unhealthy air a city experiences (Davis, 2002). Exposure to pollutants may affect you directly, or it may affect you indirectly by harming a member of your family. Exposure to toxic pollutants may even affect future generations by causing genetic mutations, or affecting sperm or egg cells, or altering hormonal levels. In short, environmental crimes of pollution are serious problems that can affect the health, well being, and longevity of you and future generations.

These arguments are not always widely accepted. For example, if we were to cite the consistent rise in rates of cancer in the United States since 1950 as evidence of this effect, naysayers might argue that this is the product of our enhanced ability to diagnose cancer. Because we are better at finding cancer than we were 30 or 40 years ago, the cancer rate has naturally increased. To be sure, there is some truth in this argument—but it is not the whole truth. Those who disagree might also state that because people now live longer, and because diseases like cancer may take decades to develop, cancers are naturally more prevalent in populations in which people live longer. Again, there is some truth to this statement, but it doesn't tell the whole story because the rise in the cancer rate is greater than can be expected from a shift in the age-structure of the population. Or, someone might argue that the rise in cancer is due to the poor diets and lifestyles of those who contract this disease. To be sure, this criticism also has some validity. None of these arguments, however, adequately explain the rise in cancer. For example, if cancer and age are related, and cancers take many decades to develop, why has there also been an increase in the cancer rate among young children over the same time period, especially in rare cancers like cancer of the brain? These criticisms also don't account for the fact that other diseases that bear a relationship to diet and lifestyle, such as heart attacks (which also bear a relationship to the age-structure of society), have been declining over the same time period while cancer rates have been rising. In short, there is something to worry about in rising cancer rates that cannot be easily explained. That something, we suggest, is the level of environmental pollution to which our society has been and is being exposed.

ENVIRONMENTAL CRIMES OF VIOLENCE VS. ORDINARY CRIMES OF VIOLENCE

Environmental crimes are not the only crimes that cause bodily harm, and many people worry much more about being the victim of a homicide. On average, over the past decade about 20,000 Americans were the victims of homicide each year. In any given year, the percentage of the U.S. population that is murdered represents about 0.2 percent of the crimes that occur in any given year, and affect only about 0.007 percent of the U.S. population. Let us put this into greater context by relating these facts about homicide to data from New York City.

During 2000, New York City police received reports of 139,664 larceny-thefts; 35,847 motor-vehicle thefts, and 37,112 burglaries. In contrast, there were 673 reports of murder and non-negligent manslaughter, meaning that you were 207 times more likely to be the victim of larceny-theft, 53 times more likely to have your vehicle stolen, or 55 times more likely to have been burglarized (assuming each person in the population has equal odds of being the victim of any of these crimes) than to have been murdered. These odds, however, are affected by age (decrease with age), race (whites are less likely than non-whites to be victims), gender (males are more likely than females to be victims), and social class (victimization increases as social class declines, with few exceptions). In short, homicide is a rare form of violence. Despite this fact, we worry a great deal about being murdered. It is much more likely, however, that you will be the victim of an environmental crime of violence.

Each year in the United States, three times as many people die from diseases contracted in the workplace that are the result of exposure to environmental contamination or workplace pollution than by homicide (Leigh et al., 2000). And, as Leigh and colleagues point out, their estimate of work-related disease deaths is underestimated because of problems linking causes of death to exposure to toxins that may have occurred decades earlier, and the unwillingness of physicians to list occupational exposure as a probable or possible cause of death. This figure could, in other words, be substantially higher than the estimate provided by Leigh and colleagues. This figure, however, doesn't tell the whole story. We need to add to this figure the number of people who die each year from exposure to toxic pollution outside the workplace. Unfortunately, there is no reliable estimate of this figure. Nevertheless, since the workforce is about one-half of the U.S. population, and workplace exposure is limited to one-third of five days each week (40 hours), we can assume that at least an equivalent number of people may die from exposure to toxic pollution outside the workplace. (One-half the population works, and may be exposed to 40 hours of workplace toxins and 128 hours of non-workplace toxins. The other half of the population—the nonworking population is exposed to a potential 168 hours of non-workplace toxins. In this simple example, we do not attempt to account for variations in exposure across occupations or residencies of non-working or working populations).

Since workplace environmentally related disease deaths are probably under-reported, we can assume the same about non-workplace environmentally related disease deaths. Further, it is probably even less likely that non-workplace deaths are rightfully attributed to environmental pollutants given the vast number of potential sources of exposure. Thus, we will assume that the average person is 8 to 10 times more likely to die from exposure to environmental toxins than by homicide, or that 160,000 to 200,000 people die each year from exposure to toxic pollution inside and outside of work compared to the 20,000 people who die from homicide each year. In a city the size of New York, this means there are up to 6730 deaths annually that can be attributed to exposure to environmental pollution. This is certainly something to worry about, and we have not even addressed the serious illnesses, which number in the millions, that may be attributed to exposure to environmental pollution in and outside of the workplace (see Leigh et al., 2000 for discussion).

Viewed relative to serious acts of violence that we ordinarily fear, such as homicide, it is clear why the violence caused by environmental pollution is important; more so than homicide, your life is threatened by environmental crimes of pollution. But these crimes have an even greater impact—they may be threatening the world's ecosystem, causing an unprecedented decline in species, from the smallest to the largest, while impacting the entire web of life through related phenomenon like global warming. For instance, during 2002 alone, the Arctic and Greenland ice caps receded by 650,000 square miles, while glaciers in Alaska were found to be melting at twice the rate previously assumed (Whitty, 2003).

Increased global temperatures have raised ocean levels and altered weather patterns, threatening the existence of island-based nations, such as Tuvalu, home to about 9,000 human inhabitants (Whitty, 2003). This is why the U.N.'s global warming treaty, the Kyoto Protocol (which the U.S. and Australia, the two largest per capita greenhouse gas producers, have failed to endorse) is so important. In short, crimes that we don't fear, like environmental crimes, possess the potential to destroy the world. Ordinary crimes, while having negative impacts on society, have yet to threaten the world, even though these latter crimes have existed for millenniums.

Our point in making these comparisons and bringing this information to your attention is not to be mellow-dramatic, but to force you to seriously consider the relative nature of the violent threats posed to you and society by common crimes and environmental crimes. Environmental crimes cause more financial and physical harm, are treated less seriously, and are more likely to be ignored than street crimes. They are committed by the most socially and economically powerful people in our society rather than by the powerless.

In making these points, we are not attempting to scare you; we are trying to change the way you perceive the world around you, and those behaviors that pose the greatest threats to you. Thus, for example, the next time you hear a politician give a "get tough on crime" speech in an effort to sway your vote, raise your voice and ask him/her what they are planning to do about the serious threat posed to society by environmental crimes and criminals. Since most major politicians are financially supported by persons maintaining an association to organizations that commit environmental crimes (such as the oil and gas, chemical, and automobile industries), they are unlikely to address your questions in any meaningful manner. As an example, consider the

George W. Bush administration's stance on global warming and the Kyoto Protocol, or air pollution, or water pollution standards. The Bush administration has strong ties to industries, such as the oil and energy industries, that make the most significant contributions to global warming. In each case, the Bush administration has sided with the industries that are adding to, rather than solving, our pollution problems. These companies want reduced pollution standards to enhance their profits. What we should be asking them to do is find new ways to produce commodities that can also create profits (and jobs), enhance our lives, and simultaneously protect our health and well being. This is not some pie-in-the-sky idea. Companies, such as Xerox, which produces zero-waste Lake brand copiers, and Interface, which manufactures recycled carpeting, are already on the cutting edge of sustainable, low-level pollution production procedures. Offending companies can be forced to comply if our elected representatives in government hear our collective voices alert them to the fact that we want pollution standards raised. This will only happen if citizens become involved in the political process and become members of environmentally conscious groups.

TAKING ACTION

It is of the utmost importance that the general public voices their opinions regarding environmental pollution. Public opinion polls demonstrate the concern American citizens have for environmental issues. But, polls only go so far. To demonstrate that the public is concerned for the environment and is willing to act on their concerns, they must become active in the political arena.

The important role of political activism must also be played by those who study environmental crime and pollution. For too long, academics have either failed to act on the findings of their research, or downplayed the significance of the effects of corporate and environmental crime on society. This position has been recently critiqued by Potter and Miller (2002) who use James Q. Wilson's widely read work on street crime and public policy as a springboard for their discussion. Nearly 25 years earlier, a similar point was made by Jeffrey Reiman (1979) in his book, *The Rich Get Richer and the Poor Get Prison*, when he argued that our obsession with street crime committed by the powerless detracts attention and effort from the more serious crimes, like environmental crimes, committed by the powerful.

Without question, street crime is a serious problem, and it is worthwhile that people study this issue in hopes of eliminating this type of negative behavior. Although the impact of street crime on society pales in comparison to the impact of environmental crimes, most criminologists continue to busy themselves with studies of the causes and extent of street crime while neglecting the more common and dangerous acts of corporate and environmental crime that continuously occur. The number of articles published on environmental crime by criminologists, for example, numbers less than a dozen over the past five years. Many researchers offer excuses for their lack of interest in environmental and corporate crime. As noted earlier, one excuse for the lack of environmental crime research involves the claim that there is insufficient data on environmental crime to study. As we demonstrated throughout this book, such a claim is untenable given the amount of data currently available. Further, academics in other disciplines make much better use of these data than criminologists.

Those who study crime need to reorient their focus to reflect the level of harm caused by environmental crimes. This means focusing more attention on environmental crime, and less on street crime. In our view, making this change is required if criminologists want to continue laying claim to an objective approach. Objectively, it is clear that environmental crimes are more serious than street crime.

Reorienting the study of crime from street crimes to environmental and corporate crime is the first step in a process. The second step requires that social scientists become active participants in the historical struggle to eliminate and reduce the violence caused by environmental and corporate crimes. Some may read this statement and object, believing that adopting this course of action will somehow make the study of crime more subjective. However, the study of criminal behavior has always been rooted in efforts to discover policies that would effectively reduce crime. Criminologists routinely engage in policy analysis and offer suggestions about the best ways to punish, effective treatment strategies, mechanisms for enhancing social bonds, and so on. They have been leaders of the street crime policy movement, and one of the discipline's newest journals, *Crime & Public Policy*, is devoted to this focus. Therefore, it makes little sense to refute our argument by claiming that such an approach is less objective; rather, it is the norm within criminological research.

Today, criminologists remain largely absent from the war on environmental crime. Instead, that war is being waged by people in environmental organizations, and those engaged in political activism, such as the Green Party. By remaining passive observers, criminologists have chosen to side with those who defend the idea that environmental crimes are not serious or worthy of efforts to uproot.

More than passive observers, they have long sided with polluters by helping, as Jeffery Reiman pointed out, detract attention from the behavior of environmental criminals, by focusing attention on what they define as the "real" war on crime—street crime.

The community of academic criminologists possesses the potential to become a substantial agent of change in the historical struggle against environmental crime. They can either accept or reject their obligation as learned individuals to become involved in this effort to change history, which we define as the story of human action and conflict. History, in short, is the story of class struggle, and involves both the story of class struggle itself, and the attempt to move beyond class interests to promote human interests.

Corporations—or, perhaps it is more useful to say the people who benefit most from them, the ruling economic class—fear the history-making potential of the masses (and academics) and regularly engage in efforts to undermine movements that would remake history and shift power away from corporations and the status quo. Those who run corporations may do this by engaging in public relations campaigns that demonstrate a green corporate image (Lynch and Stretesky, 2003). They do so when they engage in research that questions the harms caused by environmental toxins (sometimes directly, and sometimes through "front groups" that appear to be independent of corporate interests). All of these efforts attempt to provide alternative interpretations of environmental harms by offering conflicting evidence of harm. The culmination of this endeavor enhances their ability to control the content of communication about environmental harm. In altering the "data" that enters the communication about environmental harms, corporations also take an active hand in undermining democracy, because democracy has the potential to remake history—to change the rules under which corporations do business. As Harvey Kaye (1996, p. 23) argued, history-making is "a process of struggle for freedom and for justice,...a fight for liberty, equality and democracy." What is at stake in this particular struggle is the effort to attempt to label the noxious environmental harms that corporations perpetuate as criminal acts, which would affect their legitimacy and the difference between them and the common street criminal.

Our point is that the environmental criminologists must connect research to activism and become a conscious participant in the history-making effort designed to ameliorate current levels of environmental crime that threaten the health and well being of current and future generations. The environmental criminologist must, in other words, act on what they have learned from their research efforts. Some might even claim that to do less is to act immorally.

Luckily for the academic, there are a number of options that can be selected to become an active participant in history making, and none will be required to make a supreme sacrifice like giving up their job to become a "tree-hugger." The typical academic criminologist has at their disposal, for example, the students they teach, who can become an audience for communications about environmental crime. Those with active research agendas can alter the content of their research. Active researchers are also invited to participate in policy-making discussions, conferences, and to serve as reviewers of manuscripts submitted for publication. Each of these opportunities is also an opportunity to become an active participant in the struggle against environmental crime.

A CLOSING NOTE

Rebovich (1998, p. 351) argues that "Research on the environmental crime reduction question could prove useful for determining the importance of the relationship between legislation, its enforcement, and legal waste disposal alternatives. Efforts must be made to increase the size and availability of data on environmental crime." The present work is but one small step toward addressing environmental crime concerns. It is hoped that greater public attention will focus on environmental harms and environmental crimes through encouraging researchers to seek and use available data. Ultimately, this project could expand to incorporate data and data sources from other areas with the ultimate goal of compiling a *Sourcebook of White-Collar Crime Statistics*.

Several comments should be made, and limitations noted, regarding the present work. First, many acronyms and technical terms appear that are foreign to those not overly familiar with environmental terminology, thus Appendix C provides a key for the extensive list of acronyms. Second, the purpose of this text was to provide a reference tool for those seeking to research environmental crime; not to provide actual data sets that require detailed explanations. In general, the goal was to demonstrate to researchers: (1) how to access the available data regarding environmental crime, and (2) the available environmental crime data. Footnotes are excluded from many reports/tables presented above, and partial/incomplete tables are sometimes presented. Accordingly, readers are strongly encouraged *not* to use the actual data presented in this work. Those interested in these reports/data are encouraged to visit the sources from which they were taken (references are provided for all reports).

Those familiar with the Internet likely realize that Web sites are constantly changing, and what appears online one day may be gone the next. The data presented above were gathered from reputable, credible sources that are not likely to soon disappear. However, it cannot be certain that these data will be available months from the time of this writing. Based on experience developing this work, we advise anyone interested in gathering environmental crime data to begin exploring the Web site of an appropriate agency. If this approach is unsuccessful, the next best option is to identify the appropriate contact at the agency and inquire. You may be required to become a "squeaky wheel," but your efforts will more than likely be rewarded.

As noted, the above data sets/reports are not comprehensive of what is available. The tables are by no means comprehensive, as there is too much available information for the purposes of this project. Efforts were made, however, to provide a representative sample of the data likely to be of most interest and use to environmental crime researchers. We suggest an expansion of this work to incorporate other areas in facilitating research on "non-traditional crimes," for example, in the automobile and pharmaceutical industries. Appendix A provides a list of agencies that contain information useful for accomplishing this task. We view the current work as a seed to hopefully blossom into something akin to the *Sourcebook of Criminal Justice Statistics*.

Accordingly, we envision expansion of this project to include input from other researchers, and conclude this project with an open invitation to those interested in this field to offer assistance, advice, direction, and any other helpful input. This extensive undertaking involves input from all who are interested in developing this project into something increasingly useful. We welcome positive/critical comments and/or offers for collaboration. What data sets, or areas of environmental crime are absent? What agencies have you used to gather data? How can this work be formatted to best serve environmental crime researchers? We call on those with something to offer to step forward and help advance the field, and hope that this work facilitates your study of environmental crime.

APPENDIX A

AGENCIES AND DATA SOURCES PROVIDING WHITE-COLLAR CRIME DATA

Expansion of this project should identify and include data sources from regulatory and enforcement agencies (among other entities) in other areas, such as those charged with overseeing occupational, automobile, and food and drug regulations. Below we provide a partial list of agencies to be included.

- Bureau of Land Management
- Centers for Disease Control and Prevention
- Commodity Futures Trading Commission
- Consumer Product Safety Commission
- Equal Employment Opportunity Commission
- Federal Aviation Administration
- Federal Communications Commission
- Federal Deposit Insurance Corporation
- Federal Energy Regulatory Commission
- Federal Highway Administration
- Federal Railroad Administration
- Federal Trade Commission
- Food and Drug Administration
- Internal Revenue Service
- Mine Safety and Health Administration
- National Highway Traffic Safety Administration
- National Institutes of Health
- National Park Service
- National Transportation Safety Board
- Nuclear Regulatory Commission
- Occupational Safety and Health Administration
- Securities and Exchange Commission
- U.S. Chemical Safety and Hazard Investigation Board
- U.S. Customs Service
- U.S. Department of Agriculture
- U.S. Department of Commerce
- U.S. Department of Energy
- U.S. Department of Health and Human Services
- U.S. Department of Housing and Urban Development
- U.S. Department of Labor
- U.S. Department of the Interior
- U.S. Department of Transportation
- U.S. Department of Treasury
- U.S. Fish and Wildlife Service
- U.S. International Trade Commission
- U.S. Postal Service
- U.S. Tax Court

APPENDIX B

EPA AND STATE ENVIRONMENTAL REGULATORY AGENCY CONTACT INFORMATION

EPA National Office

Standard Mailing Address
Environmental Protection Agency
Ariel Rios Building
1200 Pennsylvania Avenue, N.W.
Mail Code 3213A
Washington, DC 20460
www.epa.gov
Phone: (202) 260-2090

EPA Regional Offices

Region 1 (CT, MA, ME, NH, RI, VT)
Environmental Protection Agency
1 Congress St., Suite 1100
Boston, MA 02114-2023
www.epa.gov/region01
Phone: (617) 918-1111
Toll free: (888) 372-7341

Region 2 (NJ, NY, PR, VI)
Environmental Protection Agency
290 Broadway
New York, NY 10007-1866
www.epa.gov/region02
Phone: (212) 637-3000

Region 3 (DC, DE, MD, PA, VA, WV)
Environmental Protection Agency
1650 Arch Street
Philadelphia, PA 19103-2029
www.epa.gov/region03
Phone: (215) 814-5000
Toll free: (800) 438-2474

Region 4 (AL, FL, GA, KY, MS, NC, SC, TN)
Environmental Protection Agency
Atlanta Federal Center
61 Forsyth Street, SW
Atlanta, GA 30303-3104
www.epa.gov/region04
Phone: (404) 562-9900
Toll free: (800) 241-1754

Region 5 (IL, IN, MI, MN, OH, WI)
Environmental Protection Agency
77 West Jackson Boulevard
Chicago, IL 60604-3507
www.epa.gov/region5
Phone: (312) 353-2000
Toll free: (800) 621-8431

Region 6 (AR, LA, NM, OK, TX)

Environmental Protection Agency
Fountain Place, Suite 1200
1445 Ross Avenue
Dallas, TX 75202-2733
www.epa.gov/region06
Phone: (214) 665-2200
Toll free: (800) 887-6063

Region 7 (IA, KS, MO, NE)

Environmental Protection Agency
901 North 5th Street
Kansas City, KS 66101
www.epa.gov/region07
Phone: (913) 551-7003
Toll free: (800) 223-0425

Region 8 (CO, MT, ND, SD, UT, WY)

Environmental Protection Agency
999 18th Street, Suite 500
Denver, CO 80202-2466
www.epa.gov/region08
Phone: (303) 312-6312
Toll free: (800) 227-8917

Region 9 (AZ, CA, HI, NV)

Environmental Protection Agency
75 Hawthorne Street
San Francisco, CA 94105
www.epa.gov/region09
Phone: (415) 744-1305

Region 10 (AK, ID, OR, WA)

Environmental Protection Agency
1200 Sixth Avenue
Seattle, WA 98101
www.epa.gov/region10
Phone: (206) 553-1200
Toll free: (800) 424-4372

State Environmental Regulatory Agencies

Alabama Department of Environmental Management

1400 Coliseum Boulevard
Montgomery, AL 36110
www.adem.state.al.us
Phone: (334) 271-7700

Alaska Department of Environmental Conservation

410 Willoughby Avenue
Suite 303
Juneau, AK 99801-1795
www.state.ak.us/dec
Phone: (907) 269-7591

Arizona Department of Environmental Quality

1110 West Washington Street
Phoenix, AZ 85007-2935
www.adeq.state.az.us
Phone: (602) 771-2300

Arkansas Department of Environmental Quality

8001 National Drive
Little Rock, AR 72209
www.adeq.state.ar.us
Phone: (501) 682-0744

California Environmental Protection Agency

1001 I Street
Sacramento, CA 95814
www.calepa.ca.gov
Phone: (916) 445-3846

Colorado Department of Public Health and Environment
4300 Cherry Creek Drive S.
Denver, CO 80246-1530
www.cdphe.state.co.us
Phone: (303) 692-2035

Connecticut Department of Environmental Protection
79 Elm Street
Hartford, CT 06106-5127
www.dep.state.ct.us
Phone: (860) 424-3000

Delaware Department of Natural Resources and Environmental Control
89 Kings Highway
Dover, DE 19901
www.dnrec.state.de.us
Phone: (302) 739-5072

Florida Department of Environmental Protection
3900 Commonwealth Boulevard, M.S. 49
Tallahassee, FL 32399
www.dep.state.fl.us
Phone: (850) 245-2118

Georgia Department of Natural Resources, Environmental Protection Division
2 Martin Luther King Jr. Drive, Suite 1152 East Tower
Atlanta, GA 30334
www.dnr.state.ga.us
Phone: (404) 657-5947

Hawaii Department of Health
1250 Punchbowl Street
Honolulu, HI 96813
www.hawaii.gov/health
Phone: (808) 586-4400

Idaho Department of Environmental Quality
1410 North Hilton
Boise, ID 83706
www.state.id.us/deq
Phone: (208) 373-0502

Illinois Environmental Protection Agency
1021 North Grand Avenue East
Springfield, IL 62702
www.epa.state.il.us
Phone: (217) 782-3397

Indiana Department of Environmental Management
100 North Senate
P.O. Box 6015
Indianapolis, IN 46206-6015
www.in.gov/idem
Phone: (317) 232-8603

Iowa DNR Environmental Protection Division
Henry A. Wallace Bldg.
502 East 9th Street
Des Moines, IA 50319-0034
www.iowadnr.com
Phone: (515) 281-8973

Kansas The Division of Environment
1000 SW Jackson, Suite 420
Topeka, KS 66612-1367
www.kdhe.state.ks.us
Phone: (785) 296-1535

Kentucky Department of Environmental Protection
14 Reilly Road
Frankfort, KY 40601
www.nr.state.ky.us/nrepc/dep/dep2.htm
Phone: (502) 564-2150

Louisiana Department of Environmental Quality
7290 Bluebonnet Boulevard
Baton Rouge, LA 70810
www.deq.state.la.us
Phone: (888) 763-5424

Maine Department of Environmental Protection
17 State House Station
Augusta, ME 04333
www.state.me.us/dep
Phone: (207) 287-7688

Maryland Department of the Environment
1800 Washington Boulevard
Baltimore, MD 21230
www.mde.state.md.us
Phone: (410) 537-3000

Massachusetts Department of Environmental Protection
One Winter Street
Boston, MA 02108-4746
www.state.ma.us/dep
Phone: (617) 292-5500

Michigan Department of Environmental Quality
Constitution Hall
525 West Allegan Street
P.O. Box 30473
Lansing, MI 48909
www.michigan.gov/deq
Phone: (517) 373-7917

Minnesota Pollution Control Agency
520 Lafayette Road
St. Paul, MN 55155
www.pca.state.mn.us
Phone: (651) 296-6300

Mississippi Department of Environmental Quality
2380 Highway 80 West
Jackson, MS 39204
www.deq.state.ms.us
Phone: (888) 786-0661

Missouri Department of Natural Resources, Division of Environmental Quality
P. O. Box 176
Jefferson City, MO 65102
www.dnr.state.mo.us
Phone: (573) 751-3443

Montana Department of Environmental Quality
P.O. Box 200901
1520 East 6th Avenue
Helena, MT 59620
www.deq.state.mt.us
Phone: (406) 444-2544

Nebraska Department of Environmental Quality
1200 "N" Street, Suite 400
PO Pox 98922
Lincoln, NE 68509
www.deq.state.ne.us
Phone: (402) 471-2186

Nevada Division of Environmental Protection
333 W. Nye Lane, Room 138
Carson City, NV 89706-0851
ndep.nv.gov
Phone: (775) 687- 4670

New Hampshire Department of Environmental Services
6 Hazen Drive
P.O. Box 95
Concord, NH 03302-0095
www.des.state.nh.us
Phone: (603) 271-3503

New Jersey Department of Environmental Protection
P.O. Box 402
Trenton, NJ 08625
www.state.nj.us./dep
Phone: (609) 292-2885

New Mexico Environment Department
P.O. Box 26110
1190 St. Francis Drive
Santa Fe, NM 87502
www.nmenv.state.nm.us
Phone: (505) 822-2588

New York Department of Environmental Conservation
625 Broadway
Albany, NY 12233
www.dec.state.ny.us
Phone: (518) 402-8540

North Carolina Department of Environment, Health and Natural Resources
1601 Mail Service Center
Raleigh, NC 27699-1601
www.ehnr.state.nc.us
Phone: (919) 733-4984

North Dakota Department of Health
Environmental Health Section
1200 Missouri Avenue
P.O. Box 5520
Bismarck, ND 58506
www.health.state.nd.us/ndhd/environ
Phone: (701) 328-5150

Ohio Environmental Protection Agency
122 South Front Street
Columbus, OH 43215
www.epa.state.oh.us
Phone: (614) 644-3020

Oklahoma Department of Environmental Quality
707 North Robinson
Oklahoma City, OK 73102
www.deq.state.ok.us
Phone: (405) 702-1000

Oregon Department of Environmental Quality
811 SW Sixth Avenue
Portland, OR 97204-1390
www.deq.state.or.us
Phone: (503) 229-5696

Pennsylvania Department of Environmental Protection
16th Floor, Rachel Carson State Office Building
P.O. Box 2063
Harrisburg, PA 17105-2063
www.dep.state.pa.us
Phone: (717) 783-2300

Rhode Island Department of Environmental Management
235 Promenade Street
Providence, RI 02908-5767
www.state.ri.us/dem
Phone: (401) 222-6800

South Carolina Department of Health and Environmental Control
2600 Bull Street
Columbia, SC 29201
www.scdhec.net/eqc
Phone: (803) 896-8940

South Dakota Department of Environment and Natural Resources
Joe Foss Building
523 East Capitol
Pierre, SD 57501
www.state.sd.us/denr
Phone: (605) 773-3151

Tennessee Department of Environment and Conservation
401 Church Street, 21st Floor
Nashville, TN 37243
www.state.tn.us/environment
Phone: (615) 532-0104

Texas Commission on Environmental Quality
Building Letter
12100 Park 35 Circle
Austin, TX 78753
www.tceq.state.tx.us
Phone: (512) 239-1000

Utah Department of Environmental Quality
168 North 1950 West
Salt Lake City, UT 84116
www.eq.state.ut.us
Phone: (801) 536-4400

Vermont Department of Environmental Conservation
103 South Main Street
Waterbury, VT 05671
www.anr.state.vt.us/dec/dec
Phone: (802) 241-3800

Virginia Department of Environmental Quality
629 East Main Street
P.O. Box 10009
Richmond, VA 23240
www.deq.state.va.us
Phone: (804) 698-4000

Washington Department of Ecology
300 Desmond Drive
Lacey, WA 98503
www.ecy.wa.gov
Phone: (360) 407-6000

West Virginia Department of Environmental Protection
1356 Hansford Street
Charleston, WV 25301
www.dep.state.wv.us
Phone: (304) 558-5929

Wisconsin Department of Natural Resources
101 South Webster Street
P.O. Box 7921
Madison, WI 53707
www.dnr.state.wi.us
Phone: (608) 266-2621

Wyoming Department of Environmental Quality
122 West 25th Street
Herscheler Building
Cheyenne, WY 82002
www.deq.state.wy.us
Phone: (307) 777-7937

APPENDIX C

LIST OF ACRONYMS

ACR	Accidental Chemical Release
AFS	AIRS Facility Subsystem
AGWeb	AIRS Graphics
AHERA	Asbestos Hazard Emergency Response Act
AILESP	American Indian Lands Environmental Support Project
Air RISC	Air Risk Information Center Hotline
AIRS	Aerometric Information and Retrieval System
ALS	American Laquer & Solvents Co.
AQCR	Air Quality Control Region
AQS	Air Quality Subsystem
ARIP	Accidental Reporting Information Program
ASHAA	Asbestos School Hazard Abatement Act
ASHARA	Asbestos School Hazard Abatement Reauthorization Act
ASTER	Assessment Tools for the Evaluation of Risk
BACT	Best Available Control Technology
BASINS	Better Assessment Science Integrating Point and Nonpoint Sources
BAT	Best Available Technology
BCT	Best Conventional Pollution Control Technology
BJS	Bureau of Justice Statistics
BPT	Best Practicable Control Technology
BRS	Biannual Reporting System
CAA	Clean Air Act
CAAA	Clean Air Act Amendments
CAFE	Corporate Average Fuel Economy
CAP	Criteria Air Pollution
CAS	Chemical Abstracts Service
CATC	Clean Air Technology Center
CDCP	Centers for Disease Control and Prevention
CEAM	Center for Exposure Assessment Modeling
CEQ	Council on Environmental Quality
CERCLA	Comprehensive Environmental Response Compensation Liability Act

CERCLIS	Comprehensive Environmental Response Compensation and Liability Information System (CERCLA data)
CFC	Chloroflurocarbons
CFR	Code of Federal Regulations
CHIEF	Clearinghouse for Inventories and Emission Factors
CO	Carbon Monoxide (compound)
CO_2	Carbon Dioxide (compound)
CORR	Chemicals on Reporting Rules
CREM	Council on Regulatory Environmental Modeling
CRM	Criminal Enforcement Docket
CSMoS	Center for Subsurface Modeling Support
CWA	Clean Water Act (see also FWPCA)
DEP	Department of Environmental Protection
DMR	Discharge Monitoring Reports
DOI	Department of the Interior
DOJ	Department of Justice
DOT	Department of Transportation
ECHO	Enforcement and Compliance History Online
ECOS	Environmental Council of the States
EDR	Environmental Data Registry
EFIN	Environmental Financing Information Network
EMCI	Envirofacts Master Chemical Integrator
EPA	Environmental Protection Agency
EPCA	Energy Policy and Conservation Act
EPCRA	Emergency Planning and Community Right to Know Act
ERNS	Emergency Response Notification System
ESA	Endangered Species Act
ESDB	Endangered Species Database
ET	Ecotox Thresholds
ETS	Emissions Tracking System
FACILITY	Facility Index System
FBI	Federal Bureau of Investigation
FDF	Fundamentally Different Factor
FFDCA	Federal Food, Drug, and Cosmetic Act
FFIS	Federal Facility Information System
FIFRA	Federal Insecticide, Fungicide and Rodenticide Act
FII	Federal Identification Initiative
FIRE	Factor Information Retrieval
FMI	Flexible Market Incentives

FOIA	Freedom of Information Act
FQPA	Food Quality Protection Act
FWPCA	Federal Water Pollution Control Act
FY	Fiscal Year

GCS	Geo-Common Subsystem
GIS	Geographic Information System
GRID	Global Resource Information Database
GW	Global Warming

HAP	Hazardous Air Pollutant
HC	Hydrocarbons (chemical)
HCFC	Hydrochloroflurocarbons
HPV	High Priority Violations
HUD	Housing and Urban Development

IDEA	Integrated Data for Enforcement Analysis
IISM	Integrated Iron and Steel Mills
IMIS	Integrated Management Information System
IRIS	Integrated Risk Information System
IRPTC	International Register of Potentially Toxic Chemicals
ISMM	Iron and Steel Mini Mills

LACT	Lowest Achievable Control Technology
LDC	Legacy Data Center
LQG	Large Quantity Generators

MICE	Methods Information Communication Exchange Service
MOD	Maps on Demand
mpg	Miles per gallon
MSEE	Major Source Enforcement Effort
MSW	Municipal Solid Waste

NAAQS	National Ambient Air Quality Standards
NAFTA	North American Free Trade Agreement
NASA	National Aeronautics and Space Administration
NCDB	National Compliance Data Base
NCOD	National Contaminant Occurrence Database
NEDI	National Environmental Data Index
NEPA	National Environmental Protection Act
NESDIS	National Environmental Satellite, Data and Information Service
NESHAP	National Emission Standards for Hazardous Air Pollutants

NFMVEL	New Federal Motor Vehicle Emission Limitations
NGDC	National Geophysical Data Center
NGO	Non-Governmental Organization
NHD	National Hydrography Dataset
NHTSA	National Highway Traffic Safety Administration
NIJ	National Institute of Justice
NIMBY	"Not In My Backyard"
NOAA	National Oceanic and Atmospheric Administration
NO_x	Nitrogen Oxides (various combinations; compound)
NO_2	Nitrogen Dioxide
NPDES	National Pollutant Discharge Elimination System
NPL	National Priorities List
NRC	Nuclear Regulatory Commission
NSCEP	National Service Center for Environmental Publications
NSPS	New Source Performance Standards
NSR	New Source Review
O_3	Ozone (compound)
ODA	Ocean Dumping Act
ODES	Ocean Data Evaluation System
OECA	Office of Enforcement and Compliance Assurance
OEI	Office of Environmental Information
OEJ	Office of Environmental Justice
OPA	Oil Pollution Act
OSHA	Occupational Safety and Health Administration
Pb	Lead (element)
PCS	Permit Compliance System
PDE	Person Days in Exceedance of NAAQS
PDM	Probabilistic Dilution Model
PM	Particle Matter
PM-10	Particle Matter less than 10 microns
PM-2.5	Particle Matter less than 2.5 microns
POTW	Public Owned Treatment Work
POWT	Publicly Owned Water Treatment
PPA	Pollution Prevention Act
PPIC	Pollution Prevention Information Clearinghouse
PPIS	Pesticide Product Information System
ppm	Part per million (measure)
PRP	Potentially Responsible Party
PSD	Prevention of Significant Deterioration
PSI	Pollution Standards Index

QNCR	Quarterly Noncompliance Reports
QUAL2E	Enhanced Stream Water Quality Model, Windows
RACT	Reasonably Available Control Technology
RBLC	RACT/BACT/LAER Clearinghouse
RCRA	Resource Conservation and Recovery Act
RCRIS	Resource Conservation and Recovery Information System
RETC	Retention Curve Computer Code
RITZ	Regulatory and Investigative Treatment Zone Model
RMP	Risk Management Plan
RODS	Record of Decision System
RTK	Right-to-Know Network
RTK NET	Right-to-Know Network (EPCRA data access point)
RUP	Restricted Use Products
SARA	Superfund Amendments and Reauthorization Act
SBAP	Small Business Assistance Program
SCRAM	Support Center for Regulatory Air Models
SDWA	Safe Drinking Water Act
SDWIS	Safe Drinking Water Information System
SEC	Securities and Exchange Commission
SEP	Supplemental Environmental Projects
SETS	Site Enforcement Tracking System
SFIP	Sector Facility Indexing Project
SIP	State Implementation Plan
SIS	Superfund Information Systems
SNC	Significant Noncompliance
SO_2	Sulfur Dioxide (compound)
SQG	Small Quantity Generator
STORET	Storage and Retrieval System for Water and Biological Monitoring Data
SUV	Sport-Utility Vehicle
TCEQ	Texas Commission on Environmental Quality
TDR	Treatment, Disposal and Recycling
TECO	Tampa Electric Company
TMDL	Total Maximum Daily Loads
TNRCC	Texas Natural Resource Conservation Commission
TRI	Toxic Release Inventory
TRIS	Toxic Release Inventory System
TSCA	Toxic Substances Control Act

| TSCATS | Toxic Substances Control Act Test Submissions |
| TSD(F) | Treatment, Storage and Disposal (Facility) |

UAW	United Auto Workers
UNEP	United Nations Environment Programme
USC	United State Code
USGS	United States Geological Survey
UST	Underground Storage Tank
UV	Ultra Violet Radiation

| VOC | Volatile Organic Compound |

| WHO | World Health Organization |

References

Adler, R. W. & Lord, C. (1991). Environmental crimes: Raising the stakes. *The George Washington Law Review, 59*, 781–861.

Albanese, J. (1995). *White-collar crime in America*. Englewood Cliffs, NJ: Prentice Hall.

Allen, M. & Milbank, D. (2003, August 12). Utah Gov. named as chief of EPA; nominee wants power moved out of Washington. *The Washington Post*, p. A1.

Anderton, D., Anderson, A., Rossi, P., Oakes, J., Fraser, M., Weber, W., & Calabrese, E. (1994). Hazardous waste facilities: 'Environmental equity' issues in metropolitan areas. *Evaluation Review, 18*, 123–140.

Anderton, D. Oakes, J., & Egan, K. (1997). Environmental equity in Superfund: Demographics of the discovery and prioritization of abandoned toxic sites. *Evaluation Review, 21*(1), 3–26.

Asch, P. & Seneca, J. (1978). Some evidence on the distribution of air quality. *Land Economics, 54*, 278–298.

Athanasiou, T. (2002). *Divided planet: The ecology of rich and poor*. Athens, Georgia: University of Georgia Press.

Barkdull, J. (1998). Nixon and the marine environment. *Presidential Studies Quarterly, 28*(3), 587–605.

Barnett, H. C. (1993). Crimes against the environment: Superfund enforcement at last. *The Annals, 525*, 119–133.

Bellini, J. (1986). *High tech holocaust*. London: David & Charles.

Boer, T., Pastor, M., Sadd, J., & Snyder, L. (1997). Is there environmental racism? The demographics of hazardous waste in Los Angeles County. *Social Science Quarterly, 78*, 793–810.

Bowen, W., Salling, M., Haynes, K., & Cyran, E. (1995). Toward environmental justice: Spatial equity in Ohio and Cleveland. *Annals of the Association of American Geographers, 85*, 641–663.

Bowman, A. (1984). Intergovernmental and intersectoral tensions in environmental policy implementation: The case of hazardous waste. *Policy Studies Review, 4*, 230–244.

Brace, C. L. (1872). *The dangerous classes of New York and twenty years' work among them*. New York: Wynkoop & Hallenbeck.

Brajer, V. & Hall, J. (1992). Recent evidence on the distribution of air pollution effects. *Contemporary Policy Issues, 6*, 63–71.

Brever, J. (1993, July). Nuclear whistleblower. *The Progressive, 57*, 36.

Brown, M. H. (1980). *Laying waste: The poisoning of America by toxic chemicals*. New York: Pantheon.

Brown, M. H. (1988). *The toxic cloud: The poisoning of America's air*. New York: Harper & Row.

Brown, P. & Mikkelsen, E. J. (1990). *No safe place: Toxic waste, leukemia, and community action*. Berkeley, CA: University of California.

Bullard, R. (1990, 1994). *Dumping in Dixie: Race, class and environmental quality*. Boulder, CO: Westview.

313

Bullard, R. (1996). Environmental justice: It's more than waste facility siting. *Social Science Quarterly, 77*, 493–499.

Bullard, R. D. & Wright, B. H. (1992). The quest for environmental equity: Mobilizing the African-American community for change." In R. E. Dunlap and A. G. Mertig, (Eds.), *American environmentalism: The U.S. environmental movement, 1970–1990* (pp. 39–49). New York: Taylor and Francis.

Bullard, R. D. & Wright, B. H. (1993). Environmental justice for all: Community perspectives on health and research needs. *Technology and Industrial Health, 9*(5), 821–841.

Burby, R. J. & Strong, D. E. (1997). Coping with chemicals: Blacks, whites, planners, and industrial pollution. *Journal of the American Planning Association, 63*, 469–480.

Burns, R. (1999). Realities of automobile safety. *Transportation Quarterly, 53*(1), 83–92.

Burns, R. G. and Lynch, M. J. (2002). Another fine mess . . . : A preliminary examination of the use of fines by the National Highway Traffic Safety Administration. *Criminal Justice Review, 27*(1), 1–25.

Cable, S. & Benson, M. (1993). Acting locally: Environmental injustice and the emergence of grass–roots environmental organizations. *Social Problems, 40*(4), 464–477.

Cable, S. & Cable, C. (1995). *Environmental problems, grassroots solutions: The politics of grassroots environmental conflict.* New York: St. Martin's Press.

Caldicott, H. (1992). *If you love this planet: A plan to heal the Earth.* New York: Norton.

Cannon, L. (2000). *President Reagan: The role of a lifetime.* New York: Public Affairs.

Capek, S. M. (1993). The 'environmental justice' frame: A conceptual discussion and application. *Social Problems, 40*(1), 5–24.

Carpenter, M. (1851). *Reformatory schools for the children of the perishing and dangerous classes and for juvenile offenders.* New York: A.M. Kelly.

Carson, R. (1962). *Silent Spring.* Boston, MA: Houghton Mifflin.

Carter, T. (1998). Policing the environment. In M. Clifford (Ed.), *Environmental crime: Enforcement, policy, and social responsibility* (pp. 169–203). Gaithersburg, MD: Aspen.

Chevalier, L. (1973). *Laboring classes and dangerous classes in Paris during the first half of the nineteenth century.* New York: Fertig.

Clark, R. D., Lab, S., & Stoddard, L. (1995). "Environmental equity: A critique of the literature." *Social Pathology, 1*(3), 253–269.

Clear, T. (2001). Thinking strategically about the American Society of Criminology. *The Criminologist, 26*(1), pp. 1, 3–7.

Clifford, M. (Ed.). (1998). *Environmental crime: Enforcement, policy, and social responsibility.* Gaithersburg, MD: Aspen.

Clifford, M. & Edwards, T. (1998). Defining 'environmental crime.' In M. Clifford (Ed.), *Environmental crime: Enforcement, policy, and social responsibility* (pp. 5–30). Gaithersburg, MD: Aspen.

Cockrell, R. (1992). *A green shrouded miracle: The administrative history of the Cuyahoga Valley National Recreational Area.* Omaha, NE: National Park Service.

Cohen, B. R. (1998). Polluted agency. *National Review, 50*(14), 38–39.

Cohen, M. A. (1989). Corporate crime and punishment: A study of social harm and sentencing practices in federal courts, 1984–1987. *American Criminal Law Review, 26*, 605–662.

Cohen, M. A. (1992). Environmental crime and punishment: Legal/economic theory and empirical evidence on enforcement of environmental statutes. *The Journal of Criminal Law & Criminology, 82*, 1054–1108.

Cohen, M. A. (1998). Sentencing the environmental criminal. In M. Clifford (Ed.), *Environmental crime: Enforcement, policy, and social responsibility* (pp. 229–249). Gaithersburg, MD: Aspen.

Cohen, S. A. (1986). EPA: A qualified success. In S. Kamieniecki, R. O'Brien, & M. Clarke (Eds.), *Controversies in environmental policy* (pp. 174–198). Westport, CT: Greenwood Press.

Colborn, T., Dumanoski, D., & Myers, J. (1998). *Our stolen future: Are we threatening our fertility, intelligence and survival? A scientific detective story.* New York: Penguin.

Conca, K. (2000, Winter). American environmentalism confronts the global economy. *Dissent, 47*(1), 72–78.

Couch, S. R. & Kroll–Smith, S. (1997). Environmental movements and expert knowledge: Evidence for a new populism. *International Journal of Contemporary Sociology, 34*(2), 185–210.

Cutter, S. (1994). The burdens of toxic risks: Are they fair? *Business and Economic Review, 41*, 3–7.

Davies, J. C., III. (1970). *The politics of pollution.* New York: Bobbs-Merrill.

Davis, D. (2002). *When smoke ran like water: Tales of environmental deception and the battle against pollution.* New York: Basic Books.

Daynes, B. (1999). Bill Clinton: Environmental president. In D. L. Soden (Ed.), *The environmental presidency* (pp. 259–312). New York: State University of New York Press.

DiMento, J. F. (1990, April). Polluters beware. *The Economist, 315*, 38.

DiMento, J. F. (1993). Criminal enforcement of environmental law. *The Annals, 525*, 134–146.

Dowie, M. (1995, March/April). The fourth wave. *Mother Jones, 20*, 34–36.

Downey, L. (1998). Environmental injustice: Is race or income a better predictor? *Social Science Quarterly, 79*, 766–778.

Dunlap, R. & Mertig, A. (1992). *American environmentalism: The U.S. environmental movement, 1970–1990.* Washington, DC: Taylor and Francis.

Earickson, R. J. & Billick, I. H. (1988, January). The areal association of urban air pollutants and residential characteristics: Louisville and Detroit. *Applied Geography,* pp. 5–23.

Edwards, S. M. (1996). Environmental criminal enforcement: Efforts by the states. In S. Edwards, T. Edwards, & C. Fields (Eds.), *Environmental crime and criminality: Theoretical and practical issues* (pp. 205–244). New York: Garland.

Edwards, S. M. (1998). A history of the U.S. environmental movement. In M. Clifford (Ed.), *Environmental crime: Enforcement, policy, and social responsibility* (pp. 31–56). Gaithersburg, MD: Aspen.

Edwards, S. M., Edwards, T. D., & Fields, C. B. (1996). *Environmental crime and criminality: Theoretical and practical issues.* New York: Garland.

Ehrlich, P. H. (1969). *The population bomb.* New York: Ballantine Books.

Elkington, J. (1998). *Cannibals with forks: The triple bottom line of 21st century business.* Stony Creek, CT: New Society Publishers.

Environmental Protection Agency. (1990). *Reducing risk: Setting priorities and strategies for environmental protection.* Washington, DC: U.S. EPA.

Environmental Protection Agency. (1999). *Enforcement and compliance assurance: FY 98 accomplishments report.* Washington, DC: U.S. EPA.

Epstein, J. (1998). State and local environmental enforcement. In M. Clifford (Ed.), *Environmental crime: Enforcement, policy, and social responsibility* (pp. 145–169). Gaithersburg, MD: Aspen.

Epstein, J. & Hammett, T. (1995). Law enforcement response to environmental crime. *Issues and Practices,* Washington, DC: National Institute of Justice.

Fagin, D. & Lavelle, M. (1996). *Toxic deception.* Ontario: Birch Lane Press.

Ferkiss, V. C. (1995, June 16). Strong winds from D.C. *Commonweal, 122,* 4–5

Ferrey, S. (1997). *Environmental law: Examples and explanations.* New York: Aspen.

Findlay, R. W. & Farber, D. A. (2000). *Environmental law: In a nutshell.* St. Paul, MN: West Group.

Flippen, J. B. (1995, Summer). The Nixon administration, timber, and the call of the wild. *Environmental History Review, 19*(2), 37–54.

Flippen, J. B. (1996). Containing the urban sprawl: The Nixon administration's land use policy. *Presidential Studies Quarterly, 26*(1), 197–207.

Flippen, J. B. (2000). *Nixon and the environment.* Albuquerque: University of New Mexico Press.

Ford's Vow Ignores Fact That Beating CAFE Can Be Costly. (2003, April 28). *Automotive News,* 12.

Frank, N. & Lynch, M. J. (1992). *Corporate crime, corporate violence: A primer.* New York: Harrow & Heston.

Franz, N. (2002). Democrats slam Bush on EPA enforcement nominee. *Chemical Week, 164*(20), 11.

Friedrichs, D. O. (1996). *Trusted criminals.* Belmont, CA: Wadsworth.

Genovese, M. A. (1990). *The Nixon presidency: Power and politics in turbulent times.* Westport, CT: Greenwood.

Goldman, B. A. (1991). *The truth about where you live.* New York: Random House.

Goldstein, A. (2002, August 26). Too green for their own good? *Time, 160*(9), A58–A60.

Gottlieb, R. (1993). *Forcing the Spring: The transformation of the American environmental movement.* Washington, DC: Island Press.

Green Bush. (2001). *National Review,* 53(9), 14–16.

Greene, D. (2003, May 22). EPA chief Whitman resigns from post: GOP moderate perceived by some as lacking will, influence on environment. *The Baltimore Sun,* p. 1A.

Habicht, H. F., II. (1984, March). Justice cracks down on environmental crimes. *EPA Journal, 10*(2), 16–17.

Hamilton, J. (1993). Politics and social costs: Estimating the impact of collective action on hazardous waste facilities. *Rand Journal of Economics, 24,* 101–125.

Hamilton, J. (1995). Testing for environmental racism: Prejudice, profits, political power? *Journal of Policy Analysis and Management, 14*(1), 107–132.

Hammett, T. & Epstein, J. (1993). Local prosecution of environmental crime. *Issues and Practices.* Washington, DC: National Institute of Justice.

Hammitt, J. & Reuter, P. (1988). *Measuring and deterring illegal disposal of hazardous waste.* Santa Monica, CA: Rand Corporation.

Hays, S. P. (1959). *Conservation and the gospel of efficiency: The progressive American conservation movement, 1890–1920.* Cambridge, MA: Harvard University Press.

Hedman, S. (1991). Expressive functions of criminal sanctions in environmental law. *The George Washington Law Review, 59,* 889–899.

Helmkamp, J., Ball, R., & Townsend, K. (Eds.) (1996). *Definitional dilemma: Can and should there be a universal definition of white-collar crime?* National White-collar Crime Center.

Helvarg, D. (2001, May 7). Bush unites the enviros. *The Nation, 272*(18), 5–6.

Hess, G. (2001). New Bush budget trims EPA allowance by $500 million. *Chemical Market Reporter, 259*(16), pp. 1, 24.

Hird, J. (1993, Winter). Environmental policy and equity: The case of Superfund. *Journal of Policy Analysis and Management, 12*(2), 323–343.

Hird, J. & Reese, M. (1998). The distribution of environmental quality: An empirical analysis. *Social Science Quarterly, 79*(4), 693–716.

Hoff, J. (1994). *Nixon reconsidered.* New York: HarperCollins.

How green is the White House? (1994). *E: The Environmental Magazine, 5,* 36–41.

Humphreys, S. (1990). An enemy of the people: Prosecuting the corporate polluter as a common law criminal. *American University Law Review, 39,* 311–354.

Hunter, S. & Noonan, V. (1993). Energy, environment, and the presidential agenda. In R. Waterman (Ed.), *The presidency reconsidered* (pp. 303–305). Itasca, IL: F.E. Peacock.

Hunter, S. & Waterman, R. W. (1996). *Enforcing the law: The case of Clean Water Acts.* Armonk, NY: M. E. Sharpe.

Hyatt, B. (1998). The federal environmental regulatory structure. In M. Clifford (Ed.), *Environmental crime: Enforcement, policy, and social responsibility* (pp. 115–141). Gaithersburg, MD: Aspen.

Ireland, D. (2001). Whitman: A toxic choice. *The Nation, 272*(4), 18.

Jalley, E. M., Moores, P. B., Henninger, B. L. & Maragani, G. P. (2002). Environmental crimes. *American Criminal Law Review, 39*, 403–489.

Johnson, H. (1991). *Sleepwalking through history: America in the Reagan years.* New York: W.W. Norton.

Josephson, M. (1934). *The robber barons: The great American capitalists, 1861–1901.* NY: Harcourt, Brace and World.

Karliner, J. (1997). *The corporate planet: Ecology and politics in the age of globalization.* San Francisco: Sierra Books.

Kasperson, R. & Dow, K. (1991). Developmental and geographical equity in global environmental change: A framework for analysis. *Evaluation Review, 15*, 149–171.

Kaye, H. J. (1996). *Why do ruling classes fear history?, and other questions.* NY: St. Martin's.

Kraft, M. E. (1996). *Environmental policy and politics.* New York: HarperCollins College Publishers.

Kraft, M. E. (2001). *Environmental policy and politics* (2nd ed.). New York: Longman.

Landy, M. K., Roberts, M. J. & Thomas, S. R. (1990). *The Environmental Protection Agency: Asking the wrong questions.* Oxford: Oxford University Press.

Lappe, M. (1991). *Chemical deception, the toxic threat to health and the environment: Exposing ten myths that endanger us all.* San Francisco, CA: Sierra Club Books.

Larson, J. (1980). *Why government programs fail: Improving policy implementation.* New York: Praeger.

Lash, J., Gillman, K., & Sheridan, D. (1984). *A season of spoils: The Reagan administration's attack on the environment.* New York: Pantheon Books.

Lavalle, M. & Coyle, M. (1992, September). Unequal protection: The racial divide in environmental law: A special edition. *National Law Journal, 21*, S1–S12.

Leigh, J., Markowitz, S., Fahs, M., & Landrigan, P. (2000). *Costs of occupational injury and illness.* Ann Arbor, MI: University of Michigan Press.

Lester, J. P. (1989). *Environmental politics and policy: Theories and evidence.* Durham, NC: Duke University.

Levine, E. (2002). At the top of his lungs. *U.S. News & World Report, 133*(21), 28–29.

Lowe, P., Ward, N., Seymour, S., & Clark, J. (1996). Farm pollution as environmental crime. *Science as Culture, 25*, 588–612.

Lynch, M. J., Michalowski, R., & Groves, W. B. (2000). *The new primer in radical criminology: Critical perspectives on crime, power & identity* (3rd ed.). Monsey, NY: Criminal Justice Press.

Lynch, M. J., Nalla, M. K., & Miller, K. W. (1989). Cross cultural perceptions of deviance: The case of Bhopal. *Journal of Research in Crime and Delinquency, 26*(1), 7–35.

Lynch, M. J. & Stretesky, P. B. (1999). Conspiracy, deceit and misinformation: Standard operating procedure in the chemical industry. *The Critical Criminologist, 9*(4), 14–18.

Lynch, M. J. & Stretesky, P. B. (2001). Toxic crimes: Examining corporate victimization of the general public employing medical and epidemiological evidence. *Critical Criminology, 10*(3), 153–172.

Lynch, M. J. & Stretesky, P. B. (2003). The meaning of green: Contrasting criminological perspectives. *Theoretical Criminology, 7*(2), 217–238.

Lynch, M. J., Stretesky, P., & Hammond, P. (2000). Media coverage of chemical crime, Hillsborough County, Florida, 1987–97. *British Journal of Criminology, 40,* 112–126.

Lynch, M. J., Stretesky, P., & McGurrin, D. (2002). Toxic crimes and environmental justice: Examining the hidden dangers of hazardous waste. In G. Potter (Ed.), *Controversies in white-collar crime* (pp. 109–136). Cincinnati, OH: Anderson.

Marcus, A. A. (1980). *Promise and performance: Choosing and implementing an environmental policy.* Westport, CT: Greenwood Press.

Markham, A. (1994). *A brief history of pollution.* New York: St. Martin's.

McCarthy, T., Thompson, D., & Thornburgh, N. (2000). How green was Bill? *Time, 156*(25), 64–66.

McCormick, J. (1989). *Reclaiming paradise: The global environmental movement.* Bloomington, IN: Indiana University Press.

McMurry, R. & Ramsey, S. (1986). Environmental crime: The use of criminal sanctions in enforcing environmental laws. *Loyola of Los Angeles Law Review, 19,* 1133–1170.

Messner, S. & Rosenfeld, R. (1994). *Crime and the American dream.* Belmont, CA: Wadsworth.

Milbank, D. & Nakashima, E. (2001, March 25). Bush team has 'right' credentials: Conservative picks seen eclipsing even Reagan's. *Washington Post,* p. 1.

Mills, C. W. (1959). The sociological imagination. New York: Oxford.

Mintz, J. A. (1995). Enforcement at the EPA: High stakes and hard choices. Austin: University of Texas Press.

Mohai, P. & Bryant, B. (1992). Environmental racism: Reviewing the evidence. In B. Bryant & P. Mohai (Eds.), *Race and the incidence of environmental hazards* (pp. 163–176). Boulder, CO: Westview.

Nader, R. (1965). *Unsafe at any speed: The designed–in dangers of the American automobile.* New York: Grossman.

Nader, R., Brownstein, R. & Richard, J. (Eds.). (1981). *Who's poisoning America: Corporate polluters and their victims in the chemical age.* San Francisco, CA: Sierra Club Books.

Nash, J. L. (2000). Browner outlines environmental protection future. *Occupational Hazards, 62*(11), 19.

Nash, J. L. (2001). Whitman brings new direction to EPA. *Occupational Hazards, 63*(2), 29.

Nash, R. (1967). *Wilderness and the American mind.* New Haven, CT: Yale University.

Nash, R. (1976). *The American environment: Readings in the history of conservation* (2nd ed.). Reading, MA: Addison-Wesley.

Nash, R. (1990). *American environmentalism* (3rd ed.). New York: McGraw-Hill.

O'Riordan, T. (1995, October). Frameworks for choice: Core beliefs and the environment. *Environment, 37*, 4–9.

O'Riordan, T., Clark, W. C., & Kates, R. W. (1995). The legacy of Earth Day: Reflections at a turning point. *Environment, 37*, 6–10.

Paehlke, R. (2003). Environmental sustainability and urban life in America. In N. J. Vig & M. E. Kraft (Eds.), *Environmental policy: New directions for the twenty-first century* (5th ed., pp. 57–77). Washington, DC: CQ Press.

Pollock, P. & Vittas, E. (1995). Who bears the burdens of environmental pollution? Race, ethnicity, and environmental equity in Florida. *Social Science Quarterly, 76*, 294–310.

Postrel, V. (1990). Forget left and right, the politics of the future will be growth versus green. *UTNE Reader, 40*, 57–58.

Potter, G. W. & Miller, K. S. (2002). Thinking about white-collar crime. In G. Potter (Ed.), *Controversies in white-collar crime* (pp. 1–36). Cincinnati, OH: Anderson.

Pressman, J. & Wildavsky, A. (1973). *Implementation*. Berkeley, CA: University of California Press.

Quinney, R. (1970). *The social reality of crime*. New Brunswick, NJ: Transaction.

Rebovich, D. (1992). *Dangerous ground: The world of hazardous waste crime*. New Brunswick, NJ: Transaction.

Rebovich, D. (1996). Prosecutorial decision making and the environmental prosecutor: Reaching a crossroads for public protection. In S. M. Edwards, T. D. Edwards, & C. B. Fields (Eds.), *Environmental crime and criminality: Theoretical and practical issues* (pp. 77–98). New York: Garland.

Rebovich, D. (1998). Environmental crime research: Where we have been, where we should go. In M. Clifford (Ed.), *Environmental crime: Enforcement, policy, and social responsibility* (pp. 341–354). Gaithersburg, MD: Aspen.

Rebovich, D. (2002). Prosecuting environmental crime in the twenty-first century. In R. Muraskin & A. Roberts (Eds.), *Visions for change: Crime and justice in the twenty-first century* (3rd ed., pp. 331–350). Upper Saddle River, NJ: Prentice Hall.

Rebovich, D. & Nixon, R. T. (1994, December). Environmental crime prosecution: Results of a national survey. *Research in Brief*, Washington, DC: National Institute of Justice.

Reiman, J. (1979). *The rich get richer and the poor get prison*. Needham Heights, MA: Allyn & Bacon.

Reiman, J. (2001). *The rich get richer and the poor get prison* (6th ed.). Needham Heights, MA: Allyn & Bacon.

Ringquist, E. J. (1993). Does regulation matter?: Evaluating the effects of state air pollution control programs. *The Journal of Politics, 55*(4), 1022–1045.

Ringquist, E. J. (1997). Equity and the distribution of environmental risk: The case of TRI facilities. *Social Science Quarterly, 78,* 811–829.

Ringquist, E. (2003). Environmental justice: Normative concerns, empirical evidence, and government action. In N. J. Vig & M. E. Kraft (Eds.), *Environmental policy: New directions for the twenty-first century* (5th ed., pp. 249–273). Washington, DC: CQ Press.

Robinson, M. B. (2002). *Justice blind?: Ideals and realities of American criminal justice.* Upper Saddle River, NJ: Prentice Hall.

Rosenbaum, W. A. (2003). Still reforming after all these years: George W. Bush's 'new era' at the EPA. In N. J. Vig & M. E. Kraft (Eds.), *Environmental policy: New directions for the twenty-first century* (5th ed., pp. 175–200). Washington, DC: CQ Press.

Rosoff, S. M., Pontell, H. N., & Tillman, R. H. (2002). *Profit without honor: White-collar crime and the looting of America* (2nd ed.). Upper Saddle River, NJ: Prentice Hall.

Ross, D. (1996). A review of EPA criminal, civil and administrative enforcement data: Are the efforts measurable deterrents to environmental criminals? In S. M. Edwards, T. D. Edwards, & C. B. Fields (Eds.), *Environmental crime and criminality: Theoretical and practical issues* (pp. 55–78). New York: Garland.

Ross, E. A. (1977, original in 1907). The Criminaloid. In G. Geis & R. Meier (Eds.), *White-collar crime: Offenses in business, politics and the professions* (29–37). New York: The Free Press.

Runyan, C. & Norderhaug, M. (2002, May/June). The path to the Johannesburg summit. *World Watch, 15*(3), 30–35.

Ryan, W. (1982). *Equality.* New York: Vintage.

Sachs, A. (1993, February). Rebellious grand jurors hire lawyer. *ABA Journal, 79,* 31.

Sale, K. & Foner, E. (1993). *The green revolution: The American environmental movement, 1962–1992.* New York: Hill and Wang.

Sanger, D. E. & Kahn, J. (2001, May 18). Bush, pushing energy plan, offers scores of proposals to find new power sources. *New York Times,* p. A1.

Schaeffer, E. (2002). Clearing the air. *The Washington Monthly, 34*(7/8), 20–25.

Schindler, G. (1995, March/April). It didn't begin with Earth Day. *E: The Environment Magazine, 6,* 32–35.

Sellin, T. (1938). *Culture, crime and conflict.* NY: Social Science Research Council.

Sexton, K., Marcus, A. A., Easter, K. W., & Burkhardt, T. D. (Eds.). (1999). *Better environmental decisions: Strategies for governments, businesses, and communities.* Washington, DC: Island Press.

Shabecoff, P. (1990, February 1). Environmental groups told they are racists in hiring. *New York Times,* p. A20.

Simon, D. R. (2000, January). Corporate environmental crimes and social inequity: New directions for environmental justice. *American Behavioral Scientist, 43*(4), 633–645.

Sinclair, U. (1906). *The jungle.* New York: New America Library.

Smith, A. (1776). *The wealth of nations*. Middlesex, England: Penguin.

Soden, D. L. (1999). Presidential roles and environmental policy. In D. L. Soden (Ed.), *The environmental presidency* (pp. 1–13). Albany: State University of New York Press.

Spangler, J. & Dougherty, J. (2003, August 13). The heat's on Leavitt. *Deseret News*, p. A1.

Starr, J. W. (1991). Turbulent times at Justice and EPA: The origins of environmental criminal prosecutions and the work that remains. *The George Washington Law Review, 59*, 900–915.

Steingraber, S. (1998). *Living downstream: A scientist's personal investigation of cancer and the environment*. New York: Vintage.

Stine, J. K. (1998). Environmental policy during the Carter presidency. In G. M. Fink & H. D. Graham (Eds.), *The Carter presidency: Policy choices in the post–new deal era* (pp. 179–201). Lawrence, KS: University Press of Kansas.

Stretesky, P. & Hogan, M. (1998). Environmental justice: An analysis of Superfund sites in Florida. *Social Problems, 45*, 268–287.

Stretesky, P. & Lynch, M. J. (1999). Corporate environmental violence and racism. *Crime, Law & Social Change, 30*, 163–184.

Stretesky, P. & Lynch, M. J. (2001). The relationship between lead exposure and homicide. *Archives of Pediatrics and Adolescent Medicine, 155*, 579–582.

Strock, J. M. (1991). Environmental enforcement priorities for the 1990s. *The George Washington Law Review, 59*, 916–937.

Sutherland, E. H. (1983). *White-collar crime: The uncut version*. New Haven, CT: Yale University Press.

Switzer, J. V. & Bryner, G. (1998). *Environmental politics: Domestic and global dimensions* (2nd ed.). New York: St. Martin's Press.

Szasz, A. (1986). Organizations, organized crime and the disposal of hazardous waste: An examination of the making of a criminogenic regulatory structure. *Criminology, 24*(1), 1–27.

Tappan, P. W. (1947). Who is the criminal? *American Sociological Review, 12*, 96–102.

Taylor, J. (2002). "Greeniacs in Jo-burg." *National Review, 54*(17), 29–30.

The Rocky Flats cover-up, continued. (1992, December). *The Progressive, 57*, 36.

Thornburgh, R. (1991). Criminal enforcement of environmental laws—A national priority. *The George Washington Law Review, 59*, 775–780.

Tolchin, S. J. & Tolchin, M. (1983). *Dismantling America: The rush to deregulate*. New York: Oxford University Press.

Train, R. E. (1996). The environmental record of the Nixon administration. *Presidential Studies Quarterly, 26*, 185–196.

Tucker, W. (1982). *Progress and privilege: America in the age of environmentalism*. New York: Anchor Press/Doubleday.

U.S. Council on Environmental Quality. (1971). *Environmental quality, 1971*. Washington, DC: Government Printing Office.

Vig, N. J. (2003). Presidential leadership and the environment. In N. J. Vig & M. E. Kraft (Eds.), *Environmental policy: New directions for the twenty–first century* (5th ed., pp. 103–125). Washington, DC: CQ Press.

Vig, N. J. & Kraft, M. E. (2003). Toward sustainable development? In N. J. Vig & M. E. Kraft (Eds.), *Environmental policy: New directions for the twenty–first century* (5th ed., pp. 391–407). Washington, DC: CQ Press.

Vig, N. J. & Kraft, M. E. (Eds.). (1984). *Environmental policy in the 1980s: Reagan's new agenda.* Washington, DC: CQ Press.

Vogel, D. (2003). International trade and environmental regulation. In N. J. Vig & M. E. Kraft (Eds.), *Environmental policy: New directions for the twenty-first century* (5th ed., pp. 371–389). Washington, DC: CQ Press.

Walijassper, J. (1990). Who are the greens and what do they believe? *UTNE Reader, 40,* 58–60.

Wargo, J. (1998). *Our children's toxic legacy: How science and law fail to protect us from pesticides.* New Haven, CT: Yale University Press.

Waterman, R. W. (1989). *Presidential influence and the administrative state.* Knoxville: University of Tennessee Press.

Weidenbaum, M. L. (1986). *Business, government, and the public* (3rd ed.). Englewood Cliffs, NJ: Prentice Hall.

Whitaker, J. C. (1976). *Striking a balance: Environmental and natural resources policy in the Nixon–Ford years.* Washington, DC: American Enterprise Institute.

White, M. (2003, May 29). Whitman's EPA could have been worse, right? *Newsday (NY)*, p. A31.

Whitty, J. (2003). All the disappearing islands. *Mother Jones, 28*(4), pp. 50–55, 92–93.

William Reilly's green precision weapons. (1991, March 30). *The Economist,* 28.

Yeager, P. C. (1991). *The limits of law: The public regulation of private pollution.* Cambridge: Cambridge University.

Zimmerman, R. (1993). Social equity and environmental risk. *Risk Analysis, 12,* 649–666.

Index